HOW TO BE A

happy

Academic :)

Sara Miller McCune founded SAGE Publishing in 1965 to support the dissemination of usable knowledge and educate a global community. SAGE publishes more than 1000 journals and over 800 new books each year, spanning a wide range of subject areas. Our growing selection of library products includes archives, data, case studies and video. SAGE remains majority owned by our founder and after her lifetime will become owned by a charitable trust that secures the company's continued independence.

Los Angeles | London | New Delhi | Singapore | Washington DC | Melbourne

ALEXANDER CLARK
& BAILEY SOUSA

HOW TO BE A
happy
Academic :)

Los Angeles | London | New Delhi
Singapore | Washington DC | Melbourne

Los Angeles | London | New Delhi
Singapore | Washington DC | Melbourne

SAGE Publications Ltd
1 Oliver's Yard
55 City Road
London EC1Y 1SP

SAGE Publications Inc.
2455 Teller Road
Thousand Oaks, California 91320

SAGE Publications India Pvt Ltd
B 1/I 1 Mohan Cooperative Industrial Area
Mathura Road
New Delhi 110 044

SAGE Publications Asia-Pacific Pte Ltd
3 Church Street
#10-04 Samsung Hub
Singapore 049483

Editor: Jai Seaman
Assistant editor: Alysha Owen
Production editor: Victoria Nicholas
Proofreader: Derek Markham
Marketing manager: Susheel Gokarakonda
Cover design: Bhairvi Gudka
Typeset by: C&M Digitals (P) Ltd, Chennai, India
Printed in the UK

Library of Congress Control Number: 2017951199

British Library Cataloguing in Publication data

A catalogue record for this book is available from
the British Library

ISBN 978-1-4739-7879-9
ISBN 978-1-4739-7880-5 (pbk)

At SAGE we take sustainability seriously. Most of our products are printed in the UK using responsibly sourced
papers and boards. When we print overseas we ensure sustainable papers are used as measured by the PREPS
grading system. We undertake an annual audit to monitor our sustainability.

CONTENTS

FIGURES AND TABLES

FIGURES

TABLES

ABOUT THE AUTHORS

Alexander Clark, PhD, is Full Professor at the University of Alberta, and is a World Economic Forum Young Global Leader / Young Scientist. He fulfils leadership roles with a number of national research funding bodies across Canada. Alex regularly writes on academic career development, growth, and leadership, and has led workshops all over the world for a decade for researchers from all career stages on academic effectiveness, writing, and research. He speaks nationally and internationally to young scientists from across disciplines on academic career issues, including skills, teamwork, and mentorship. Alex's research on heart disease has been published in some of the world's most influential journals, including *The Lancet, British Medical Journal, Journal of American College of Cardiology* and *Social Science & Medicine.*

Bailey Sousa, PMP, is the Director of the International Institute for Qualitative Methodology (IIQM) based at the University of Alberta, and is an entrepreneur and workplace effectiveness advocate. Bailey has worked as a team leader, managing complex projects for over a decade in a variety of entrepreneurial ventures and roles in corporate, social enterprise, and academic settings. Her current role enables her to connect with, and provide connections among, academics internationally, giving her a global perspective on effectiveness and the challenges faced. Bailey's interests and contributions relate to workplace and academic effectiveness, leadership, and teamwork in complex settings, and she facilitates workshops all over the word in this area. In 2015, Bailey was also recognized as one of Edmonton's *Avenue Magazine's* 'Top 40 Under 40' for her contribution in her work and to her city.

ACKNOWLEDGEMENTS

Many people helped us develop and write this book. As we say, academic work is never just about the work. As we juggled our home and work lives, family and friends near and far provided the rock, not only for this book but also for all the work to which it gives expression. To Fiona, Matthew and Bronwen Clark, thank you for your daily presence, patience and efforts. These were *vital* in all ways. To Tim, Avriella and Arion Sousa, your support and understanding of the 'crazy' has been unwavering. A special thank you to the little ones, who bring laughter and fun to the days when it is needed most, and to Nana Jacks, whom 'it all' could not be done without.

The ideas and concepts described throughout have come from many rich sources both inside and outside of academia. We have benefited from the creativity and insightfulness of the many other authors whose works are used in this book. We hope that this book is a catalyst to read more widely and to discover and explore more of these wonderful contributions.

We are especially thankful for the inspiration and generosity of the other people whom we have met along the way. At our workshops and in our daily interactions, academic workers who have gifted their stories and time to share with openness and vulnerability their daily and deep experiences, fears and difficulties. They remind us that these are never just words. We appreciate all your feedback and affirmation regarding the concepts and content in *How to be a Happy Academic*. This book evolved a lot from our conversations with you and it is far better for it.

We are grateful to those who have supported this book commercially and practically, notably the team at SAGE and their reviewers. From beginning to end, you have been responsive and industrious in your support of our vision for a different kind of academic book.

Ultimately, like all academic work, even the best of ideas add up to little if the right tasks don't get done. For helping us to do these well, we thank our copyeditor, Sabina Pietrosanu, and illustrator, Janna Priest. To the rest of our team, especially to Mona and Yvette, who have stood by us through it all – thank you!

INTRODUCTION

Our hope: Every academic: effective, successful, and happy.

It's hard to think of three more important or more difficult aims than these. Demands on academic workers around teaching, research and engagement forever increase. Wherever you are in the world, contexts change apace. In the midst of all this, grappling with the complexities of 'what is known' and 'what is unknown' in academic work is endlessly challenging (Walker et al., 2008). Does being clever, having a doctorate, or a healthy dose of methodological and substantive expertise suffice? If only.

In leading hundreds of workshops all over the world, our workshops are full of talented, earnest and extremely hardworking and well-motivated scholars. People who want to be successful and respected, but also have a life beyond their job. Alas, we meet all too many people trying to succeed who feel isolated, under intense pressure and disengaged from their workplace and colleagues. We hear of many workplaces in which 'busyness' and 'office hours accrued' are the main currency, places where volume of individual achievements trumps learning, innovation, visibility, impact, or influence. Cultures in which 'keeping your head down' and your door closed is the means to survive. No one has enough time.

This book is about expecting more from your life and your job. It provides a means to see, do, and tame academic work. This work, we argue, is distinctively challenging and those charged with seeking to be effective, successful, and happy doing it will be consistently challenged to their limits. If you want an easy ride, get off now.

Effectiveness, success, and happiness are also precarious territory. This is not a book about the transformative power of self-belief, positive thinking, goal-setting, or motivation. We recognize avowedly that the challenges of academic work vary profoundly across people, countries, and disciplines. Casualization, expectations, workload, job securities, and even the status of academic workers vary markedly across the world. Such differences risk lending any text that seeks to help with academic work a degree of 'otherness'. We can already hear the laments: 'You just don't understand'. 'Naive idealists can chase fulfilment, but stress, discombobulation and disillusionment are rites of passages, even badges of honour, in the trenches of academic work'.

We respect but disagree with this thinking. Instead, we cast light on how academic workers can set expectations for effectiveness, success, and happiness and engage in the reflections and actions that can help to facilitate these ends. From a doctoral student to a senior professor, academic workers grapple with the messy realities of this work: who you are, what you stand for and how you seek to change the world through your work. Effectiveness, success, and happiness in academic work tie in to some of the most troublesome and profound questions that occur to many of us over our careers, such as:

- How can I do my best academic work?
- How can my life and work be and stay more balanced?
- How can I be authentically engaged in and at my work?
- How can I be successful at work and happy in my life?

EVERY ACADEMIC: EFFECTIVE, SUCCESSFUL, AND HAPPY

WHY HAPPY?

While we include whole chapters focused on effectiveness and success, here we deal with happiness and what we mean by 'happy'. Indeed, we waivered particularly about whether to focus on 'happy' in the book's title. Yet, putting 'happy' forward as a vital consideration for today's and tomorrow's academic workers has proved to be the main and most surprising impetus for this book. Initially, in our workshops, we mentioned 'happiness' more in passing because happy had no ready place in workplace mission statements or resumes. Could the seriousness of academic work make open talk of happy seem heresy? However, in response we noticed unexpected but immediate and palpable waves of relief and excitement, reactions that were consistently so warm and intense. Whereas our talk about success and effectiveness evoked avid intellectual determination, reactions to happy were heady: strong and exhilarated. Happiness in academic work, it transpired, was about something more. Something deeper.

Happiness in academic work has since become a sustaining catalyst for our work and this book. This motivation has only increased from hearing more about the struggles, optimism, challenges, and growth of academic workers around their lives and work. We continue to be inspired by the talented academic workers worldwide striving to bring their best to the immense challenges of academic work and careers in workplaces in which 'happy' seems taboo. We have also come to understand more fully that 'happy' for academic workers is as diverse as it is important. This is why, despite this centrality, we won't operationalize and define what happy, success, or effective should mean for you.

The reluctance of today's academic workers and workplaces to openly address and acknowledge aspects of happiness stands starkly in contrast to the millennia of scholarship which has been devoted to happiness. Ironically, far from being trite or trivial, throughout history, considerations of happiness have remained one of the most prominent scholarly topics. Scholarship around happiness is confined neither to religion (e.g. in Buddhism, Hinduism, and Judaism) or modern preoccupations with pleasure and wealth (McMahon, 2006). Indeed, the first book of Western literature, 'The History of Herodotus', details the Lydian king Croesus's quest to reach happiness in life via his search for the happiest man in the world (McMahon, 2006). The nature of and paths to happiness are also prominent in the work of Socrates, Plato, Aristotle, the Epicureans, the Stoics, the Romantics...and more recently in: Bentham, Marx, Rousseau, Nietzsche, Klimt, Freud, Beckett, and Atwood amongst many (McMahon, 2006; Irvine, 2008; Brown, 2016). If happiness is good enough for this cast, avowedly its consideration and aspiration has legitimate place for academic workers.

Further, for millennia, this scholarship constantly reiterates the intimate communion of happiness with difficulties and abject toil (McMahon, 2006). Time and again, it is not the absence of difficult events, circumstances, or people that makes happiness legitimate or viable – but rather it's the very presence of such fearsome challenges that renders happiness important (Irvine, 2008). It is because today's academic workers, work, and workplaces are so beset with challenges, our thoughts and actions around happiness are needed.

WHY IS THIS BOOK NEEDED?

We see this book as being useful for those seeking an academic position and progressing their academic work over time, and as a means of ongoing development. All three aims address the nature of modern academic work and workplaces.

Getting an academic position requires years of tenacity and output – and decades more to progress thereafter. We knew that we would have to teach and write (and work long hours to do so), but academic outputs are tracked at every turn with both old and new metrics. Tensions are ubiquitous between quality, quantity, and visibility of academic output, and these vary markedly across departments, disciplines, and countries. Obtaining funding is ever more competitive and work is increasingly done, not only with a myriad of academic colleagues but also in teams, with 'stakeholders', members of the public, and mass and social media audiences.

More established academics – tenured, promoted or otherwise on their way – can use this book and knowledge of The Core as a means to mentor, help and support their students and junior colleagues. However, many of us have emerged, often weary and wary, into established academic careers feeling overburdened, excessively busy and tired. Ourselves and our scholarship have suffered and risk suffering more. The course and compromises of our careers did not turn out as we expected them to. Amidst all the constraints of academic workplaces, it is tempting to see progress in these ends as 'coming, if only ...' If only we had more time, if only people understood us or our work better, if only our colleagues, students, and organizations left us alone. Paradoxically, success as an academic worker comes in many different packages and via many different paths. Amidst this diversity, irrespective of career stage, we should each periodically take quality time to step back, pause and reflect on how to fully realize our visions for our scholarship.

Academic workplaces – as axioms of student, public, government and professional interest – are 'supercomplex' (Barnett, 2000). This is not unlikely to lessen. Perspectives on academic work from the 1980s convey a far simpler life, free from stress, with a high level of autonomy, reasonable demands, forthcoming respect, and supportive colleagues (Kinman, 2014). While this 'golden age' account likely downplays historical change in university life over the last 50 years (Barnett, 2011), modern academic life is replete with ongoing challenges, including:

- Lack of collegiality (Ryan, 2012).
- Corporatization (Woodhouse, 2009).
- Falling academic standards (Cote and Allahar, 2007).
- Bullying, low morale, and long working hours (Kinman, 2014).
- Pressure for high volumes of quick work (Berg and Seeber, 2016).

The harms created by these demands are telling. High levels of stress are common. A notably large survey of 14,500 academics from the United Kingdom identified that nearly 75 per cent of them viewed their jobs as 'stressful', with 50 per cent perceiving this stress to be 'high' or 'very high' (Kinman, 2014). Other negative consequences include burnout, poor physical and mental health, and lack of balance (ibid.). Asked what they find most stressful in their academic work, while less than a third reported unachievable deadlines, almost 80 per cent reported working intensively and more than 50 per cent felt pressured to work fast and to work long hours (ibid.). Our workplaces are also commonly places of inherent tensions, reconciliations and trade-offs, and departmental and methodological politics. For good or for ill, we are drawn into career comparisons with others and are quick to judge those who are different or choose different paths. The successes of others have never been more in our face, not only in the success narratives of résumés and publications but also via social and mass media. Animosities, fear, and small differences can come to characterize the ongoing academic project. This world can lead us to recoil and resentment.

While today's academic jobs appear to need the skills of 'superheroes' (Pitt and Mewburn, 2016), training and support has not increased. A 'learning-on-the-job' ethos dominates that is seen to be 'acceptable and enough' despite being dramatically out of step with the intense demands, range and depth of academic work (Smith, 2010). Doctoral education too often remains focused on developing individual 'technical skills' around substantive and methodological knowledge, despite subsequent academic work-life being characterized by competition, interpersonal work and uncertainty (Bogle et al., 2010).

GET THE MOST FROM THIS BOOK

This book provides a technical way to see and do academic work. More than this, academic work is always personal and, in this book, we seek to honour and reflect this. It is about you: who you are, your fears, your values, your hopes, and your aspirations. Accordingly, we place this ignored but pivotal personal part of academic work centre stage.

ACADEMIC WORK IS ALWAYS PERSONAL

Reflection, openness, and empathy

Using this book should not be uniformly comfortable: when you feel your thoughts, fear or ire start to really kick in, we urge openness to these sensations. Take time out. Reflect on your thoughts, emotions, and physical sensations. What has triggered them? What do they indicate about you and your work? What is *really* going on? Be prepared to trace your intellectual objections back to underlying fears, experiences, and vulnerabilities. These may be hard to face up to or acknowledge but offer opportunities because our reactions, particularly intense ones, are telling and warrant what Brené Brown (2012) describes as 'the courage of vulnerability' to explore.

Being overly harsh about others or even ourselves is tempting but seldom productive. It's all too common to bemoan, ruminate, or strike out at the work, motivations, actions, aspirations, theories and reputations of other academic workers or even ourselves. Outcomes, relationships and projects go awry in academic work for many reasons. Holding harsh judgements (and all manner of other negative thoughts) of both yourself and others in check generates more space for your own reflections and development. Accordingly, we urge you to honour your and others' values and positive intent. Have empathy, but be slow to presume that you understand the burdens and difficulties that others carry. Also, be kind to yourself.

Recognizing it's personal

We are not just academic workers, but sons, daughters, partners, spouses, sisters, brothers, parents, friends, and colleagues, too. Our work and our lives are blurred – sometimes to the point of inseparability. These intersections affect our values for work and life. We write this book as two people who have families, children, bad days, good days, great days, and whole histories and trajectories of how we got here and where we try to make our work fit.

> **Alex:** I grew up in Scotland, completing doctoral and postdoctoral studies of social dimensions of heart disease before moving to Canada for an entry-level teaching and research position in 2003. With two children and a wife on a new continent, life was very different from back home in Scotland. Spare time became filled with home life, coaching
>
> *(Continued)*

soccer (football!) and learning the ropes of both academic and Canadian life. My biggest struggles have been with keeping boundaries between work and home – particularly over the recent years when I was an associate dean who was trying also to retain a credible research programme – without support from the family and friends who were close to hand for most of my life. I have had challenges keeping my own research on track but also dealing with worries over my career being off-track, of my research being one step away from crisis. I worry too much what others think of me. My favourite part of being an academic worker is getting to 'connect the dots' around interesting ideas – to bring in fresh and new insights to my research from far-flung fields. I really enjoy working with, around, and in messiness, which may explain why my work has evolved in qualitative research, complex interventions, complexity, and realist theory, and academic leadership and development.

Bailey: I grew up in Canada, in both Alberta and Nova Scotia (both in Canada but 5000 km apart) at various points in my life. Post-university I began my foray into entrepreneurship, initiating various start-ups and owning a number of small- and mid-sized businesses. I thrived on the excitement of the fast-paced changes and challenges, and learned much from experiencing both great success and great failure, but moreover, learned how to create 'successful failure'. My personal interests led to memberships on many advisory boards and furthered my work with and around leadership, project management, workplace success and effectiveness, and teams in complex settings. After the birth of my first child (I now have two), I came to work within academia by luck (yes, I love what I do!). In addition to being the Director of a self-sustaining, interdisciplinary, and international university institute, I am passionate about using my skills and sharing my experiences in other sectors to co-create a vision, models, and resources in order to help academic workers succeed in their own challenging environments. For me, effectiveness is an ongoing practise – sometimes two steps forward and sometimes two steps back – but I have found focusing on concepts of 'practise' and 'growth' key. My values are most challenged in the spaces where work and life collide, especially in the context of being a working mother who frequently travels internationally as part of my work. I am vulnerable around the questions: Can I 'do it all'? and What does 'it all' even look like in terms of success and happiness for me?

Over the last 10 years, in providing workshops for academics on different aspects of effectiveness, success, and happiness, we have had the privilege of meeting many people at every stage of their academic journey: from graduate students through to deans. We have met:

- Academics focused intently on meeting the challenges of role expectations and being truly and deeply fulfilled.
- Academics who strive to put the principles of effectiveness detailed in this book into practice but have then been met with harsh judgement, skepticism, and condescension from colleagues, to the point where they elect to remain in the 'effectiveness closet' instead of being open about their true values and practices.

- Students and new academics with dizzying fears about sky-high expectations and unpredictable or unfair feedback from un-empathetic others.
- Many who feel angry, isolated, or confused by their work and the settings in which it is done. This leads to antipathy to aspects of their jobs and animosity toward their colleagues and administration.

We have heard stories of mothers striving to hold their family and lives together in the midst of juggling the intense and seemingly competing expectations of their employer and family commitments, and their own needs for health and well-being. Stories from fathers dealing with coaching sports, being a fully engaged husband and dad, while trying to get the next grant submitted and successful. Prospective academics paralyzed by uncertainty – put off from following academic career trajectories because they don't want to end up divorced, burnt out, or bitter like so many other academics they know. PhD students grappling with disengaged supervisors, tight timelines, and career make-or-break. Beyond everything, we consistently hear stories from academics with demanding lives: heavy workloads, high expectations, unhelpful work contexts and, all the while, dealing with rejection. It is because of these challenges that we wrote this book.

DOING THE RIGHT THINGS RIGHT: THE SUCCESS PYRAMID AND THE CORE

Unlike other resources for doing academic work, common in both books and on social media, we provide an approach in this book that is *integrated* and *in-depth*. Our approach is integrated in that, instead of providing separate chapterized nuggets on different parts of academic work, we provide a unified and cohesive means of conceiving and then working on academic work. After addressing the nature of academic work as 'extreme knowledge work' (Chapter 1), Section One addresses 'The Success Pyramid' – a systematic means founded on values (Chapter 2) that informs our conceptions of success (Chapter 3), which can then be used to formulate priorities and strategies (Chapter 4), set goals and do the right task(s) (Chapter 5).

In the next section, we describe 'The Core' – the range of underlying deeper skills that can help to do these *right* things *right*. This approach is efficient: deliberatively developing practises and aptitudes that transcend discrete tasks. As these differ so much by context, country, and discipline, The Core focuses on deep elements that underpin academic work, including chapters on: Creativity (Chapter 6), Human Work and Self-Work (Chapter 7), Learning (Chapter 8), Influence (Chapter 9), Writing (Chapter 10) and Habits and Systems (Chapter 11).

Finally, we bring The Core and The Success Pyramid together in some worked examples, featuring real academic workers' experiences (Section Three) before speculating on the future of academic work and some of our own growth in writing the book (Chapter 12).

Feeling uncomfortable? Let's begin

It's good to say early and clearly that: we understand that the mere mention of 'effectiveness', 'success' and 'happiness' will raise concerns for some around vocabulary, identity, and autonomy. Discomfort is often the norm when we truly face academic work. We developed The Success Pyramid and The Core in over 100 workshops with colleagues at all career stages across the world. Throughout, we have witnessed at firsthand the gamut of responses to these aims. Is effectiveness the right way to describe what we should seek to do in universities? Who has the right to dictate what success in academic work is? Is it right for academic workers to expect or want to be happy? Indeed, this is not language or ends commonly used around academic work.

Historically, battle lines have been drawn between a workplace nomenclature of 'expectations' and 'excellence' versus workers' autonomy, freedom and scholarship. In some countries, the autonomy of academic workers is declining as casualization of contracts increases. Such developments raise concerns regarding dependence on and independence from government and funding bodies, the declining stature of academic workers and the risks of vested interests steering academic work. The academic worker, in the mire, should rightly feel wary of trite framing and solutions that serve only the needs of workplaces. We don't doubt that these are problems or the political actions to slow or redress these trends. However, our main aim here is to support academic workers to do their work.

While others propose single solutions – most notably, recent pleas for 'slower academic work' (Berg and Seeber, 2016) – we have sought to ground our approach in a detailed conception of the distinctive nature of academic work and the large body of research, theory and other contributions useful to support this work.

We acknowledge but disagree with accusations that seeking to be effective, successful, or happy in academic work is inherently privileged. This is not to dismiss the reality that some academic workers have poor conditions, are oppressed or marginalized by vent, for example, of gender, discipline, or affiliations. We hunger for academic workers to fight these injustices but also reclaim the possibility of effectiveness, success, and happiness in their own work. 'Diversity' scarcely begins to capture the pervasiveness and depth of differences that abound across the different academic work done by different academic workers. Recommendations for academic work that are unresponsive to context will ultimately be ineffective. To address this challenge, The Success Pyramid and The Core provide a means of seeing and 'working through' your own work that takes account of individual context rather than dictate what that work should look like or how you should respond.

LANGUAGE AND TERMINOLOGY ISSUES

To the practicalities of language: many different types of people are engaged in academic work today. The range of recognized 'disciplines' continues to grow, while advances in technology expand the very fields of what research is even possible. This academic work focuses on every conceivable facet of the universe, from the most micro to the most macro, from high theorizing about the most abstract to researching the most applied. Within disciplines, all manner of cultural norms are implicit, played out and enforced about what is considered to be rigourous, important and timely (Dolby, 1996). These and other norms guide the micro-cultures in individual departments and the behaviours of those in them – whole different 'worlds' exist and are played out next to each other in academic workplaces (Swales, 2009).

Many different labels are used to describe academic workers. Terminology can be confusing. 'Professors' in the UK are the most senior of successful and seasoned academics, while 'professors' in North America may be on their first day of the job after taking a tenure-track position following their PhD. Different job titles abound, including: lecturers, senior lecturers, readers, fellows, research or teaching fellows, researchers, research associates, research coordinators, and so on. Most of these people are doing academic work from, if not located in, traditional academic workplaces, like universities and colleges. Wide variations are also obvious in seniority. Students doing higher degrees are not only intensively engaged in working with their research but also in forming their identity, values and vision (Kamler and Thomson, 2008). Senior professors may be as intensely involved in their own research but working extensively to preserve their values and vision amidst workplaces and funding contexts that increasingly challenge these. Wide and meaningful variations are everywhere in people's portfolios and tasks.

To deal with these manifold differences in this book, we will use the term 'academic worker' to describe all of those engaged in academic work, irrespective of career stage, seniority, qualifications, function, or title. From this perspective, from the higher degree student doing research in their master's degree to the most senior of professors – all share the common purpose of engaging in academic work. This is not to say or imply that academic workers are the same. Indeed, academic work and workers are so defined by diversity that we need a common term to avoid confusion and extensive qualification. By using this term, we do not intend to rob anyone of their achievements or progression, but to recognize that there are clear commonalities beyond the wide diversity of academic work that academic workers do: that all academic work, as we will show in the next chapter, is knowledge work and, moreover, that this work is extreme knowledge work.

THEORETICAL BASIS AND FEATURES

Like ice cream, atheoretical 'tricks-and-tips' approaches to academic work have an allure that cannot ultimately sustain us, given the immense diversity of academic workers, their work, workplaces, countries and aspirations (Kamler and Thomson, 2008; Koay, 2015). As such, throughout the book, we draw on insights from complexity and genre theory to present considerations for academic work that are expressed in The Success Pyramid and The Core. While recognizing the nature, diversity, and complexity of academic work, our primary gaze keeps returning to the self. This reflects the ancient Stoical truth that the only thing that one can control with certainty is oneself (Irvine, 2008). This profound insight reflects in other work on performance and self-awareness that we draw on from Steve Peters (2013), Jamie Catto (2016) and Brené Brown (2012).

Reflecting on this personal focus and range, throughout the chapters, we include 'Over to You' sections that address not only how elements of The Success Pyramid and The Core can be thought about and developed – but also how elements can be refined, re-energized and refocused. Some readers will likely want to commit their reflections to their personal journals, while others will be content to reflect in the moment. Do what works best for you.

Many of the topics that this book covers are addressed by other entire books from many and various fields. There are a huge number of these books to read and few of us make the time, spend the energy, or have the inclination to sift through this mountain for the really useful ones. We will refer to some of the best ones in 'Remarkable Resources' boxes throughout the text. As very few of these books are actually focused on academic careers and jobs – which we view (discussed in Chapter 1) as being similar yet also different to other jobs – we will address the applicability of these to academic workplaces and workers. Recognizing the new world in which scholarship operates similarly, insights to workplace effectiveness are commonly covered on social media (try searching Twitter for #worksmarter or #workhacks). These are useful, but in isolation from bigger and broader directions and approaches represent a textbook example of placing tasks before strategy. The Core allows you to use such resources, but within a broader and more integrated approach.

In closing this introduction, we hope that wherever you have come from and wherever you are going on your academic journey, this book helps. We hope that for those in their early career, the book fosters optimism and insights for the challenges ahead. For those with more years behind them than ahead, we hope that it helps rekindle memories of why you chose academic work and proves useful for the time that remains. Academic workplaces, those in them and the work they do, are different and special. While our journeys are very different, few are easy, but we believe that they should and can be more effective, more successful, and happier. So, let's go!

1

ACADEMIC KNOWLEDGE WORK AS EXTREME KNOWLEDGE WORK

> The most valuable assets of a 20th-century company was its production equipment.
> The most valuable asset of a 21st-century institution (whether business or nonbusiness)
> will be its knowledge workers and their productivity.
>
> (Drucker, 1999: 79)

How did you end up in academic work? Why? What pieces of golden advice have helped you most in your work so far? Which were the feeblest irrelevant misfires? Few of us work in academic workplaces because we are indifferent to learning, education or knowledge. Our place in this work has its origins in deep thoughts, motivations, decisions, and sometimes wild serendipity. Yet, academic work across and between academic workplaces and workers is defined mostly by difference. How then to make any comments – let alone steps for effectiveness, success and happiness – when diversity so dominates?

This chapter is about the nature of academic workers, workplaces, and work, but it also dwells on that which more deeply unites this academic work. In it, we shall show why academic work – fully and completely – is extreme knowledge work, and we shall consider the implications of this for those who do this work. We make space, too, for you to reflect on your own view of academic knowledge work and your place within it. Finally, we conclude that it is important for those seeking to be more successful, effective, and happy in academic work to understand and approach this academic work, not as mere tasks, inputs, or hours expended but as *extreme knowledge work*. The conception of academic work as extreme knowledge work is a foundation of this book.

Sounds all too uniform? Indeed, differences abound between academic work, workers, and workplaces. The UK, Australia, and Italy have national performance assessment exercises for research and teaching, while other countries have none. Public universities are the norm in some places but the exception in others. Academic workers have more job security than almost any other type of worker in some parts of the world, whereas management can hire and fire academic workers relatively easily in other parts of the world. Profound variations extend to the nature of the work that academic workers do. Academic work stretches from bench science to population-based qualitative research. Good luck getting consensus on what success looks like, for example between the relative esteem of teaching versus research or of books, journals, and patents. Daily work patterns can vary markedly around individual autonomy, managerial involvement, and workplace expectations.

Such issues touch the daily lives of almost all academic workers, from doctoral students to university presidents, from issues of whether comics represent a viable genre for doctoral theses to how student teaching can be evaluated at the institutional level. What shape does work need to be in order to step across from casual contracts to permanent work? What are the rewards for spending the next hour writing a definitive teaching textbook versus writing another journal manuscript? How much should you focus on improving your student feedback versus improving your next publication? We could go on and on and on ... every working hour of every working day of the academic worker, variation upon variation. The immense diversity of academic work, workers, and workplaces raises immediate and unavoidable challenges, which make conclusions and comparisons precarious, and produce manifold tensions and pushes and pulls for individual academic workers, their workplaces and societies. Across all of these variations, what then is academic work?

WHAT IS ACADEMIC KNOWLEDGE WORK?

'Academic knowledge work' is extreme knowledge work done by academic workers. To consider what this means, we first consider the nature of knowledge work.

What is knowledge work?

Peter Drucker (1967) first popularized the term 'knowledge worker' to describe professionals whose work involves a rich mix of thinking, problem-solving, action, and interactions with others. Unlike manufacturing work, knowledge work requires technical and people skills. As inputs bring no guarantees of outputs in knowledge work, its success is determined only by what is produced: years can be spent working to no discernable success, while a mere moment of insight can be ground-breaking. Knowledge work is far less routinized than manufacturing work and requires workers who are highly educated and autonomous (ibid.). Knowledge itself – rather than machines of manufacturing – are the means of production in knowledge work (Arthur et al., 2008).

More recently, knowledge workers have been defined as those who create, distribute and apply knowledge (ibid.) – a definition with immediate resonance with academic work. Knowledge workers use: *know why*, *know how*, and *know whom*. They have a clear, personal and sometimes deep sense of values: they *know why* they do the work (Drucker, 1999; Arthur et al., 2008). They *know how* to get work done in both technical and interpersonal realms: what methods to use but also how to go about their work and *with whom* to work with – the other people in teams, organizations or communities (Arthur et al., 2008). The effectiveness of the knowledge worker depends then, not only on the individual but also on those with whom they work and interact. In knowledge work, other people can make doing the right things difficult, very time-consuming, or even impossible.

The success of knowledge work depends on *getting the right things done*, then acquiring the knowledge to do the next right thing (Drucker, 1967). Due to the demands of others, time is always insufficient for knowledge workers to do all that could be done. Success involves making the right choice of what to do. This sounds deceptively easy. Yet, choosing the right things to do from the infinite gamut of all that could be done is actually very difficult because the world is replete with known knowns, unknown knowns, known unknowns, and also unknown unknowns (Rumsfeld quoted in Department of Defense, 2002). How then to select what is the right thing to do?

Success in knowledge work is evident from outcomes – not inputs or processes. The knowledge worker should always seek to be effective: that is, to get the right things done (ibid.). Work success is not defined by the workers' quantity of work hours or even by the quantity of work, but simply by whether the work achieves the desired ends. For the academic worker, what paper will be written next and why? How best can student feedback or study recruitment be improved? What research grant should be worked on most? Decisions proliferate but the right next thing to do does not self-identify. Work needing attention does not even clearly label itself as being a problem of a particular type: the academic worker perceived by others (but not by themselves) as a bully may assume wrongly that having a more visible office will render them more approachable to others. Understanding, framing, and perception influence not only how problems are solved but even if or how problems are seen in the first place.

Yet, doing the right things is achieved far more by good habits than talent or skills (ibid.). Indeed, Drucker (ibid.) argued that all manner of intellectually brilliant people are also wildly ineffective as knowledge workers. They did things right – but they did the wrong things. In the face of academic work, many caution that academic work is too immense in variety and volume, too complex in nature and too mired in institutional, contractual, or country-based differences to be tamed into effectiveness. We disagree. More of the right work can be done right in academic workplaces but this won't happen by magic. In future chapters, we propose that The Success Pyramid can help this happen by better identification of what the right tasks are to do, while The Core can help you to do these well. First, though, we move to a deeper consideration of the nature of academic knowledge work as extreme knowledge work.

THE NATURE OF ACADEMIC KNOWLEDGE WORK

Academic knowledge work is clearly and completely knowledge work. Let's consider this in relation to the main types of academic work: research, teaching, and engagement work.

Research as academic knowledge work

The most common route into academic work is via the undertaking of a higher degree with a research component, usually a thesis or dissertation. This research could be exclusively philosophical, but more commonly involves the use of an overt method to collect data either from primary sources (for example, human beings, other animals, or the world) or secondary sources (from existing other research as with systematic reviews). Throughout their career, many types of academic workers are expected to have research in their work portfolio – research is to be done, published and hopefully used by others. Research work is knowledge work in source, impetus, means, and ends. Knowledge is used to justify, guide, undertake and, in turn, is then produced by research.

Research is accomplished using both skills and knowledge to produce knowledge. During doctoral degrees, academic workers become aware of existing knowledge ('literatures') in their areas, become proficient in the methods needed to complete their degree, and apply their skills accordingly to read, think, collect data, philosophize, problem-solve, work with supervisors and, crucially, write to complete their degrees.

New knowledge is the product of research but is then also applied in various forms (knowing how, who and why) throughout the process of doing research. Existing knowledge is applied during the course of research, from how to effectively manage and relate to other staff and students, to the application of theories to interpret research. Consider the skills now needed to undertake a systematic review of literature. This involves 'know how' skills in forming researchable questions from abstract thoughts and of the substantive literature and the patterns that exist therein – a task that has been memorably termed 'forcing the octopus into the jar' (Kamler and Thomson, 2014).

'Know how' and 'know who' skills are needed. Work with librarians is required to develop the systematic search (including the right key terms, combinations and databases) based on the question. Interpretation skills are needed to assess the quality of papers using different methods. Skills associated with supervising a research assistant to carry out the work and provide useful feedback to increase their performance may be employed. Knowledge of the principles of high-quality systematic reviews are used to ensure that the review contains only the studies that it should. All manner of processing and language skills are used to interpret the often messy, incomplete and meaningless data that are found. The meaning of the reviewed data, the conclusions, and caveats emerge from the integration of interpretations, principles and considerations. Meaning does not inherently jump out from the data but emerges from working with the data. All the while, 'knowing why' the review is being done may be important: What need it meets for whom?

The lack of a relationship between inputs and outputs is evident in research. Some academic workers labour for years exploring various research cul-de-sacs before suddenly and unexpectedly making profound contributions. Others work harder for longer but never make their intended breakthroughs at all. Further still, lucky others stumble on major developments serendipitously.

Teaching as academic knowledge work

Historically, teaching – not research – defined academic workplaces. Teaching in academic workplaces encompasses giving formal lectures or facilitating seminars or individual student supervision. Some academic workers only teach, while others do little or no formal teaching altogether.

Teaching, though diverse, is also academic knowledge work – involving knowing how, who and why. In the past, approaches to teaching methods tended to be normative, guiding teachers to organize knowledge into patterns, presenting facts and generalizations clearly, and fostering understanding and fair assessment (Ricca, 2012). However, these principles do not take account of differences in students' experiences, backgrounds, cultures, and learning (ibid.). This placed further demands on the educator to individualize, contextualize, and personalize their teaching.

Variations abound around teaching in different workplaces with markedly different amounts of teaching in terms of time, mode (for example, face-to-face versus online), course numbers or student numbers, levels of autonomy, support and prescription of teaching methods to be employed. Quality of knowledge work around teaching remains contested. Student evaluation is useful and important, but also does not necessarily measure actual teaching quality (Spooren et al., 2013).

For academic workers, teaching can be challenging, difficult, and exhilarating. Many have progressed through doctoral studies with limited formal educational qualifications and skills but are then expected to teach and engage students in a wide range of classroom settings, from small groups to large lectures.

As with research, inputs and outputs are not proportional. A single exquisitely crafted example could yield more understanding in a student than a three-hour lecture. More assessment is not necessarily better assessment, particularly when assessments are not discriminating or do not have clear objectives. Knowledge remains the source, means and ends of teaching – wherein knowledge is applied to impart content or understanding of key concepts to students in order to increase their knowledge. More clearly than research work, teaching academic work involves 'knowing who', an interpersonal and direct connection between teacher and learner.

Engagement as academic knowledge work

In addition to teaching and research, the presence and influence of academic workers outside of their workplaces has become increasingly legitimate and important. In past decades, academic work in this area has focused more on communicating the results of research to other academics and students. However, over the last 10 years, a much greater focus has been placed on the social impact of research (Bornmann, 2013), commercialization via spin-off companies, patents and engagement via many diverse means. Consequently, engagement can now occur in all manner of ways and to all manner of groups. Research can be communicated to the public and to practitioners in applied fields through a variety of means, including mass media (like newspapers, radio, internet, and television) and social media (including platforms such as blogs, Twitter, Snapchat, Facebook, and Instagram). Reviews can be done for journals, conferences can be organized and appraisals of others' research can be done for grant review panels. Once more, this challenges the skillset of the traditional academic worker trained to communicate with other, similar, researchers.

All this work is knowledge work. Some of this work may be allocated or 'suggested' by other more senior academic workers such as heads of department, but great flexibility remains for most academic workers to choose the 'engagement' work that they take on, how they choose to do this work and how it synergizes with their teaching and research.

In summary, of course, it is impossible to even begin to capture the richness and diversity of knowledge work that occurs in research, teaching, and engagement. Yet, across each of these realms, academic knowledge work offers the supreme example of knowledge applied to itself. In teaching and research, this knowledge even produces new knowledge. In academic work, knowledge is the beginning, the end, and the means.

THE CHALLENGE OF 'EXTREME KNOWLEDGE WORK' FOR ACADEMIC WORKERS

Knowledge work is then everywhere and almost everything in academic work (Cortada, 1998b). Given the sheer ubiquity of workers now labelled as 'knowledge workers' (ibid., 1998a), has the term lost its special significance? Still, we see academic work as being different from this more general picture of knowledge work. More particularly, we see academic knowledge work as an extreme manifestation or form of knowledge work.

ACADEMIC WORK IS EXTREME KNOWLEDGE WORK

Completely knowledge work

Knowledge is the source, motivation, means, and product of academic work. While this raises challenges over 'what isn't knowledge' (Blackler, 1995), nevertheless, by even the most restrictive definitions, knowledge is ubiquitous in academic work in research, education, and engagement. It is the work of the head, not of the hand (Defillippi et al., 2006).

As academic workers' careers progress, demands on their skills and knowledge broaden and deepen. Whereas expectations of students (as expressed in their submitted theses, dissertations and oral defences) focus on methodological proficiency and substantive knowledge (Bogle et al., 2010), career progression in research places more demands on 'softer skills' such as working with people, leading diverse teams, and resolving conflict. More complex demands relate to the ability of the academic worker to be highly creative under pressure, to sustain teams, to work effectively in ambiguous contexts, and to reconcile their ethical and personal conduct with the perceived need to get or to keep a job or to be seen as successful. Training and support to do this in academic workplaces is the exception rather than the norm.

Highly educated

Despite declining social status, salaries and job security, entry qualifications and ongoing competitiveness around academic work has not declined. Most salaried academic workers are required not only to have an undergraduate degree but usually a higher degree as well – often a doctorate. In some countries and disciplines, a period of postdoctoral experience is seen to be a necessary for independent research. Even then, it takes about a decade to be seen as progressing from being 'junior'. As knowledge workers, academic workers are unusually highly educated in terms of years and standards, and this shows little sign of abating.

Most of this education is in formal qualifications rather than job-related skills. While doctoral education has focused predominantly on developing extensive and deep methodological and substantive knowledge, the actual demands of academic work extend far wider to encompass workplace skills, approaches and reactions to uncertainty, leading teams and managing people – amongst many, many other things (Bogle et al., 2010). This can create difficulties when academic workers confuse an expertise in substantive and methodological domains with a proficiency across all work domains.

Establishing, leading and sustaining teams around teaching and research is a common need in academic work (Lungeanu et al., 2014). Research is increasingly interdisciplinary and the academic workers' ability to work with others outside of their disciplines is important. Increasingly, research funding bodies now specifically call for team-based research approaches. Out of all the research program announcements made by the National Institute of Health and the National Science Foundation in 2010 in the USA, 46 per cent specifically called for either 'interdisciplinary' or 'multidisciplinary' research approaches or both (Begg and Vaughan, 2011). The proportion of papers published by teams has increased from 17.5 per cent in 1955 to 51.5 per cent in 2000, with team size growing from an average of 1.9 to 3.5 authors per paper in the same period (Wuchty et al., 2007). Despite a growing expectation of working in teams, academic workers remain educated, evaluated, and discussed mostly as individuals. Yet, how many of these research teams have the characteristics of high-performing teams? How many are mere lists of people? While necessary, being highly educated and proficient in substantive and methodological domains is insufficient for academic work. 'Highly educated for what ...?' one might ask.

High autonomy

Autonomy in academic work is a place of marked concern and contention. Academic workers increasingly bemoan ongoing reductions in their freedom to teach, research, and engage at both the institutional and individual level (Henkel, 2005 and 2007). Flexibility around academic work patterns and work content mitigates the stress associated with longer working hours and high demands, particularly in relation to working from home or at flexible times of the day (Darabi et al., 2017). Despite these benefits, the perceived growth of audit and managerial cultures in academic workplaces has led to concerns in some countries about the perceived decline in the autonomy and freedom of academic workers (Henkel, 2005). While historical interpretations of what constituted autonomy in academic work were varied and academic workers in more research-intensive workplaces have preserved high autonomy, autonomy in academic work is no longer a perceived right (Henkel, 2007; Kok et al., 2010) but is a contested and variable practise, which is often codified in more prescriptive contractual terms and shorter or otherwise less permanent academic positions (Musselin, 2013). Critical literature around these developments – variously labelled as managerialist, neo-liberalist, or corporatization – has raised issue of whether trends toward lowered autonomy represent reasonable societal checks and balances versus harmful ideological tools of power and oppression (Woodhouse, 2009; Barnett, 2011; Rolfe, 2013).

Where does this increased casualization and move away from autonomy leave academic workers? In absolute terms, the autonomy of the vast majority of academic workers in different countries has declined in the last 30 years (Musselin, 2013). The glass is, indeed, emptier than it has been historically. Academic workers are, in the main, evaluated more often, steered to teach well and attain high teaching evaluations, publish in journals of higher impact or visibility, move graduate students through to success against particular timelines and, in some disciplines, apply and obtain peer-reviewed grant funding.

That said, considerable absolute and relative advantages around freedoms still remain for academic workers. At the individual level, very few other types of knowledge workers function in the absence of any external constraints, reporting requirements or incentives. Indeed, unlike academic workers, many types of knowledge workers are assigned work projects and deadlines and – even in highly innovative organizations – have only a small proportion of their time for discretionary projects. It is entirely normal for knowledge workers to have to work toward particular defined ends, have to record and report their work or have some parameters placed on the processes through which work is attained. While concerns around low autonomy in academic work are understandable, these reflect the more autonomous past as much as the challenges of the present.

Seared with personal values

A commonality across many academic workers is that their academic work, in their eyes, cannot be reduced to simple 'tasks' that are performed or hollow platitudes about 'excellence' in academic work (Wood and Su, 2017). This work instead expresses deeper values and motivations (Darabi et al., 2017). These are often intertwined around broader aspects of identity related to particular aspects of the academic worker role, notably teaching (van Lankveld et al., 2017), gender (Bostock, 2014) or generational affiliation (Darabi et al., 2017).

To teach new nurses, doctors, or engineers, to teach new technologies, to make a difference, to cure a disease, to continue the legacy of past pioneers, to help particular communities, to develop a discipline – all manner of values and aspirations are played out in and through research work. Due to the nature of knowledge work and the especially high autonomy of academic workers, academic knowledge workers are particularly motivated by their personal values and volitions.

The place of values in academic work is incredibly important and we will discuss this in more detail in Chapter 2. Values help motivate and guide decisions on the work that is taken on board and completed, can inform career choices and contribute to the rich diversity of academic workers and work. Values also allow academic workers to fulfil their scholarly visions, to approach and understand academic work with a deeper and more profound understanding of 'why': why take on the challenge of supervising a challenging student, why seek to be published in a particular journal, why choose to teach in a new innovative way when it makes you uncomfortable? Values are essential to academic work.

Critical of organization, loyal to discipline

The individual attitudes that academic workers have, of course, vary widely. However, compared to other types of knowledge workers, academic knowledge workers tend to be more critical of their immediate employers, while being more loyal to and furthering the interests of their discipline (Deem, 2004). This represents the opposite of other types of knowledge workers, who tend to be less attached to their discipline (Arthur et al., 2008).

This can create challenges for those who seek to lead or manage academic workers, especially taking account of the high autonomy, education, and value-laden nature of academic work. Government and senior management often challenge those in leadership or management roles in academic workplaces, with expectations to provide and deliver around specific activities and indicators. This is what makes these roles both fascinating and also extremely challenging.

No upper thresholds

Academic work has both inputs and outputs like any other kind of work. However, in terms of outputs, academic work remains devoid of clear maximum output expectations. The quality of teaching resources can never be perfected. There is no upper threshold to how 'big' one's research can become; there is always another paper that can be published, grant proposal written or activity engaged in.

Yet, major contributions to knowledge occur only over the long term, usually after many failures and often in uncertain contexts. Historical accounts of academic workers, such as pioneering scientists, tend to write out this blur, and the doubts, insecurities and fears that it brings (Clark and Thompson, 2013). In the midst of this, how do academic workers manage the volume, time, energy, and quality of their work? The issues around this are key aspects of effectiveness, success, and happiness in this book.

Academic research work occurs in the world replete with organizational, governmental and fiscal change, conflicts, and constraints. It occurs through the thoughts and actions of knowledge workers, who are influenced by emotions, thoughts, and often doubts. The lack of upper thresholds in academic work and the difficulties around how quality and success should be judged can lead to high levels of ambiguity and even self-doubt.

Variations in academic knowledge work and workers

The brief overviews of research, teaching, and engagement that we have provided cannot begin to do justice to the diversity of the work done by academic workers. This work is also ever changing, raising interesting challenges. Must academic work, for example, be confined to universities and colleges? How should academic work be approached and evaluated in ways that comprehend and respect its immense diversity, scope, and depth?

There is some extremely rich and thought-provoking work on the nature, evolution, and purposes of academic places (Boulton and Lucas, 2008; Barnett, 2011). While many of those working in academic workplaces have grown accustomed to ongoing change and some lament a past era of stasis and stability, the last 300 years of academic workplaces are characterized by ongoing change (Barnett, 2011). Change is not new but defines the growth and evolution of the sector. What, too, of those conducting academic work outside of traditional academic settings? While research is clearly carried out by all manner of different corporate and non-corporate organizations, our focus here is on those carrying out academic work under the auspices, if not the roofs, of academic workplaces. Differences even in these different institutions, old and new, abound in focus, philosophies, priorities, and academic worker attitudes (Kok et al., 2010).

Tasks and overall job portfolios differ, too. The degree to which academic workers can make choices around their research, teaching and engagement work – expressing their values, expertise and preferences, and reflecting their seniority and locality – generates an impressively wide diversity of work across different people, departments, and disciplines. Some academics focus predominantly or even exclusively on teaching in their roles, while others mostly do research. Some focus intently on external functions, such as community engagement or social media, while others barely give this a second of consideration or effort. Selective academics take administrative roles, acting as heads of departments, some become research chairs, whereas others delight in teaching students throughout their whole career. Diversity is also everywhere in terms of function.

The tremendous range and scope of work that an academic worker does or could do in research, teaching, and engagement raises distinctive challenges for those seeking to evaluate their own or others' academic work. For example, while most academics would agree that quality of research is important, disagreements proliferate on what this looks like, how it should be measured or whether it is measurable at all. What success should and does look like is prone to stunningly wide variation. Quality of research, teaching, and engagement remains hard to define and measure and is notoriously contested around the importance of quality, quantity, and visibility of outputs. How much merit is ascribed to publishing a single definitive book or five published papers in impactful journals versus 10 in any journals? How many presentations of the research should be made, to whom and at what venues, meetings and conferences? To what degree are teaching evaluations from students key to evaluating teaching quality? Is attending departmental talks and meetings expected or truly optional? Variations across disciplines also abound in the perceived value of different kinds of outputs, measures, and citation practises. Such questions go on and on ...

Clearly, not all research, teaching, and engagement efforts are of similar quality, but how is this quality to be discriminated, measured, and compared? Does diversity of academic knowledge work and its links to skills and expertise (Blackler, 1995; Alvesson, 2001; Arthur et al., 2008;) render futile attempts to evaluate quality? Given that quality can be contested so much, even knowledge workers themselves come to question their competency (Alvesson, 2001): *Am I any good?* Doubt, fear, and vulnerability, as we cover in Chapters 7 and 8, all too frequently accompany academic work, particularly in the face of failure. In the context of the high autonomy of academic knowledge workers, this scope creates challenges for developing standards, categories or expected outcomes (such as in job or promotion applications and annual reviews). Confusion and anxiety results around expectations, excellence, and career progress. The challenge of evaluating work around quality is not an unusual predicament for knowledge workers but creates challenges for those seeking to evaluate and compare the relative merits of academic work and workers across disciplines, fields, and departments.

This diversity immediately questions the wisdom and veracity of anyone seeking to say anything universal or even widely applicable about academic work, workers, and workplaces. To do so undermines or downplays the manifold complexities and nuances of each. A challenge, indeed, for any book, workshop, or resource that seeks the noble ends of making academic workers more successful, effective, and happy! Herein lies the unavoidable problem with universalistic, prescriptive, and immensely alluring 'tricks-and-tips' approaches to academic life: these assume wrongly that norms, standards, and even cultures are similar and static across different fields, disciplines, and departments (Kamler and Thomson, 2008). We may well know what will work in our 'world' but whether this holds in the next department is a whole different matter. As such, this book focuses throughout on tools, resources, and insights that should be applied to personal situations. While some generalities are inevitable and useful, we try at all times to take account of and be responsive to variations in aspiration, context, and norms across disciplines, countries, and organizations.

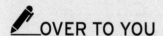 OVER TO YOU

Knowledge Work and You

Academic work is extreme knowledge work but because of this it can also be extremely challenging. Think about the following questions.

For everyone

1. Why did you choose to do academic work? What were your initial reasons or motivations?

(Continued)

2. What are the three biggest challenges that you grapple with in the academic work that you currently do?

3. What challenges did you least expect?

4. Which challenges were you best prepared to address? How?

5. Which challenges were you least well prepared to address?

6. What scares or worries you most about your future?

Mid- and senior career academic workers

1. What has most helped you to do academic work effectively over the course of your career?

2. What has most hindered your capacity and ability to do academic work effectively over the course of your career?

3. What achievement or action has made you most proud in your academic work?

4. What is your biggest regret about your academic journey so far?

━━━━ REMARKABLE RESOURCES ━━━━

Imagining the University by Ronald Barnett

What are academic workplaces and what could they be? Ronald Barnett's (2013) extraordinary book is no dull treatise on the purpose of academic workplaces but a creative,

(Continued)

expansive, and optimistic vision of the work and possible places of publicly funded academic workplaces in modern societies.

Key messages

- The academic workplace has always been changing. Change is nothing new there.
- Academic workplaces are extremely diverse, conceivably with over 100 different functions.
- Aspiration is vital to academic workplaces – imagine and attempt to create *feasible utopias* to truly push toward what can be done and achieved individually and collectively in academic workplaces, in amidst the macro-structural and contextual factors in which they now must operate.

Key applications

- Argues for the importance and contribution of positive visioning in academic work, challenging academic workers to envision work positively and creatively, beyond seemingly constrictive academic workplace structures.
- Gives insights into the immense diversity and potentiality of academic work and workplaces beyond the entrepreneurial university, with a vast array of different conceptions of academic workplaces.
- Challenges via the concept of 'feasible utopia' in order to conceive academic work that strongly aligns imaginative personal values with realistic external expectations. Where can this sweet spot be in your academic work?

SECTION 1

CHOOSING THE RIGHT ACADEMIC WORK

The Success Pyramid

I am a great admirer of mystery and magic. Look at this life - all mystery and magic.

(Harry Houdini)

Doing the right academic work is essential but far from easy. Sometimes, we are in a place where everything just flows: motivation comes easily, and other people welcome us and the contribution of our work. *This* is why we do academic work. Other times, academic work isn't like this. We feel resigned to doing too much and too much of the 'wrong' work. Doubt, disenfranchisement and hollowness may dominate. We may even question whether academic work is right for our career. Further still, others may be dismissive, hostile or apathetic to our work, but we are doing the right work, nevertheless. All these scenarios occur because academic work, as extreme knowledge work, incorporates our values and our judgement of what constitutes success.

Selecting the right work to do *and then* doing it well are pivotal to being successful, effective, and happy in academic work. That said, selecting the right work to do does not happen by magic. What does this mean? What looks smooth actually requires lots of underlying work behind the scenes to do the right thing well.

DOING THE 'RIGHT' WORK DOES NOT HAPPEN BY MAGIC

At one level, this very un-magical 'law' brings us back to the realities of academic work as extreme knowledge work, in which inputs don't map to or equate with outputs and choices abound. Further still, the right work is not necessarily the easier work, the obvious work, or the popular work. The right work *and* its underlying selection must be based on conscious, deliberated, mindful choices. If we are not selecting the right thing to do in the first place, all manner of efforts may be wasted – even if those things are done well. They are quite simply the wrong things, done right.

The chapters in this section address how to select what this right academic work is. That is, how to select that work that needs to be done first, who can determine this and what this process should take into account.To help with the process of selecting the right work, we will introduce a key tool: 'The Success Pyramid'. The chapters will then break down the pyramid's levels or strata into its interlinked parts related to: success and its indicators, priorities, goals, and tasks.

GETTING THE MOST FROM THE SUCCESS PYRAMID

Before we move to specifics, it's useful to understand the nature and purpose of The Success Pyramid (S1.1).

Purpose of The Success Pyramid

'The Success Pyramid' helps to select the right work to be done from all that can be done. It offers a way of seeing and approaching work that can be used to identify the right work to do. Using the pyramid requires the active input, thought, reflection, perceptions, and skills of each person who uses it. Consequently, throughout this book, we have provided various iterations of The Success Pyramid that you can personalize.

Nature of The Success Pyramid

The Success Pyramid consists of a number of linked strata that collectively and individually serve the overall purpose of selecting the right work. The pyramid does this for academic work by offering a means to integrate personal values with a deliberate specification of what success is ('success indicators'). This identification then informs what should be: prioritized ('priorities'), sought ('goals') and done ('tasks').

We will address each of these strata in the subsequent chapters in this section. These different strata respectively relate to:

- *Success indicators*: Valid and intended aspiration(s) for academic work.
- *Priorities*: That which should be done first to meet a success indicator(s).
- *Goals*: The shorter-term ends needed to further priorities.
- *Tasks*: The actions needed to meet goals.

In our final chapter of this section, we will consider why and how to link between the strata of The Success Pyramid and between multiple pyramids. We call this 'strategy'.

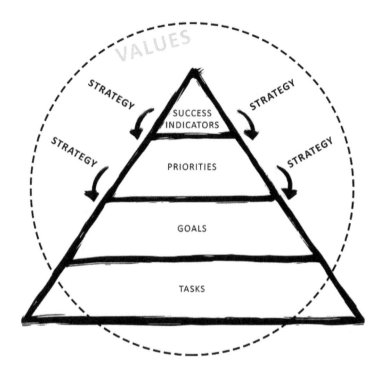

S1.1   The Success Pyramid

Use of The Success Pyramid

Use of The Success Pyramid is in itself straightforward. An appraisal of values (and external factors) informs the selection of success indicators, which then leads to the identification of priorities. These inform the selection of goals and then tasks. As such, there should be a clear and readily perceivable flow from success indicators through to priorities, which should then map to goals and tasks. Problems, as we shall identify in the following chapters, arise when success indicators are not set in the first place, strata are confused or when strata are insufficiently linked.

The content of the pyramid is very personal because academic work is always personal and value-laden. We pointedly recognize that academic workers in different places and at different stages have different levels of autonomy, self-determination, and privilege. More prescribed or fixed aspects set by a line manager or supervisor can also be incorporated into the pyramid.

We also suggest that each academic worker usually should set multiple success indicators for their work. A doctoral student may seek to complete their thesis and also to publish credibly during their doctoral studies. Because of this, we suggest that separate pyramids be used for each success indicator. With time and practise using The Success Pyramid, those using multiple pyramids may be able to select common priorities, goals, and tasks across them – we view this as the epitome of 'good strategy'. However, for now, it is important to realize that each pyramid should not contain too much or relate to more than one success indicator.

COMMON CHALLENGES WITH THE SUCCESS PYRAMID

The Success Pyramid is both easy and challenging. Many workshops have demonstrated to us that coming up with the right things for each strata can be intellectually difficult, provocative and personally vexing. The most common challenges with using it are as follows.

Content is hard to specify

It can sometimes be difficult to readily specify the content of different strata in the pyramid. For example, some academic workers struggle with addressing the big picture questions around success indicators. To them, success is not immediately obvious because they have not stepped away to think about this for a long time. Dealing with the next project, or paper, or class, they have not stepped back to ask themselves what larger purposes these serve.

When it is difficult to select and specify such content, we strongly urge taking time away to reflect, read and even be distracted by other things. This will help, as later chapters will explain, to select the right success indicators, priorities, goals, and tasks. Given that academic work is extreme knowledge work, at any one point (or stratum) there is usually a bewildering – even sometimes paralyzing – array of choices of what could be done. Taking time (even a long time) to identify which priority is 'most right' is more important and far more valuable than quickly throwing oneself behind an alluring but ultimately misplaced end.

Confusing levels

It is not uncommon to confuse different levels of the pyramid. Most commonly, this occurs when 'goals' are conflated with 'success indicators'. For example, a new professor who mislabels the 'goal' of publishing three papers per year as a 'success indicator' fails to specify the bigger, longer-term aim(s) that publishing with such frequency will serve. In this case the 'success indicator' could be to publish continuously, credibly, and visibly, or to become known in one's field.

Coming back to the definition that we have provided for each level of The Success Pyrimid and understanding the worked examples in this book should help to clearly separate the nature of the different strata and how they link to each other.

Values are omitted

The value-laden nature of academic work reflects the nature of extreme knowledge work, provides an important ethical compass for academic work, and helps facilitate long-term engagement and motivation with this work.

Yet, immersed in the practical demands of getting or keeping an academic job or a viable career, it is easy to leave one's values behind. In the next chapter, we will outline some of the harms of this for ourselves, our workplaces, and for society's trust in academic workers.

As it addresses extreme knowledge work, we recommend that personal values inform work with The Success Pyramid. Even in instances in which success indicators and priorities seem fixed by supervisors or workplaces, academic work (as extreme knowledge work) still leaves scope for individuality and the incorporation of values. The Success Pyramid is not merely a cognitive tool but is also a means to thread values through and across one's academic work more determinedly and mindfully.

Believing that the right work is selected by magic

We are all eager sometimes to do the wrong things right and get that alluring sense of ready satisfaction and achievement that more completed tasks yield. Emails take precedence over writing, or organizing our office over having a difficult conversation with a colleague: very human responses, but ones that will not help effectiveness. Consequently, we have seen our workshop attendees underestimate the necessity of carefully going through the pyramid from 'success indicators' right through to tasks.

Yet, this careful step-by-step exposition opens up space to consider if one is really engaged in the right work. Resistance to going through this process is often more about avoiding the dawning and destabilizing brute realization that one has wasted past efforts or is on the wrong track. Being open to the questions that The Success Pyramid poses is vital to doing the right work. As we often say at our workshops: If specifying your success indicators, priorities, goals, and tasks feels hard, this is because it is.

2

VALUES IN ACADEMIC WORK

If you don't know why, you can't know how.

(Sinek, 2009: 70)

'I just felt an academic job was not for me …,' Paul, a final-year doctoral student, confides about his impending choice to leave academia on completion of his thesis. Difficulties and tensions between his supervisors had blighted his progress. Petty squabbles seemed to him to trump the importance of his research and the issues that it sought to address. Academic workers, in Paul's, eyes were fretful, fearful, and overworked, motivated by a system that promoted vain insecurity, personal fear, and pettiness. The academic path was not for him. It was the antithesis, Paul explained, of the openness, dynamism, and confidence that he had expected to find in a university. Resigned and disappointed, he was now pursuing career options outside of academia. The contributions that will be missed by this decision will never be known.

VALUES AND IDENTITY IN ACADEMIC WORK AND WORKERS

What drives your academic work? Who are you and what do you stand for? Who do you stand with? Most academic workers come into this work for conscious reasons. During our workshops and in our own jobs, we observe a vast range of different values guiding academic work. Whether related to influencing or improving other people's lives, addressing social justice, challenging orthodoxy or wonderment over complexity, a career in academic work usually requires substantial ongoing reasons to seek, start, and stay on the path. These motivations are bound up in how people see themselves, what is important to them and to their personality and predilections. We see such factors coming together to influence the values that guide academic work. It is these values that we address in this chapter.

Values are about the 'why' of academic work. These values come from and are entwined in identities and can provide a deep rationale for academic work and self-expression. Drawing on Simon Sinek's book on workplace motivation, *Starting with Why* (2009), the 'why' fundamentally differs from considering the 'how', the 'who' and the 'what' of work. Indeed, the 'why'; of our work connects with the 'what' through the 'how' (Figure 2.1). These facets relate to the people, relationships, outcomes, processes, and tasks of what is needed to do work and what that work looks like. Conversely, the 'why' of work relates to deeper questions: 'By why … what is your purpose, cause or belief? … Why do you get out of bed in the morning? And WHY should anyone care?' (ibid.: 39). Throughout this chapter, we position this 'why' about academic work as being expressed in the *values* that guide this work and the *identities* and *motivations* of those who do this work: how we each see ourselves and what transcending values we identify with ourselves that motivate what we do.

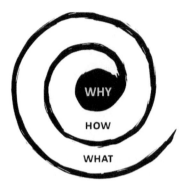

Figure 2.1   The Why, How, and What of Work

Source: Adapted from Sinek (2009)

As extreme knowledge workers, individual academic workers can and should bring their values to their work in teaching, research, and engagement (Table 2.1). Accordingly, academic work can and should be viewed not only in terms of how, who, and what, but also 'why'.

Table 2.1   Examples of the What, the How, and the Why of Academic Work

	What-focused	**How-focused**	**Why-focused**
Teaching	Teaching a four-hour class	Developing visual aids for teaching	Influencing a future generation
Research	Writing a research grant application	Obtaining research funding	Improving the lives of people with heart disease
Engagement	Attending external meetings	Serving on the local community ethics committee	Helping the homeless to be more respected and get better support

This 'why' piece in relation to work strikes a chord with something more basic in us, which is perhaps why values and identity are so closely linked. Sinek's TED Talk on the importance of 'why' has been viewed over 33 million times and his book on starting with 'why' has been used across a myriad of fields, including leadership, marketing, sales, and organizational wellness. Most workers (and workplaces), Sinek argues, just do not spend enough time and effort considering 'why' they do what they do: what the deeper purpose, cause, or beliefs are of their work. This is because the answers to 'why' tend to be seen as 'fuzzy', soft, contested, and tacit in organizations. Yet, it is the *why* that really inspires, motivates, and sustains us. It connects with something deeper, more transcending and more profound in us as human beings.

There is good evidence that over the duration of their careers, academic workers consider and deal extensively with their identity and values. This is partly because these are expressed and so closely related to writing (Lea and Stierer, 2011). Research with doctoral students shows that they engage in this identity-forming values-work, expressed when they undertake and write up their final thesis (Kamler and Thomson, 2008). The doctorate assumes, reflects and is oriented around disciplinary conventions, supervisor expectations and institutional policies but is also the first step toward forming and expressing identity and values relative to scholarship: finding and stating your place in the scholarly world.

The academic workers studied by Archer (2008) exemplify some of the ways in which the why of academic work is addressed: Embodying the development of a 'principled personal project' – an ongoing project of formation, generation and regeneration in the self that captured and expressed who they were and what they stood for in their research and teaching – is what discipline workers associated with and how they furthered its ends (Becher and Trowler, 2001). Similarly, a senior academic studied by Lea and Stierer (2011) informed his work as the head of his academic workplace with strong concepts of engagement, collaboration, and freedom that he saw as characterizing academic work and his workplace: this informed how he wrote about his institution in his high-level reports for the senior administration. Identity and values work can be channelled in other directions beyond writing: in approaches to teaching; in external committees served on; in the presence (or absence) of social media activity; and in the focus, process, and very aims of research. Values and identity are everywhere in academic work.

EXPLORING YOUR VALUES

While values are everywhere in academic work, they always and ever start with each of us individually. The values that we hold are at the centre of who we are and are influenced by our past experiences and with what we have identified. In short, we can't differentiate between 'work values' and 'life values'. Using a values inventory can help us identify with and position ourselves relative to those values that we hold most centrally: our core values. Completing an inventory can also help to identify the values that we don't identify with, those which may even cause us distress at the very thought of them. While there may be particular values that we hold that transcend all or most situations, values can also be situationally specific, with some values being more or less important to us in particular situations. For example, while valuing 'competition' might be very useful when seeking motivation for pursuing promotion, it can also be harmful when engaging in collegial relationships with others in your department. We might be ashamed of some of our values. The presence and implications of valuing 'being liked' may cause us distress when we need to fail a student or give negative feedback. Indeed, such feelings of discomfort are actually a clue as to the presence and influence of what we value even when we may not be aware that a value is so important to us. Those feelings point to what our values really are and sometimes they can be difficult to discern and acknowledge.

✎ OVER TO YOU

Exploring Your Values

Using the Values Inventory provided in Appendix 1:

1. My top five Core Values are:
* Select the values that you most identify with, those you wouldn't be you without:

2. The five values I least identify with are:

3. Why do I think that I have these Core Values? Where did they originate from?

4. What are the possible or likely conflicts between any of my Core Values?

VALUES AND INTEGRITY

Values that guide our academic work may be manifest in stated principles and priorities or more subtly in thoughts and perceptions. More than this, values are not just stated philosophical principles or theoretical ideas but, as we will cover later, are expressed in what actions and tasks should be prioritized. Values frame everything: not only whether we are successful, but what we believe success even is. Values should therefore be pervasive throughout and across academic work and unless such values are to be cast as mere ideals, values should influence how we see things and, crucially, our actions. Thus, values can have expression in a variety of ways in everyday academic work (Table 2.2).

Table 2.2 Examples of Values Guiding Academic Work

Values	Explanation	Possible expression
Innovation	Challenges conventional thought and assumptions	Lead research to re-conceptualize basic concepts Liberate and empower students to challenge basic assumptions
Giving back	Prioritizes progressing knowledge in the public over personal or corporate interests	Engage with public via mass and social media
Creativity	Vehicle of self-expression, freedom and unboundedness	Undertake research and teaching that draws and expresses divergent thinking Draw from unusual sources to adopt new approaches
Making a difference	Prioritizes influence	Undertake research highly likely to be quoted or adopted by the most organizations or people
Order/ Control	Strong adherence to principles of method and procedure	Undertake research that is of the highest methodological quality over speed or hurried advancement Strict adherence to teaching procedures and regulations
Equity	Furthers the needs and interests of vulnerable or excluded populations	Lead research to raise awareness about vulnerable populations Teach students in all fields about inequalities and principles of social justice

When values and actions align, this reflects what the academic Brené Brown terms 'integrity', to choose 'courage over comfort;...what is right over what is fun, fast or easy; and...to practice our values rather than simply professing them' (2017: 98).

Integrity, the wide pervasiveness of values across academic work, and the deep and meaningful link between values and the very identities of academic workers lead to immense, intense, and ongoing challenges. These challenges relate partly to the need to work alongside academic workers who hold markedly different values, for example around, ambition and duty, or collaboration and independence. Because academic work is extreme knowledge work and much of this work is done with other people in larger workplaces (who also have their own stated organizational values and identities), the values of the individual academic worker always exist in the context of those held by others who may be and usually are different. How do we react and respond to the values that impinge on us?

Moreover, academic workers function in workplaces that are the axis for what has been an increasing range of pressures that are also value-laden and challenge their identities. In many countries, over the last 20 years, this has been associated with increasing accountability to governments and students for quality and relevance of teaching and research, reductions in autonomy, declining resources, increasing workloads, and performance assessment. For example, the principled projects of new academic workers described by Archer (2008) were seen to be squeezed from the outset. On the one hand, these workers sought to embody values of intellectual rigour, criticality, ethics, and professionalism but also felt under strain from a range of internal and external factors related to self-identified age, sex, class, and race, their staff categorization (rank and contract type) and conceptions of success.

Yet, academic identities remain at the centre of these forces and, arguably, as Lea and Stierer contend, are slower to respond because 'the political, economic, and institutional circumstances in which academics work have changed dramatically in recent years, but the essence of academic identity has largely remained fixed, resulting in acute tensions and dislocations' (2011: 608). How well academic workers' principled personal projects can endure, respond, and thrive in the midst of all these pushes and pulls remains key.

These challenges are very real. The academic workers studied by Ylijoki (2013) viewed success in academic work as requiring intense personal commitment, and found the time and energy required was increasingly incompatible with their other values, notably to be a good mother or father. Values do not necessarily always tally even when these coexist in the same person. Kuntz's (2012) account of academic workers illustrates both their perceived need for solitude to do their academic work and their lament that academic workplaces are too often deserted and un-collaborative. While holding incompatible values is likely to be very difficult, values are often in tension.

Values and identity in academic workers are intellectual: they are based on principles and can be defended through reason and argument. However, crucially, many academic workers also have intense passions around their values and identity. This arises because academic work is a particular kind of extreme knowledge work. As such, values and identity cannot only be situated in terms of the intellect but also have emotional and physical dimensions.

While some academic workers may readily dismiss the place of such 'feelings-based' elements in and to their work (you know who you are!), the very annoyance, sensations and intensity of likely reactions from some of you to this suggestion illustrates the very point: values and identity do not just function intellectually but can produce feelings, emotions and tension. These physical sensations and emotions can promote open intellectual questioning and reflection but also close-minded defensiveness. How can we deal with threat or tension around our values, yet preserve enough of our own 'why'? People do differ in their respective emphasis or reliance on these two domains; sometimes, such differences are terms to be associated with the 'left brain' versus the 'right brain'. Daniel H. Pink (2005) suggests that both are important in helping us to think in broader ways and make better decisions. It is important then to see reason and emotion – the physical and cognitive – as working together to help each other, rather than being in conflict.

One of the most common examples around emotions associated with values that we have heard in our workshops from academic workers, relates to their family/personal life and work life. While we may value collaboration, contribution and efficiency at work, we feel that these values are called into question when we express our values of commitment, parenting, and family when we need to leave a meeting that has run late to pick up our children from school. Seldom are these values issues overtly discussed but they tend to bubble under and manifest in unsidious comments and actions.

REACTIONS TO VALUE CONFLICTS IN ACADEMIC WORKPLACES

We now move to discuss some common scenarios in which values are played out in academic settings and to discuss the most common reactions and consequences of this. As we shall see, a range of reactions are common.

Values absent

Values can be too absent from academic work. In our experience, this mostly arises when academic workers do not recognize that it's 'okay,' 'normal', or 'acceptable' to draw on your values in academic work. More than this, we think that not only is it okay, but necessary and needed. More on this later. There may be many reasons for trying to keep your values out of your academic work: moving into academic work from other industries in which personal values are not seen to have a place in work, or situations in which research is carried out for other people and, as such, there is little sense of personal investment or influence over the work. Some academic jobs ostensibly provide no means of expressing personal academic values, such as contract research positions or those in workplaces that have highly centralized and prescribed performance expectations and evaluation. In such instances, the values of the institution seem to trump and drown out those held from within. That said, the sense of values being absent from academic work is also evident in established academics. Kuntz's (2012) interviews revealed the presence of firm boundaries between the highly value-laden research work undertaken by the academic workers in his study (which they termed 'my work') and the seemingly value-less engagement work done teaching students, on committees and with students within the physical workplace. Moreover, he concludes that the academic workers' 'connection to work practises took on an inverse relation to their proximity to their actual campus. Faculty felt most distant from work activities performed on campus and most aligned with work performed away from campus' (ibid.: 775).

The benefits of keeping your values absent from some or all of your academic work may well be a degree of self-preservation in the face of work that has been allocated to you. However, as Kuntz's account conveys, this tends to take academic workers away from their campus communities, thereby reducing the social capital, camaraderie, and mutual support that accrues from human contact during work. It also places teaching and research in opposition and reduces personal commitment to the former, while reducing social accountability for the latter.

Values eclipsed

'Staying honest,' author on scientific failure Stuart Firestein concludes, 'is the whole point of science' (2016: 149). Yet, a consequence of the subservience, separation, or removal of values from academic work is that other influences tend to take hold. During the past decade, there have been hundreds of well-publicized instances in which the conduct of individual academic workers in relation to their research has been questionable, dubious, and fraudulent. While there have been a number of high-profile instances of academic workers simply 'making up' data and/or results, the term *questionable research practices* has been coined (John et al., 2012) to describe the various underhand or 'grey' techniques that some academic workers have used to increase the perceived impact and significance of their research (Banks et al., 2016). These tactics include: selective reporting of data, finishing studies early, intentionally deceptive analysis or ignoring some data entirely (John et al., 2012). Some startling analyses have reported that *most* academic workers in some fields have done such actions (ibid.). While it is tempting to dismiss the methods of such studies (Fiedler and Schwarz, 2016) and attribute these practises to poor skills, the majority appear to be calculated and deliberate and as common in experienced academic workers (DuBois et al., 2013). Why do clever, seemingly well-established people engage in such practises? Despite the practises undermining academic workers and research in almost every way imaginable, the conduct is also a consequence of a broader context in which publishing pressures are very high (Banks et al., 2016), newsworthiness and highly cited papers are given disproportionate emphasis (Clark et al., 2015), and secure permanent academic jobs in many fields are scarce (ibid.). Career progression and economic necessity come to dominate and trump all manner of scholarly values associated with methodological rigour, ethics, and standards.

Subtler still are instances in which tensions between career and rigour in academic work play out, leading to a slight, yet firm, resistance to difference. Conflicts of interest can arise when individuals are overly vested in the results of their research due to their need to preserve or consolidate a perceived career foundation, stream of work or legacy. Personal drive and ambition to be known for or associated with a particular argument or to pioneer an individual approach can lead to a palpable defensiveness and resistance to competing arguments, people, and data. This blurs the line that can exist between being an advocate and being a scientist or scholar (Clark et al., 2015). Values associated with career, politics, personal, or disciplinary affiliations and ties, and costs of 'going against the grain', come to eclipse values associated with scholarship. Too often, these workers appear closed to competing models, play down inconsistencies in results, questioning the approaches that they advocate, and criticize contrary results for all manner of fairly common methodological flaws (Clark and Thompson, 2012). Likewise, some senior academic workers can come to view their role as advocating for particular interventions or approaches at the cost of suppressing students.

To some degree, all academic research deals with conflicts between personal interests and those of society, scholarship and science: this reflects the social nature of research and knowledge development and dissemination. In his fascinating account of knowledge creation, the philosopher R.G.A. Dolby (1996) describes such tensions as being very common in the social process of knowledge creation. In this way, certain questions are written out by the very way in which academic work is done in departments, groups, and institutions. Individuals' hunches, data, and framing come to be filtered and altered step-by-step between the academic workers' thoughts and what is written, contributed, shared, and discussed at local, national, and international realms. How truly open can we be to arguments that go against those we have made in the past? This question cuts to the nub of where research and values meet. While the social nature of research is incontestable, placing exclusive focus on this context as a determinant of questionable research practices downplays the responsibility that individuals have for reflecting on and working through tensions in values.

Yet, tensions are common and serious. Sometimes, scholarly values come under direct strain from powerful and influential forces that lead to direct decisions that may harm academic careers and progression. The scientist Marc Edwards publicly reported in 2015 that the water supply in Flint in the USA contained unsafe amounts of lead. His research identified that high levels were not just isolated 'one-off' measures but reflected a 'systemic problem' that had been seemingly ignored by the state's own scientists. Yet, many aspects of academic culture would have incentivized Edwards not to act on this discovery. In his own words, he reports being:

> very concerned about the culture of academia in this country and the perverse incentives that are given to young faculty. The pressures to get funding are just extraordinary. We're all on this hedonistic treadmill - pursuing funding, pursuing fame, pursuing h-index - and the idea of science as a public good is being lost … In Flint the agencies paid to protect these people weren't solving the problem. They were the problem. What faculty person out there is going to take on their state, the Michigan Department of Environmental Quality, and the US Environmental Protection Agency? … I don't blame anyone, because I know the culture of academia. You are your funding network as a professor. You can destroy that network that took you 25 years to build with one word. I've done it. When was the last time you heard anyone in academia publicly criticize a funding agency, no matter how outrageous their behavior? We just don't do these things. (Quoted in Kolowich, 2016)

Issues in which the values of academics can be overly compromised are not mere academic matters but have huge public relevancy and implications. Academics and institutions that have accepted funding from large corporate bodies with a vested interest in research results or whose work promotes the credibility or priorities of such bodies have been labelled as being 'up for sale' (Matthews, 2015). Scenarios in which clear conflicts of interests have occurred have not only been featured in the academic press more frequently (Clark et al., 2015; Matthews, 2015) but have also been on the front page of the *New York Times* (Lipton, 2015) and in Oscar-winning documentaries like *Inside Job*. These show that academics can move from their roles as academics to being 'actors in lobbying and corporate public relations campaigns' (ibid.).

Values abdicated

As awareness of values in academic work becomes more widespread and most academic workers begin to establish this awareness in their early substantial pieces of work, it is far more likely that *value conflict* will occur and is even inevitable. Almost half of the academic workers whom Smith (2010) interviewed experienced considerable threats to their values from their early experiences in academic jobs. Anger, in Smith's words, 'permeates their talk' (ibid.: 585) as their workplaces were perceived to be far less supportive, and processes and career progression were 'bureaucratic and unfathomable' (ibid.: 584). It is not the mere presence of values conflict that defines this but reactions to that conflict. These academic workers felt a lack of connection with their workplace's mission, were more personally isolated, felt un-helped by senior colleagues and untrusted by their departmental heads. This group of new academics perceived that their academic identities were threatened by their academic workplaces. They experienced reduced productivity related to low morale and were often actively looking for other career options.

Indeed, many of the critical accounts of academic workplaces in the last 30 years are characterized by value conflict leading to value abdication: ongoing tensions between the values of workers and the academic workplace that have led these workers to abdicate their values. Due to pressures on universities from governments to be more accountable and productive, academic workers have been cast as becoming: 'zombified' (Ryan, 2012), 'McDonaldized' (Nadolny and Ryan, 2013), withdrawn (Ryan, 2012), deskilled and reluctant (Cote and Allahar, 2007). This value vacuum occurs when academic work is seen to be externally imposed. As elements of passive governance, audit and an acquiescent leadership coalesce, academic workers become 'zombified' – living an undead existence, separated from their values in order to survive (Ryan, 2012).

Common practical consequences of alienation from values is a lack of community orientation or action, disengagement, an intense focus on the self, worry, and a lack of fulfilment in academic work. Accordingly, early-career academic workers often report high insecurity, uncertainty, vulnerability and 'inauthenticity'. Chasing research money is seen to be 'soul-destroying' and unfulfilling, and rejection for this work and that of publications, painful, (Archer, 2008). Those in senior roles at the academic workplaces can be cast *en masse* as part of the problem. As Kimber and Ehrich conclude: 'the introduction and spread of managerialism in higher education institutions in Australia and the United Kingdom have resulted in schisms between academic managers and managed academics ... The former group, for example heads of schools, have internalised the values of managerialism and therefore have value congruence with the organisation' (2015: 86). In this way, when we abdicate our own values, we can view others through an excessively simple and jaded lens: it's tempting to see those with different values as negative, always acting through malevolent means to foster their own or an ulterior agenda to oppress scholarship, diversity and various other entirely wholesome ends with which we associate ourselves. This makes us feel better about ourselves, but polarizes thinking, risks being judgemental of others and their intentions, reduces empathy and promotes isolation.

Values suppressed

An alternative reaction in the face of values conflict is to shut down and back off. A colleague voices the importance of publishing in high-impact journals, a senior department head gives you feedback that you need to increase your external committee involvement or a student questions the validity of your long-standing theoretical framework – all scenarios entwined with values and a test of our true openness to different values. While mission statements, platitudes, and meetings may give rise to talk of diversity, how truly open are we to hearing and respecting values different to our own? How much easier it is to label, dismiss, and criticize under the guise of freedom-fighting against all manner of evils?

In such situations, it is tempting to remove ourselves (and our values) from these conflict situations by 'throwing all our cards in' and seemingly ceding, while also continuing to find alternative outlets for expressing our displeasure and disgruntlement. We both disengage and seek to get even. Ostensibly, we might say, 'What the heck!', 'It's fine!' or 'I don't care anyway,' but feel angry, shut down and vent frustration in other directions.

In academic workplaces, negative behavioural reactions to suppressing our own values can take many and often extreme forms (Twale and De Luca, 2008), including simple contrariness; being overly critical, 'two-faced' or passive aggressive; engaging in personal gossip; exploitation; making consistent negative comments about someone's personality, teaching, research, or workstyle; and extreme forms of bullying and intimidation. Workplaces that have culture and practices that support or enable such reactions become prone to bullying and fear, and respect for differences around absent values is replaced by a lack of empathy, harsh prejudgement and fear.

Why does this happen? There are very human and understandable reactions. They are reactions that the researcher Bréné Brown would view as resulting because those involved do not feel heard, respected, or valued (2007). We would like to pretend that it's all about the work or scholarship but, sometimes, it just isn't. There are many complicated cultural and individual reasons as to why academic workers engage in such conduct (Twale and De Luca, 2008). When we see and feel conflict in values in any part of our life, Brown argues that it is natural and expected to feel annoyed, frustrated or even threatened (2007). We not only intellectually object but can physically feel our 'buttons being pressed', our anger bubbles up and our fuses shorten. In part, it is because academic work is extreme knowledge work and the values expressed in and through it involve years of effort, high personal investment and are closely linked to identity. Academic workers often care deeply about what they do but also see success in this as fleeting and temporary (Archer, 2008), leading to a high sense of vulnerability.

Values in workable strain

Academic workers can reach a kind of uncomfortable harmony between their own values and those of others and their workplace. In our own work with academic workers, and also in the literature, there are accounts of this kind of paradoxical state of poised disequilibrium (Smith, 2010). This state is about a full openness to the inevitable trade-offs and compromises that arise when doing extreme knowledge work in complex organizations that are prone to a gamut of local, national and international pressures, expectations, and influences.

Compared to the other reactions to values conflict described, this may appear to be a scenario in which values are least clear and most compromised. However, we propose that this stage requires an acute and critical awareness of personal values and a fuller openness to the range of other values at play. This is a place where we truly feel strain between these values and those of others and/or our workplace. But, instead of suppressing this strain, we seek to acknowledge and be open to it, and even view it as an inevitable consequence of many good things, notably of the richness and range of academic workers and work. This is a place of tension but also of higher awareness and healthy self-regard not to shut down. However, also because of these, this is a place of greater listening, openness, and frankness.

This is also a place in which our identities are not simplistically stereotyped or overly universal. A number of authors have pointed to the importance of a coherent fluidity in academic workers' identities evident amongst those who can consistently feel engaged in the changing academic workplace (Archer, 2008). As Taylor reconceptualizes:

> Rather than identity as a claim that decontextualises and unites the academic workforce (against the forces of corporatism and managerialism), it might be productive to see academic identities as context-specific assemblages that draw on a shared but open repertoire of traits, beliefs and allegiances – a creative commons for identity assemblage ... more representative of 'supercomplexity'. (2008: 38)

Is this approach one that naively subjugates the academic worker to forces that are widely decried as dangerous? We don't think so because it is based on a fuller awareness of scholarly values and identity, a greater openness to the nature of the values held by others, and of a more conscious need to work through value conflicts. It is about the strength of vulnerability (Brown, 2007) that comes from recognizing that only with a higher awareness and acceptance of ourselves and our limitations can we do our best to find the right balance between our own values and those of others. Academic workers who find workable strains and have spent time considering and reflecting on aspects of their identity are firmly aware of the broader forces and factors influencing their workplace. They have a sense of influencing those aspects that they can change and an acceptance of those that they cannot. An equilibrium is struck which sees the individual academic worker being able to accept compromises as inevitable but never compromising too much or around too many aspects.

We have presented different scenarios that result from values conflict in academic workers – a state that we see as inevitable and desirable. We will now consider what academic workers can do to set the best stage for incorporating values in their work and ensuring that they can have both high awareness and openness around these. This process increases our values literacy and our awareness of what our values are and why we have them.

FIRST STEPS TO WORKABLE STRAIN: INCREASE YOUR VALUES LITERACY

Sometimes academic life can overwhelm and frustrate. Values can be sustaining and inspiring but the need to hold onto them and draw on them also causes inevitable difficulties, conflict, and personal tension. This is because all workplaces contain different people and different people have different values. Many academic workers can recall instances in which other people, issues, or situations make them particularly annoyed, angry, or tense. We see these reactions less as intellectual than as being about values. How individual academic workers react to their colleagues' approaches, interactions and successes speaks to their own values. Situations in which some facets of scholarship are seemingly esteemed over others by colleagues or workplaces asks questions about our own values. Receiving repeated rejections for grants, publications or our ideas makes us reflect on our values and others' reactions to them.

While we may wish tensions in values between academic workers and their workplaces would go away or be easily reconciled, irrespective of career stage, places, or time – they won't.

The pressures on academic workers (and the implications and costs of these) are undoubtable and not likely to dissipate anytime soon. Tensions in values don't stop with/or at particular career stages, milestones, or other work boundaries. These tensions are an inevitable consequence not only of doing academic work but, more fundamentally, of being engaged in extreme knowledge work. In order to promote integrity, it is not advisable to aspire to leaving your values at the office or classroom door in academic work. While the concept of keeping your own values in parentheses may seem like a ready solution to the conflicts in values caused by academic work, this path of least resistance downplays and dismisses the complexity of academic work. Values form an essential part of academic work. Without them guiding individual work, over the longer term, passivity, disenfranchisement, and ineffectiveness is likely to set in. However, by being more aware of what our own values are and how these link to our scholarly identities, and being more open to the discomfort caused by value tension, we can be in a better place to handle our values and avoid these being eclipsed, suppressed, or absent.

The values guiding academic work can be informed by many things: our experiences growing up, by particular positive or negative single events, by especially influential other people, such as role models, mentors and even those who have affected us adversely. For example, as an undergraduate, I (Alex) quickly realized in my second year that I wanted to pursue a doctorate. This would have remained something of a speculative dream were it not for the proactivity, accessibility, and thoughtfulness of an established academic who reached out and encouraged me to see that this was a natural step that could be taken, even if it seemed impossible to me at the time. This support from an established academic means that encouraging others, irrespective of age or career stage, has always been very important to me. I can always find time, no matter how busy or pressed, to meet with, encourage, and support undergraduates to take a research path.

To foster greater awareness and critical awareness of what your values are, and to develop the ability for intense and authentic reflection, self-scrutiny, and openness around values in yourself and others, we need to be more values literate. Like emotional literacy (Steiner and Perry, 1997), values literacy requires us to know ourselves better, develop greater capacity for empathy for the values of others, and learn to manage our own tensions around values better. Increased 'values literacy' allows academic workers to understand these reactions better because they understand their own values more.

Values literacy is important because values are inevitably different and often in tension in academic workplaces. Differences can be large and obvious: for example, those whose values are entwined in their research on animals and those whose research seeks to protect and preserve animals. Usually, however, differences are smaller and less obvious: for example, between academic workers who grade students relatively in their class versus those who grade them absolutely; those who prioritize quantity of research outputs over quality; those who advocate for applied work versus those who advocate for theoretical work; and those who seek their research to promote local changes versus knowledge generation.

These might seem like fairly straightforward 'intellectual' points of choice; however, they usually feel like a lot more than that and come to colour broader reactions to people and issues across situations. Indeed, seemingly small value differences can lead to all manner of interpersonal conflict, acrimony, nastiness, infighting, and stereotyping. Even small differences within a particular seemingly close set of similar values can lead to disproportionate conflict.

While on the one hand recognizing the imperative of values in academic work adds vital depth, on the other hand this, of course, also brings diversity and difference. It remains far easier to make vague platitudes about respecting diversity in values than to truly embrace people whose values are different or in seeming conflict to our own. These tensions are inevitable and important. Being more values literate will not remove them but can help this extremely challenging movement to greater openness.

WHAT PRINCIPLES, ASPIRATIONS AND FACTORS DO WE WISH TO GUIDE OUR ACADEMIC WORK?

Awareness and critical awareness of values

The first step to increased values literacy is more values awareness. Can we develop more *awareness* of which values guide our work? What principles, aspirations, and factors do we wish to guide our academic work? Unless you can be clear on what values guide your work, it's hard to really understand why sometimes our reactions to others are tense or negative. Usually, we are only roughly aware of what our values are but have not devoted time to writing them down specifically and reflecting on them carefully. Moreover, we also need a critical awareness of why these values are held, how they are or can be expressed, and what the impact or evidence of this would be. This very clear, critical awareness provides, Brown argues, a vital first step not only in understanding what is important to us but also our reactions to other people and our own feelings around conflict (2007).

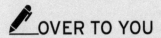 OVER TO YOU

Values Literacy

1. What behaviours cause you most annoyance or discomfort in your academic workplace? What values do they represent that are in conflict with your own?
*Think back to the situations in which these occurred. Put yourself back there.

2.   What feelings have you had when these conflicting values impinged on you?

*Try to give specific labels to what the feelings were.

3.   How did you navigate these feelings? What helped and what made things worse?

——— REMARKABLE RESOURCES ———

How Great Leaders Inspire Action by Simon Sinek (TED Talk)

In this TED Talk, which has been viewed over 33 million times, Simon Sinek brings us back to why 'why' is so much more important in our work than 'how' or 'what' (2000).

Key messages

- The why of work gives vital motivation, passion, and drive to all manner of facets of personal and working life.
- The why of your work is vital during tough times: when teamwork is needed, challenges are demanding and success does not come readily.
- Always underpin your work with a clear, strong, and enduring sense of your bigger purpose.

Key applications

- Take time to reflect and pinpoint why you do academic work and how this has changed over time.
- Academic work is too demanding not to think of why you do your work. When times are busy, or you feel alone or futile, prioritize time to reacquaint yourself with the why of your work.

3

SUCCESS AND ITS INDICATORS

I have learned to define success on my own terms and to focus my work where possible on the areas where I can make the most effective contributions.

(Ruth Cameron quoted in Bostock, 2014: 9)

I want to break the mould of what you need to be like to be successful.

(Ottoline Leyser quoted in Bostock, 2014: 12)

I have never seen work as the main element in my life. It's very important and I give it my all when I'm there, but life is about much, much more.

(Laurie Friday quoted in Bostock, 2014: 18)

Gaining personal promotion was a real vindication of the effort that I had put in - despite one colleague telling me, 'It was just because they needed to promote women.'

(Anon quoted in Bostock, 2014: 23)

What is success in academic work (Bostock, 2014)? Who doesn't want to be successful, right? References to success are everywhere in academia. Papers published, doctorates attained, large and small grants won, teaching awards accrued, student feedback received: all documented in résumés, trumpeted in talks, regaled on webpages and tweets and wedged into seemingly causal corridor conversations.

Success is accordingly integral to how academic workers see themselves and are seen by peers. Reputations, credibility, job offers, promotion, awards, relationships, and collaborations are all founded on success (Bostock, 2014). If a newly employed academic worker does not address, consider or otherwise work toward success, a career can quickly drift and stall. If an established academic worker, firmly in their mid- or later career, does not actively consider the nature of success, disengagement and disappointment, a prevailing apathy can result. Considering success and incorporating what being successful 'is' into academic work is therefore key.

REFERENCES TO SUCCESS ARE EVERYWHERE IN ACADEMIA

Yet, despite the centrality of success, it is also slippery. We will consider some of this slipperiness and elusiveness in this chapter. As extreme knowledge work, academic work is immensely diverse. Values and identity are both expressed and formed in successes; variations abound by person, discipline, career stage, and country. Academic workplaces also claim successes for the people who work in them to further institutional reputation and sustainability. Indeed, who should define and evaluate success, from what basis should this be done and with what implications? These are profound and difficult, yet key, questions.

This reflects a challenge we hear repeatedly about in our workshops: a perceived lack of fit between the success indicators which academic workers aspire to and those of today's academic workplaces. Commonly, this potential disjoint is grounded in concerns not only for career progression but also around more fundamental conflicts between academic worker and employer values. Many perceive these conflicts around values and success indicators not only to exist and be prevalent across workplaces but also to be inevitable. While we disagree, reconciling these often palpable tensions seldom happens without deliberate thought and calculated action. Incorporating our own passions and talents with a careful and nuanced analysis of what employers wants and broader needs is vital. This can provide a means to identify your purpose, ikigai (Garcia and Miralles, 2017), or 'sweet spot' (Figure 3.1) – a fit between ourselves and our workplaces that ensures there is less conflict and more mutual benefit from academic work.

While specifying success can seem straightforward, such as completing a doctorate, success can also seem too lofty. A recent analysis of adverts for starting academic positions (Pitt and Mewburn, 2016) identified that academic workplaces increasingly demand that workers publish work in the most reputable journals in their fields; be accessible, organized, and engaging teachers; communicate well with peers and public alike, directly and via social and mass media; organize and lead teams, projects, and work initiatives; manage people, budgets, and heavy workloads; mentor students and junior colleagues ... and on and on. The demands and skills required of such academic workers to be successful across these domains are, indeed, immense. The supercomplexity of the academic workplace (Barnett, 2011) is transposed into a supercomplexity of expectations for academic workers.

So, it is on this challenging basis that this chapter considers success and its indicators in academia. Our approach aims for inclusivity and optimism about success in academic workers

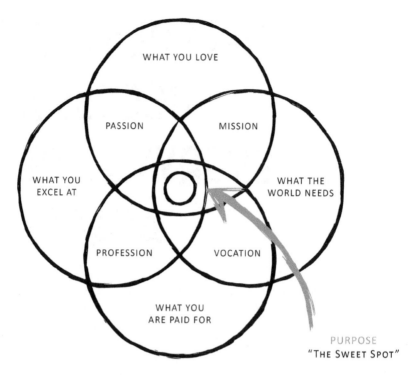

Figure 3.1   What is Your Purpose?

Source: Adapted from multiple online sources

and workplaces but not naively, subjectively or indulgently so. In approaching success, we seek to be personal but not prescriptive, and to recognize elusiveness, diversity, and standards in success. For, while there is so much variation, success should be the end, the reference point and horizon for everything an academic worker should do.

Despite growing pressures in some countries to codify and centralize success (for example, through national research performance assessment exercises), success is, nevertheless, easier to recognize than to describe, define, and codify. Inescapably, what success looks like depends on who defines it, what values guide this and also at what cost. Like so many facets of modern academic workplaces, the difficulties of adequately defining success in academic work is a blessing and a curse.

WHAT SUCCESS LOOKS LIKE IN ACADEMIC WORK

While success seems taken for granted in academic work, it is also contested. 'Success' thus demands a more detailed and careful consideration here.

Success varies but needs values

Success in academic work can come through research, teaching, and engagement, takes a plethora of different forms and can be achieved in so many ways via so many paths.

The nature of extreme knowledge work of academic workers means that success is and will always be contested and context-bound. Sometimes, success is visible and extremely tangible: getting your first academic job, completing a doctorate in five years, publishing a key paper in a target impact journal or getting favourable teaching evaluations from students. Sometimes, success is also when nothing ostensibly happens: when personal burnout is avoided or a long-term project with a troublesome team is completed without damaging relationships. For some of us, the reality is that success during some periods is getting by: holding life and work together and paying the bills. For others, success is the Nobel Prize, international recognition, curing disease and redressing social ills.

Different views of academic success can also vary by many other factors. Female academic workers in the UK report that, while conventional measures of academic success, such as promotion, publications and reputation are important, so, too, are broader factors, such as the inherent merits of the work itself, the states of one's wider life and being an important and influential colleague (Bostock, 2014).

Success can also vary around values. Our own personal favourite papers may not be those that are most cited or used by colleagues or make the biggest media splash. A department chair may frown on an academic worker spending three years writing a definitive textbook, worried that this work will not be counted in the department's national research assessment. Teaching that challenges students' assumptions may lead the students to be discombobulated and nervous before they work through this to new insights. Views of success can and are often in conflict, especially when we move beyond academic workers to address the views of success espoused by academic workplaces, governments at various levels, the media and the public.

As it pertains to extreme knowledge work, the more open we can be intellectually and emotionally to consider different views of academic success, the better. As with values, if talk of academic 'success' provokes intense reactions in you – particularly strongly dismissive or hostile reactions – that in itself is a clear impetus for further reflection. For example, despite huge potential variations in what success can look like for academic workers, some academic workers aggressively shun references or framing of their work around 'success'. Usually, this is a reaction to supposed external or 'corporate' standards of promotion or evaluation that invoke concepts of 'impact' and 'influence' or 'satisfaction' and short-termism or other seemingly pejorative standards.

This apparent rejection of 'success' is itself a stance on success taken to symbolize the lack of power academic workers and even their workplaces often have in modern societies. While a university president may appear dynamic, striding and all-conquering to those working within a university, in terms of external political influence of decisions by government, they usually have despairingly little sway (Tuchman, 2011).

SUCCESS IS NOT EQUAL (ESPECIALLY AROUND GENDER)

Perhaps men are just naturally better at research than women. (Savigny, 2014)

Concepts of academic success are contested and influential, though hopefully misconceptions, such as the one above are now long dispelled. While national assessments of research impact influence institutional funding in many countries, these exercises tend to esteem work more likely to be done by some groups over others (Back, 2015; Smith and Stewart, 2016a). Academic success is not a fair playing-field – particularly around gender. There is persuasive consistent evidence that female academic workers are: underrepresented in paid academic roles in many disciplines and countries (but especially in the sciences and in senior roles) (Metcalfe and Gonzalez, 2013; Henley, 2015; Equality Challenge Unit, 2016), publish less (Aiston and Jung, 2015), and are even less likely to receive grant funding in some competitions (Payne, 2016). Female academic workers also get paid less (Equality Challenge Unit, 2016).

Many factors contribute to these inequalities. The difficult experiences and challenges that female academic workers face in this work have been documented for over 30 years (Aisenberg and Harrington, 1988). A more recent study of 26 successful senior female academic workers at the University of Cambridge (Bostock, 2014) highlighted continued awareness of gender-based inequalities in opportunities and outcomes of academic work but also evolving conceptions of what success is and can be. Success for these extremely successful academic workers was seen to be consistently challenging, not only around their gender but also because academic work is difficult. Gender-based challenges came from every realm: from family demands outside of work to an enduring imposter syndrome about ongoing success. While some contributing factors are well known, others are startling, such as the tendency for male academic workers to cite their own work 70 per cent more often than females (King et al., 2016).

These challenges can seem dizzying, but faced with them as Sheryl Sandberg reminds us, women must be forceful in maintaining high aspirations for their progression:

> In addition to the external barriers erected by society … we (women) hold ourselves back in ways both big and small, by lacking self-confidence, by not raising our hands, and by pulling back when we should be leaning in. We internalize the negative messages we get throughout our lives - the messages that say it's wrong to be outspoken, aggressive, more powerful than men. We lower our own expectations of what we achieve. We continue to do the majority of the housework and child care. We compromise our career goals to make room for partners and children who may not even exist yet. Compared to our male colleagues, fewer of us aspire to senior positions. (2015: 8)

It's because of the distinctive challenges that academic work sets for women that the tools, approaches and resources here are so important. Women must be all the more clear on their values and their own definitions of success. While there are many and varied remedies to address these challenges and inequity institutionally – including examining types of contracts that are less accessible to different categories of academic workers, reviewing hiring and promotion procedures and doing institution-wide pay audits – this is a complex issue. But what is clear is that success is not just a matter of your abilities, natural talent, or efforts.

SUCCESS IS ABOUT WORK *AND* LIFE

Success for academic workers is always personal. It interfaces with personal values and life. Work can both impinge on wider life and be affected by it. 'Work–life balance' is an issue for academic workers of all ages. For example, research with academic workers born in the late 1960s and 1970s (so-called 'Generation X-ers') report a high degree of commitment to their careers but also strong desires to live balanced lives that emphasize quality over quantity of work and express values around pursuing stimulating and interesting research in more prestigious journals. Work success, for them, is not defined by face time 'in the office' but on using time effectively:

> There's really nothing to be gained by closing your door and working until 11:00 o'clock at night, other than the tenure hurdle that is somewhere out there. If you want to pole vault over it, you go right ahead, but no one here is going to back up the Brinks truck and start dumping all this cash on you, simply because you've decided to work like you have three jobs. So that's the approach I take – sometimes you have to know when there's this point of diminishing return, where if I keep pounding at this one front, then yes, I may nail it, but at the same time, it will then be for a very high cost in other areas. (Helms, 2010: 9)

In her book drawing together the accounts on their life and work of 11 Generation X academic workers, Elwood Watson contrasts the views of success implicit in these views:

> many of us are not willing to sacrifice our family, health, or private life simply to obtain certain goals. The desire of many … to maintain a healthy personal life while climbing the company ladder is not due to a sense of narcissism; it is due to a rational concern. Many of us have seen the price that too many of our peers, as well as a number of our Boomer and in some cases Silent Generation coworkers, have paid by putting family second to career or failing to maintain valuable personal relationships. (2013: xiii)

Despite these strains, most academic workers desire and seek more balance in their life but also want to be successful in both personal and work realms (whatever that might look like) (Helms, 2010). All the participants interviewed by Helms (ibid.) indicated that at least some aspect of their work–life balance was unsatisfactory.

Too often, this desire for more balanced 'life-work' success is less a reluctant compromise than an empowered informed trade-off. As an academic worker expressed in her response to a call for female workers not to 'opt for the less stressful and challenging role for an easy life':

> My decision not to try and climb higher on the academic ladder comes down to precisely this – I don't want the stress, thanks. I want to have a life outside my job. Those of my colleagues (male or female) who are getting to the higher positions are those who spend all their waking hours working. This is a problem with the culture of academia as a whole; I don't think women (or men) who reject it should be criticised. The whole culture should shift. (Guardian Higher Education Network, 2014)

As numerous delegates from our workshops have reminded us, the challenges posed with reconciling balance in 'life' and 'work' defy age and career stage. Children, siblings, parents, and all manner of other family and friends exhert wider social demands for our care, time, and presence. Discussions over what success should look like will come later but, for now, our conception of success is firmly that academic life and personal life (and their attendant 'successes') are so inextricably linked that they should be seen as either symbiotic or even unified. As success in academic work links to wider values and personal life, including family, relationships and well-being, 'work–life balance' has become an important and difficult challenge for most academic workers.

SUCCESS AND QUALITY ARE DIFFERENT

Academic work may appear similar in nature, but as with wine and whisky, we all know that quality matters. Yet, what quality is or how it can be inferred is far less obvious. Success links to quality but in indirect ways. Peer acclaim, awards, social kudos, reason: all can be invoked to claim or signify success. This risks negating the importance of values in academic work. What may constitute success for different academic workers may, therefore, be very different.

Should academic workers focus on success or quality in their work? While an academic worker has a strong role in determining the inherent quality of their work, their influence on its success is less direct. Quality is, arguably, neither necessary nor sufficient for success. Some academic workers can take lower-quality work and squeeze every ounce of 'success potential' out of it. It garners influence on the world, not through its quality but via the positioning of the academic worker to ensure that it influences policymakers or government (Smith and Stewart, 2016b). A department may privilege a volume of papers published over their visibility or quality, thereby giving a localized success – albeit likely at the cost of external reputation. Citations and acclaim can also be out of step with the quality of the work (Greenhalgh and Fahy, 2015). Similarly, our own personal sense of 'our best papers' often differs from those of our peers, based on citations, downloads, and awareness. Work that provides an incremental but definite shift to a new way of seeing may get lost in a flood of new papers by others. With growth in the number of journals in which research can be published, some have argued that there is just too much 'research' out there – most of it of insufficient quality (Bornmann and Mutz, 2015), and published in so-called 'predatory' journals that lack basic peer-review and quality standards. An agenda on 'more outputs' can lead to expedience, with more substantial work being chopped up, demarcated and compromised to ensure that more papers are published.

Many academic workers are supportive of the concept that good work is influential work but sceptical of narrow conceptions of success with quality (Smith and Stewart, 2016b): academic research can be influential despite its low quality, superficial attractiveness to the mass media or its ready applicability. Conceptions of influence themselves can be too simplistic, such as equating influencing a guideline or policy with *really* influencing the world (Greenhalgh and Fahy, 2015). Moreover, success of research in influencing this world may be less about the quality of the research per se than the positioning of the academic workers(s) involved, particularly in relation to forms of privilege, such as time, positioning, and proximity to power (Smith and Stewart, 2016b). This further raises deeper issues about the degree to which academic work should address the interests of society and government or retain a strong sense of independence and academic freedom from these interests. In both teaching and research, distinctions need to be drawn between short-term and longer success (ibid.).

High-quality teaching may impact on students over the long term, but receive weaker student feedback at the immediate end of a course.

IS SUCCESS SUBJECTIVE OR OBJECTIVE?

Academic success is, like culture, both very real yet simultaneously very tricky. While success may immediately seem as real and as concrete as the chair you are sitting on, on closer examination it is a lot more elusive and socially bounded. Peer reviewers of scholarship and funding applications will discuss and often argue at length around the relative success of an applicant's career based on their academic outputs. Factors such as career stage, disruptions and method, all come into play. Furthermore, conventions around academic work vary so much across disciplines. John Swales (2009) captured these differences in astounding detail in his qualitative research ('ethnography') of a single three-storey-high university building at the University of Michigan. In the building, he uncovered the nuances of three areas of work there: the Herbarium (a place of research for systemic botany using dried plants), the English Language Institute (helping students and staff with English) and a centralized computer support facility. While clearly the nature of the work is different, the nature of success was very different, too, along with the practises, conventions, norms, preoccupations, and annoyances in what amounted to three different scholarly worlds.

Such differences mean that success is best approached as a social construct. While success incorporates personal values, it is not mind-determined – one cannot become successful in academic work just because one believes that one is successful. Rather, success is 'out there' as a form of social perception and is influenced by many social factors, many of which particular groups or individuals will disagree with. For example, degrees of success in academic work can be inferred by examining the work against contextual standards and conventions, but these tend to be specific to disciplines, organizations, and countries. Judgements can be made regarding the quality of teaching against peers' assessments or the amount of innovation in research or from quantified metrics of teaching quality, citations, and impact. Yet, many are sceptical of the simplistic use of such measures. How much can these incorporate the nuances of knowledge development in particular fields, let alone the values of the individual academic worker? More basic conceptions of success are still contested. Governments are consistently seeking for academic workplaces to broaden their conceptions of success (Bornmann, 2013). Research is increasingly evaluated, less in terms of publications and more in terms of 'returns on investment', 'innovations accrued' and 'societal impact' including, 'third stream activities, societal benefits, societal quality, usefulness, public values, knowledge transfer, and societal relevance' (ibid.: 217).

Success in this way involves the diverse perspectives of multiple stakeholders, agendas, and conventions. Sometimes, these variations create conflict between types of research, notably applied research (with seemingly more ready application) versus 'basic' or discovery science that may take decades to be influential, if at all (Bornmann, 2013). Similarly, research that may have a high degree of local application and according influence may not receive many citations or recognition as a contribution to knowledge by national and international peers (Smith and Stewart, 2016b).

While success in academic workplaces is slippery, neither is it wholly subjective. Not everything becomes successful just because it is produced or done, nor does something become successful because an individual perceives it as such, wants this or believes this to be. Many of us, I am sure, know of colleagues whose views of their own relative success are at odds with those of their wider peers. An academic worker does not become successful just because they set goals and meet them. Nor can they be deemed to be successful simply because they see themselves as being 'successful'. The new PhD graduate may believe that their thesis will revolutionize their discipline but this does not make it so. It is important, too, for success not to be too parochial. Van Gogh's society during his lifetime did not recognize him as a successful painter. Was he then not successful? Few would argue that this is the case. His success could not be appreciated in his lifetime. Similarly, academic workers who collaborate with commercial organizations will quickly realize that success comes in many forms beyond the academic realm, including products sold and intellectual property protected. The researcher may lament: 'But does it actually work?!' while the profit-focused retailer gleefully counts the units sold.

Success in any field is then neither totally in the 'eye of the beholder' nor objectively 'out there' for all to see and agree with. Success will ultimately be determined via a complex fusion of factors, easier to see in their specifics but hard to define in generalities.

APPROACHING SUCCESS IN ACADEMIC KNOWLEDGE WORK: OCCLUDED GAMES AND GENRES

We live fairly effortlessly with elusive social concepts every day of our lives and quite readily make trade-offs in decisions about quality, quantity, and visibility around all manner of things. Should I buy one expensive pair of designer shoes (like Bailey) or three bargain-bin pairs (like Alex!)? Of course, a lot depends on what we value, what we need these things for, and the perceived financial and social costs of your choices. Nor is there one inherent 'right answer'. Even though some people may have strong opinions, there can be a wrong choice for each of us, depending on circumstances, but there is no one inherent right choice for all of us.

We can choose to pretend that this ambiguity and social dimension does not exist or always seek bland moderation. Academic approaches that provide tricks and tips for success can hold such normative assumptions about what success in academic work should look like. We don't believe that this reflects the nature of academic work as extreme knowledge work, particularly around the place of values in it. How then can we best approach how we work toward success in our academic work? Approaching academic work as a series of 'semi-occluded' games is the best framing that we have come across for conveying the challenge of doing academic work successfully.

Hermann Hesse describes The Glass Bead Game in his novel of the same name. This game is played in a fictional place around about the twenty-fifth century and involves an isolated community of intellectual scholars who devote their time to running a school for boys and mastering and playing The Glass Bead Game, the main challenge of which is that rules are never specifically stated but can only be inferred. The game involves a synthesis of knowledge from the arts and sciences with progress dependent on making deep connections between various often seemingly unrelated topics. The challenges of playing The Glass Bead Game well are similar to those in being successful in academic work (Swales, 2004; Christensen and Eyring, 2011). Many of the rules can only be inferred from the behaviour of others and consequent successes or failures in the game. There seem to be manifold exceptions and considerations to take into account when playing.

Mastering the game is challenging enough, but in the absence of entirely clear explicit formal rules, being successful can be extremely difficult. There are many occluded games in academic work. Swales (2004) concludes that these extend to include the genres represented in academic book and grant proposals; journal reviews; examiner discussions; book and proposal reviews; peer evaluations; all manner of letters for applications, responses, and invitations; even phone calls and emails. The ability of emerging academic workers to tune into the stated and unstated rules of academic games and genres that they navigate is key to being successful at these games. Crucially, games and genres differ in different settings; what makes for clear success in one setting may not be as successful in another. Mastering success in academia is about mastering its games and its genres – mysterious, challenging, and infuriating as they sometimes are. Again, this is why tricks-and-tips approaches to academic writing and work are limited: they simply cannot deal with the scope and range of variations at play across disciplines, organizations, countries, and … and … and … and ultimately people. However, pointedly we also say that at any one time, each and every academic worker should be aware of what success in their research, teaching, and engagement should look like: what, in short, is indicated by success indicators.

SUCCESS INDICATORS AND THE SUCCESS PYRAMID

Success indicators are at the apex of The Success Pyramid. For every phase of their work, academic workers should specify, work toward and evaluate their progress against their own success indicators. These indicators identify what will stand for success; they allow for the nature of success to be specified and its presence to be determined and are long term, transcending and responsive to career stages. Your success indicators can and should also express many different facets. The foci of indicators can be more within the walls of academia and academic workplaces (such as being the national authority in a particular approach to teaching or finishing your PhD) or more outside in other communities or organizations, such as influencing national policy or practice in an applied discipline you work in. Motivations can be intrinsic: related to the qualities of doing good academic work for good work's sake or because of your passion for the kind of academic work you do. They can also be focused on extrinsic motivations: financial reward, reputation in your field or status from peers. Most academic workers consciously either make a choice to prioritize a focus on teaching, research or engagement, or to mix the three into a viable set of success indicators. Motivations can be very personal (such as self-improvement) or focused more externally on influencing disciplines or other organizations, including one's own academic workplace. Success indicators are also likely to vary in terms of attainability and ambition, which may, in turn, be dependent on individual attitudes to workload preferences, personal energy levels, life circumstances, vision, and/or motivation.

The appropriateness of one's own success indicators around all of these factors is very dependent on personal context and values. Choices about indicators and our approach to them are not 'zero-sum' games; indicators may leverage or otherwise help each other.

Nevertheless, understanding that we need to make choices around what success looks like is important. It is the vital first step to developing a plan using The Success Pyramid to taking actions to further success.

These indicators should be specific, stated, and unambiguous enough to directly inform the selection of priorities. While successes clearly can happen in the short term ('I answered all my emails today!'), in The Success Pyramid, these short-term successes are better conceived as 'tasks' that, when completed, indicate progress toward the meeting of subsequent goals and priorities and ultimately *attaining or furthering* one's success indicators. As such, success indicators should reflect longer phases of academic work lasting 3–30 years and are verifiable. Success indicators are essential to help evaluate, map, and monitor success. While such indicators can also exist at the department and institutional level, the focus here is on the personal. What does success look like for you, at this time and at *your* career stage?

SUCCESS INDICATORS OVER ACADEMIC CAREERS

Determining what constitutes or can help us to be successful in academic work is vital but also challenging. We are consciously wary throughout this book of being too prescriptive about what success should or must look like in academic workers. It is not for us to say what *your* success should look like. Some academic workers are conscious of entirely assimilating the seeming goals of academic workplaces – and react against these – while others pragmatically assimilate to these workplace success indicators almost intuitively. Each has implications, trade-offs, and potential benefits, harms, and costs.

What factors should academic workers consider when specifying their success indicators? It is almost impossible here to provide an exhaustive list – our values, contexts, disciplines, countries, and aspirations are so diverse. To be successful in academia requires a mindful tuning into the games and genres involved within your 'academic worlds' (Table 3.1).

Table 3.1   Example Success Indicators over Career

Success indicators by career stage

Emerging	Establishing	Established
• Attain my doctorate • Build a distinct area of expertise • Impact, enrich, and support my students • Become a leader in my faculty/department	• Be nationally known in defined research area • Impact, enrich, and support my students and mentees • Become a leader externally	• Be internationally known in a defined research area • Impact, enrich, and support my students and mentees • Do work I love that impacts _____ • Obtain a senior administrative role within my institution

Success for the emerging academic worker

For doctoral students and early career academic workers, success indicators are often clearer and more consistent. The doctorate remains the common requirement for achieving career progression in most countries, and in many countries is the entry qualification for the academic worker. However, it is increasingly becoming an expectation, too, that students will already have had work published when their doctorates are finished; in some disciplines, this involves a significant number of papers and independent funding (Semenza, 2014). As noted, the expectations for many even early career academic jobs are considerable to the point of intimidation (Pitt and Mewburn, 2016).

As such, for doctoral students, getting their doctorate is likely to be the primary and vital success indicator of this period, but is increasingly accompanied by other success indicators related to teaching, publications, and leadership. In relation to values, the period of graduate study is when emerging academic workers often start to establish their scholarly identities: their personal sense of who they are, what their work seeks to do, and what they will stand for in their work (McAlpine et al., 2008). However, in many circumstances, it is also a time of establishing evidence of credibility in meeting the challenges that come during careers around publishing, grants, engagement, and service. Almost immediately, in the face of these demands, choices need to be made regarding time, effort, and energy – this is why success indicators need to be set early in academic careers. We know, too, that many (sometimes most) doctoral students do not intend or subsequently choose academic career paths. This is important and can also be embraced at this stage with the aim of tuning into the success indicators required for work in any particular field, industry, or job.

To develop the right success indicators at this stage, it's essential (and often challenging) to try to establish even basic elements, such as whether to aim for an academic career. While there are variations across disciplines and countries, attaining first-rung jobs in academic workplaces usually involves the demonstration of an early credibility in teaching and research. It is not uncommon for PhD students in the medical sciences to need around 10 publications with some grant-funding successes to be competitive for postdoctoral funding, whereas other fields will look for publications only from the doctorate. Likely, the best insights for choosing success indicators will come from talking to more experienced academic workers, supervisors, and mentors – particularly those who are well placed to comment via sitting on review and selection panels. They have special exposure to the occluded games that go on there around productivity and competency discussions.

Success for establishing academic workers

Yet, as careers progress, scholarly identity continues to evolve, success gets murkier (and messier), and the facets that are essential or necessary to academic work and workers becomes less clear and arguably more diverse. This reflects the diversity of activities (and roles) in academic workplaces and the nature of the extreme knowledge work that academic workers engage in with increasing independence over time.

It is difficult to argue that academic workers with research in their roles should not publish. But whereas, traditionally, this has meant writing books and manuscript articles, emphasis on each differs by discipline. Furthermore, dissemination can also now occur through a myriad of other channels via blogs, social media, and mass media. Success for academic workers still involves writing, but where and how this occurs is varied and contested. This realization comes even before the relative success of particular types of publications are considered within these realms. Some disciplines place extremely high emphasis for manuscript success on journal impact factors, whereas other disciplines place little emphasis on this. Success in teaching is also diverse: while institutions routinely measure teaching quality via student satisfaction, such measures are done in the short term and may struggle to capture the quality of teaching that is challenging, disruptive to core beliefs or otherwise transformative. The ways in which academic workers engage with internal and external communities becomes more diverse with career progression. Expectations within disciplines tend to increase around both volume of work and visibility. As careers progress and diversify, success becomes ever more diverse. At this stage, the degree to which success indicators assimilate or reflect those of the workplace is a matter of individual choice. But even when a career is framed as a triumph of personal academic freedom over external pressures (and attendant institutionalized oppression), this is itself a success claim. Academic work is never mere activity but is always predicated on assumptions about success.

While those at this stage are likely to have transgressed and been involved in a wide range of the occluded games and genres of academic work, mysteries remain to be uncovered and risks taken. Membership of committees that decide on promotion and funding may influence many factors of importance for this stage, but also be closed until some success has also been demonstrated in these. This catch-22 is challenging but can often be offset via wider relationships and networks that position the individual better for being included, including perceived successes in other areas and/or other perceptions of competency and relationships. Talking to others, listening and tuning into the formal written and informal hidden rules and conventions of the games and genres is key.

Success for established academic workers

Academics who have been in positions for longer tend to produce more papers of lower quality and impact (Gingras et al., 2008; Ebadi and Schiffauerov, 2016). Academic workers in full-time salaried positions for over 10 years face different challenges than those who are emerging or establishing. Progress is likely to have been made in skills, learning, and confidence in teaching, research and engagement activities. Promotion, career progress, and other notoriety as an expert and/or mentor may be evident. More deeply, scholarly identity is established with a clearer sense of what the scholarship should stand for, aspire to, and be founded on. All so easy? Reasons for variations in academic work over generations include availability of funding, the ease of creating collaboration (for example, before social media or email versus after) but also because success indicators are different.

Leadership or administration roles and their attendant complexities and challenges are likely to be far more common in this group. So are academic workers who want to change course from one focus to another, or to leave the academic workforce entirely. Likely, the peaks and troughs of academic life may be respectively less high and less low, but demands, expectations and responsibilities abound for this senior group. The challenge of staying true to one's values and scholarly identity are likely to be particularly tested with these roles. Demotivation is more likely less due to employment fears than facing and tackling seemingly similar barriers to progress and success over weeks, months, and decades.

Academic workers at this stage are likely to be well placed at being adept at the various games and genres associated with academic success, and also at gaining access to seemingly 'closed' groups to master new ones. High-level lobbying, persuasion, and relationships are likely to be influential at this stage. Reputation can be harnessed and leveraged to further ends. With reduced motivation not uncommon at this stage, wanting to play academic games at all is likely more the issue than how to do so well.

CHALLENGES IN SELECTING SUCCESS INDICATORS

Selecting success indicators is the first step in deciding what the right thing to do is. However, it is not easy, and those you choose should reflect your values but also take account of your career stage, context, and circumstances. Once you have established your success indicators, these can then inform your priorities, goals, and tasks. There, nevertheless, remain a number of common pitfalls around success indicators.

Confusing success indicators with goals or tasks

The most common mistake we see when academic workers attempt to set success indicators is confusing these overriding aspirations with smaller, shorter-term goals. While achievements like 'answering all my emails', 'keeping Monday free for my research', or 'developing teaching skills' may be important, they themselves cannot represent larger success indicators. This confusion often occurs because, at that time, these smaller issues are the ones preoccupying time and attention, but their resolution does not, in any reasonable form, represent an indicator of career success.

Success indicators are too safe

While success indicators in academia are both personal and personalized, academic workers have a wider societal obligation to seek acceptable standards for their teaching, research, and engagement. Yet, this can look very different, cannot necessarily be judged in the short term, and should respond to personal circumstances. Spending extensive periods reading and thinking may be exactly the sort of preparation needed for a consequent substantial work breakthrough. Nevertheless, success indicators that are boringly safe, parochial, or lacking in ambition risk appearing to be indicators of anything but success. Success indicators should make you excited and feel renewed passion for your work. Being challenged and even uncomfortable is part of setting appropriate success indicators. The wide prevalence of failure across and throughout academic work can also lead us to set moderate success indicators that don't stretch us. We will address failure in a later chapter, but an openness to being challenged by the prospect of failure is important in setting indicators. It is normal for appropriate success indicators to lead to feelings of fear, consternation, or challenge.

Not incorporating your values

Academic work is so far from being easy. The work itself is very challenging in its nature and diversity, jobs, funding, and publication are extremely competitive. These factors and others exert many heavy pressures on academic workers but in themselves do not produce success or help identify success indicators. In some situations, dwelling extensively on these pressures (real though they are) can lead us to develop success indicators that do not sufficiently represent our values. This may bring success in the shorter term, but over the longer term risks demotivation and burnout, particularly at the cost of other things that we may value such as family, friends, leisure time, or hobbies.

We recognize that for some academic workers this urgency to incorporate personal values in work may appear 'privileged'. Nevertheless, as extreme knowledge work, wherever and whenever you can, it's important to try to incorporate your values in your academic work. Failing to do this excessively downplays how academic work is done, its intense demands on creativity, endurance, skills, and time; in short, its status as extreme knowledge workers – characteristics that hold across disciplines and locations (Helms, 2010). Concerned claims that academic work has become routinized (so-called 'McJobs') do not stand up when compared to the reality of most academic workers' daily lives (Nadolny and Ryan, 2013). Of 14,600 academic workers surveyed by Kinman and Wray (2013), 79 per cent report always or often having to work 'very intensely' but with high autonomy: 92 per cent at least sometimes can decide how to do their work; 82 per cent at least sometimes decide what they do; and 93 per cent have a say over the way they work, while 86 per cent view their work time as being flexible. Indeed, there is good evidence that academic workers can do their work in private space (usually the home) away from the formal academic workplace (Kuntz, 2012). Freedom in how to achieve success, for now, appears to be more common than not.

Success indicators are not really about success

As entry and progression in academic workplaces involves being successful at occluded academic games involving occluded genres, knowing what success is is not even always straightforward. While it may be easier for emerging academics to specify indicators, such as getting a doctorate or permanent position within a particular timeline, for established academic workers without such major milestones, specifying success can be a lot more slippery. Success indicators can come to reflect less the academic work we do than our own needs for safety, stability, smoothness, and even control. Context can influence this, too. Workplaces that, for example, tolerate or even reward publishing in predatory journals may unintentionally foster concepts of success that are at odds with how success is conventionally conceived in academic settings. It is important that the success indicators selected are credible both internally and externally against norms and reasonable expectations of academic work.

Indicators are unclear or unstated

Success is always at stake in success indicators. It is easy to race to doing tasks before we are clear on what success for us should be. Take time to hone your indicators to ensure that they are overarching, unambiguous, verifiable, and explicit enough. In our experience, avoiding the 'trouble-to-task trap' is particularly difficult when people are faced with situations around which there are perceived social norms or expectations on academic workers that make them feel compelled to act hastily or be seen to 'do something'. Emotion, adrenaline, and ethics come into play. As you develop your success indicators, take time to step back and consider them more objectively. Comments and input from credible insiders in the occluded games of academic work, including colleagues, supervisors, mentors, and trusted others, may all help ensure that success indicators are sufficiently clear. Academic work must, by nature, consider its success. It is not mere activity but is always a *focused* activity that should take account of its bigger purpose for students, society, the discipline/knowledge community, the workplace, and your values and circumstances.

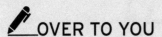 OVER TO YOU

Set Your Success Indicators

Work through The Success Pyramids (Figure 3.2). Use them to consider and specify what your three main success indicators will be for the next phase of your career. Taking account of your values and career stage, note down your top three success indicators and place one in each of the pyramids provided. Make the indicators individualized, real, responsive, and reflective of your values, career aspirations, and circumstances. Later in this book, you will again revisit The Success Pyramid and the success indicators that you noted here as you then work to set priorities, goals, and tasks based on them.

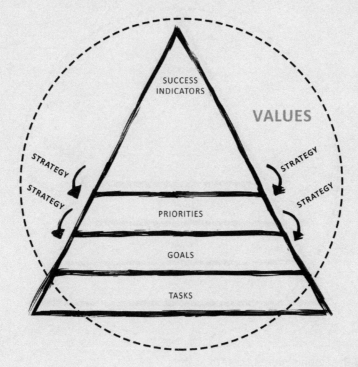

(Continued)

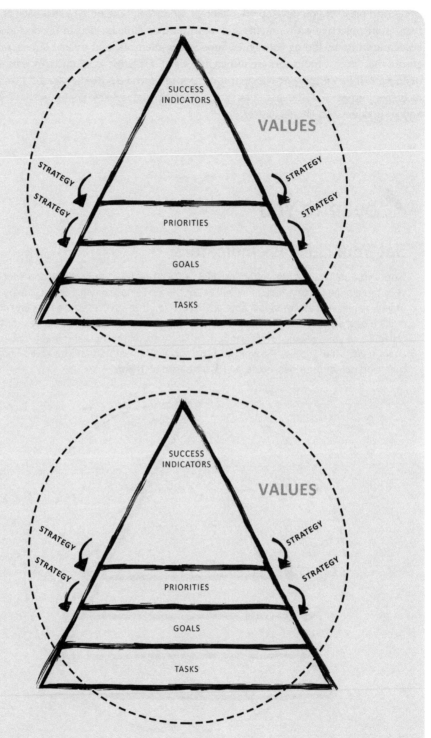

Figure 3.2 Setting Your Success Indicators

Now that you've spent some time noting down your success indicators, it's good to reflect on their appropriateness and come back to them periodically for revision.

REMARKABLE RESOURCES

Winners by Alastair Campbell

One of the UK's most connected commentators across politics, sport, business, and public life, Alastair Campbell (2015) distils the key mindsets, approaches, and reactions that characterize those who succeed in some of life's most competitive and demanding spheres and activities, including sport, business, and politics.

Key messages

- To be successful, a clear view of what constitutes success is necessary.
- Your strategy, priorities and actions must all align.
- Responding effectively to setbacks is as important as doing the right things.
- Many factors relating to your mindset, teamwork, leadership, and reactions to your use of data can help your success.

Key applications

- Inspiration and insights for academic work can be taken from success across many other fields.
- Make sure that an enduring focus on your success indicators inform your actions in your daily work.
- Don't get distracted by the noise of others' success indicators: reflection and clarity but ultimately a decisive focus will serve you well.

Leading by Alex Ferguson and Michael Moritz

Arguably the world's most successful football manager, Alex Ferguson and Michael Moritz (2015) share lessons on what it takes to achieve a quarter of a century of ongoing success in one of the world's most competitive sports.

Key messages

- Don't underestimate the importance of listening, reading, and observing to making yourself successful; talking is overrated.
- Set higher standards for success and owning these in your conduct; daily interactions and conduct is vital.

(Continued)

- Success is heavily dependent on consistently remaining hungry for success and working very hard, while avoiding complacency and drift.
- Focus and good use of time and failure are integral to success.

Key applications

- So much about success is not about wanting it but about your values, working patterns, and reactions. Ensure these reflect the best of you.
- To be more successful, read widely, find other interests, listen, and watch more.
- Try to react well to failure, distractions, time constraints, and criticism: all are potentially vital for future success.

4

DOING THE RIGHT THINGS I
EFFECTIVENESS, PRIORITIES, AND STRATEGY

We were very pleased. Our newly established professional development library, with its bookshelves overflowing with shiny, useful, and enticing tomes, was now available to anyone in our organization. If there was one lament we heard our academic colleagues make time and time again it was not having enough time to do all the cool research and writing they wanted. As we presented the curated array of the world's most insightful wisdom on effectiveness from its most pre-eminent authorities, collated and collected here in our workplace for the first time, our newly-hired colleague looked puzzled and replied: 'Oh that's great. I just don't have enough time to read any of them.' And there, in that moment, something in each of us slowly died.

One simple phrase contains everything necessary for success in academic work. And, incidentally, for success in war, marriage, friendship, and business. Like the best games, this phrase can be understood in a moment and yet offer a lifetime's worth of challenge and fascination. It has implications that are supremely practical for time, effort, and money, but is also striking to behold. Indeed, there are few more powerful or elusive words as Peter Drucker's famous paean to 'get the right things done' (1967: 1).

In this chapter, we uncover the clarity and usefulness of getting the right things done in academic work. We explain why this is so necessary and explore how doing so links to prioritization and strategy in academic work.

GET THE RIGHT THINGS DONE

EFFECTIVENESS: DOING THE RIGHT THINGS IN ACADEMIC WORK

I heard that a colleague characterised me as 'someone who didn't work weekends'. This description was not meant as a compliment ...

(Schell, 2014)

Effectiveness in academic work is about getting the right things done. In the previous chapters, we identified two vital considerations for academic work: selecting the right success indicators and ensuring that your values are sufficiently integrated or reflected in these indicators. Effectiveness allows us to consider what needs to be done in order to achieve success indicators. As we have said before, the right academic work does not happen by magic. Effectiveness is the vital first step to ensuring that the right work gets done, but let's first address the most common missteps to ensuring the right academic work gets done: tasks, time, and pressure.

Don't start with tasks

Reflecting on Drucker's plea to do the right things, with success indicators in mind, it's time to move to tasks now, right? To dive into the minutiae of academic work: to create plans and lists of teaching tasks to do, papers to write, people to see. To get sucked in and feel the satisfaction of getting things done. Wholeheartedly, we say: 'No.'

Before precious resources, including time, can be devoted to actions, first ascertain what the right things to do are. This stepping back from action can be disconcerting. Who doesn't like the reassurance and excitement of getting tasks done? It tells us that we are making progress and are good at what we do. However, like ice cream, while this may be immediately alluring to our senses and emotions, it is not necessarily the right thing to do in the longer term.

To fully realize why this follows, let's unpack what 'doing the right things' *really* means. Doing the right thing fundamentally is not about doing the wrong thing right. You have to first consider whether any action will help you move toward or meet your success indicator. Doing the right things means doing the right thing right – and ideally in the right time. Who would invest their precious time and energy into doing the wrong thing? Many of us. Ever had problems recruiting for a study, getting your published paper noticed by key people or received horrific student evaluations? All these commonly result less from inaction by an academic worker but from doing the wrong things. Even doing those wrong things right. However, we should not determine our effectiveness as academic workers by the tasks we do but rather the effectiveness of these on our success indicators. Effectiveness must come first.

Why do we feel so compelled to act in our academic work? Many factors explain industriousness in academic work: high levels of diverse demands from diverse sources, work ethic, wide reading, and knowledge ... there is always so much that we see and feel we could and should do.

These possibilities are at the heart of what makes academic work so varied, rich and rewarding but also can create a sense of malaise at the apex of all of these factors. The most common reaction that we see in academic workers is then approaching this work principally through the frame of reference or lens of time. This is very understandable. We have a strong sense of time being in short supply in academic work in opposition to these demands. Time is so tight in our lives that not only does it seem that we *never* have enough to do our tasks but we often feel cornered, squeezed, or eviscerated by the sheer pressure to do things and the lack of time to do so. This sense of lack is not just a cold intellectual conclusion – it's a real physical feeling of the walls closing in, of the impossibility of keeping up and the perilousness of what will happen if we fail. Moreover, we see ourselves as failing not just as academic workers, but as wives, husbands, partners, mothers, sons, and friends.

Indeed, large national surveys find the majority of academic workers experience high levels of stress similar to health professionals (Kinman and Wray, 2013; Kinman, 2014). Reviews show that these pressures are particularly prominent in academic workers who are younger, female, and have higher teaching workloads (Watt and Robertson, 2011). Increasing casualization of academic jobs compound these pressures and are not likely to relent.

'Stress,' 'anxiety', 'burnout', and 'fatigue' aren't just words; they exert real damage to ourselves and our relationships. Indeed, higher stress directly links in academic workers to a lowered perception of work–life balance (Kinman, 2014) and most academic workers report having problems setting boundaries between life and work (ibid.). The most common response in academic workers is to work harder and longer, losing boundaries of work and home in our lives as we add extra hours on at the end of the working day to get by. Indeed, up to two-thirds of academic workers in the UK have the perception that they simply spend too much time on work, with a similar proportion indicating low levels of well-being and half-report health-damaging effects (Times Higher Education University Workplace Survey, 2016). This time-pressed predicament is so unpleasant not only because academic work is so challenging, but also because we care so much about our academic work in this situation. There just NEVER seems to be *enough* time.

Don't start with time

This seemingly ubiquitous scarcity of time reflects the nature this resource. Kevin Kruse (2015) explains that on his desk he has a simple note with the magic number 1440 typed on it in 300-point font.

1440

When others make work requests, chat or ask for meetings – even if these would only take a minute – he knows that every minute spent away from doing his actual work is one less than the total number of 1440 minutes he has in that day. He could never get a single one of those minutes back.

Time is, Kruse explains, a unique resource. Irrespective of our status, wealth, gender, or context – whether a cleaner, royalty, celebrity, or academic worker – each of us has 1440 minutes in our day (2015). Unlike money, time cannot itself be sacrificed short-term for longer-term gain, hoarded for big 'rainy day' splurges when the need arises, or borrowed from others when we need it. Unlike health, time cannot be lost and then regained. Time is non-renewable and is neither re-spendable nor actually saveable. With time, we are on our own on an equal playing field with the human race (ibid.). As Drucker summarizes:

> The supply of time is totally inelastic. No matter how high the demand, the supply will not go up ... Everything requires time. It is the only truly universal condition. All work takes place in time and uses up time. Yet most people take for granted this unique irreplaceable, and necessary resource. Nothing else, perhaps, distinguishes effective executives as much as their tender loving care of time ... (1967: 26)

Doing starts with external pressures

There are so many pressures in academic work to do more in less time. Preoccupation and 'worry' about time in academic work is difficult to resist. These start early, with high expectations to publish extensively even during completion of the doctorate or to maintain high levels of academic performance across all areas of teaching, research and engagement every single year. In the face of these demands, we have heard time and time again (ironically) about the importance of 'good time management' and the seeming stigma around time and life choices. It can be very difficult to be seen by colleagues as putting family before work, to say 'No,' or pass on an attractive work prospect that comes our way. Due to the nature of the ways in which academic work is done, many things can affect the time we have to do it. For example, the availability of time for research is at least partially responsible for gender and race-based inequalities in academic career trajectories (Metcalfe and Gonzalez, 2013; Aiston and Jung, 2015; Jones et al., 2015). High teaching demands can constrain how much time spent on research and vice versa. In many societies and communities, women have high social demands outside of work. The actions of colleagues (junior and senior), students and professional staff who work with us can markedly affect what we spend our time doing. However, to be effective in doing the right academic work externally, we sometimes also have to do the hard personal internal work that is needed to give ourselves permission to make these choices around these pressures. It is this work that we now turn to.

If effectiveness in academic work is about getting the right things done, we can see already that this does not happen by magic. Tasks, time, and pressures immediately cloud the picture. Conversely, being effective requires a fusion of intellectual, emotional and personal factors to make the right choices.

We cannot say here what effectiveness must or will look like for you. Ultimately, doing the right things is about what is right for you based on the trade-offs and sacrifices that you are willing to make around your success indicators: being comfortable resisting external pressures, time scarcity, and tasks, but also not reacting against them. It is more about identifying what is right for you personally and what will help you achieve your success indicators during possibly decades of academic work.

PRIORITIES: THE KEY TO EFFECTIVENESS

Doing the right things is primarily about deliberately choosing the right things to do and which of these things to then do first. In other words, effectiveness is about working to priorities.

Setting and working to priorities in academic work is pivotal to doing effective academic work because it is extreme knowledge work. We have to be exceptional at prioritizing because even taking account of our success indicators, personal career trajectories or aspirations, we cannot even begin to do everything that we each could do in each area of teaching, research, and engagement.

Effectiveness is not about time but about setting the right priorities for your time. Indeed, shifting from time management – a 'time lens' – to priority management – a 'priority lens' – characterizes the approaches of luminaries from Peter Drucker (1967) to John Maxwell (2011) to Mark Horstman (2016):

> Time management is a fallacy, we like to say. Time doesn't need you to 'manage' it - it's been getting along just fine without you for billions of years. We can't manage time. But what we CAN manage is what we do with that time. (Manager Tools, 2016a)

Thinking in this way moves our gaze from time and inputs to thinking about what is most important and the possible results of our actions for these priorities. The mind shift in thinking about effectiveness from time to priorities has a resonance that risks being self-evident: we nod approvingly and comfort ourselves that, 'of course, I get that already!' However, if you ever catch yourself saying, 'I don't have enough time to ...,' know that you have not fully embraced the profundity of thinking of your day less in terms of time and more in terms of being a blank canvas of doing what is most important and meaningful to you. Saying you 'don't have enough time' is akin to saying 'it's not a priority'. The perils of this come when we don't allocate time to do those things that are *really* most important.

'I DON'T HAVE ENOUGH TIME' = 'IT'S NOT A PRIORITY'

What are priorities?

The best book on priorities that we have ever read is *Essentialism* by Greg McKeown (2014). To read it is to be challenged on almost every page. McKeown (ibid.) paints a picture of modern life that many academic workers would readily recognize: there are too many choices of what we could do, too much social pressure to be so connected and a myth from advertising and the media that 'you can have it all'. Yet, as he traces the etymology of the word 'priority', he finds that it only came into usage in English in the 1400s – and only then in relation to the singular, first and most important thing: *the priority*. It took another 500 years for this word to morph into the plural 'priorities' to refer to multiple first things. More recently, 'priorities' seems to be used in relation to anything that could be done to affect an outcome. Thus, organizational plans come to have 20, 30 or 40 *priorities*. Conversely, Drucker (1967) reflected that an effective knowledge worker could have a maximum of three.

Setting priorities in academic work is so important because it is extreme knowledge work. It can take so many different forms and follow so many different paths. Available in a couple of clicks, it's hard in our fields even to keep up with published research and writing – researchers estimate that this doubles every nine years (Bornmann and Mutz, 2015).

Yet, too much academic work is about the undisciplined pursuit of more, whereas prioritization in academic work is about the disciplined pursuit of what really matters (McKeown, 2014). Our highest priority should be to protect our ability to prioritize (ibid.). But how, in the sound and fury and fog of academic workplaces, can we cut out the trivial many and the noise to focus down and make choices to work only on that which matters most in our academic work? Setting the right priorities does not happen by magic, it necessitates making hard choices consciously, yet, in our workshops, we find that academic workers are consistently challenged by what the right things are that they should do. Which opportunities to take or reject? What sacrifices are worth taking? Doing the right things remains one of the most challenging, vexing, and elusive of ends.

How to prioritize?

Take on the priority lens

Adopting a 'priority lens' to approach academic work compared to a 'time lens' leads to different thoughts, actions, and outcomes (Table 4.1). A 'priority lens' is based on recognizing this work as extreme knowledge work and demands seeing almost all of what we could do in our academic work as being that which we should not do. We then have to make deliberate choices to spend as little time on this as we can.

Taking on this priority lens is likely to lead to doing fewer things and having to say 'no' to others' work requests far more. It is a mindset that is about honing in on what matters most for your work and deliberately making choices, and accepting the trade-offs to focus down on these. If your personal sense of competency or worthiness is based on work volume, always doing work when asked, or the hours you spend working, then this priority lens can be disturbing and unnerving. A time lens; however, is a principle cause in academic work of stress, overwork, lack of boundaries, and even of poor quality.

Adopting this priority lens makes some of our academic work practises seem readily more questionable. Around 30 per cent of full-time employed academic workers' schedules are spent in meetings and on email (Ziker, 2014). While these are necessary to modern academic workplaces, few academic workers declare these to be central to their work, résumés, job satisfaction, or success indicators.

Table 4.1 Time vs. Priority Lens

	Time lens	Priority lens
Thinks	**All things to everyone**	**Less but better**
	I have to ...	I choose to ...
	It's all important	Only select things that matter most
	How can I do it all?	What are the trade-offs?
Does	**The undisciplined pursuit of more**	**The disciplined pursuit of less**
	Reacts to the most pressing	Pauses to discern what really matters
	Says 'yes' quicker	Says 'no' to everything that is not essential
Gets	**Less satisfying**	**More meaning**
	Takes on too much, exhausting	Chooses carefully to do great work
	Feels out of control	Feels more in control
	Unsure if the right things got done	Gets the right things done

Source: Adapted from McKeown (2014)

Spending 30 per cent of your daily time on activities that don't directly contribute to your success is perilous to priorities. Conversely, reading is vital to academic workers' teaching and research but we spend less time reading any one article than ever previously (Ware and Mabe, 2015). Reading and thinking has often become what we do when everything else has been done or when we are too tired to do everything else. Alas, usually this doesn't happen because 'everything else' is never done.

It often takes more courage to stop doing things you are already doing than to say 'no' to taking on new things. Those in less secure academic jobs or with particularly prescriptive or opinionated senior colleagues may feel that true prioritization of academic work is not realistic – at least not if you want to keep your job. Thinking in terms of hours worked, efforts expended, and tasks done is actually fairly common for people across all different levels of job security (McKeown, 2014). It often occurs in organizations in which senior management would actually prefer academic workers to focus down more and do really meaningful work of the highest possible quality. If we really care about quality in our academic work, however, irrespective of circumstances, a priority lens is less about being better, results, and true quality in work. This is vital in knowledge work because we know that working more and harder on more does not necessarily lead to better teaching, research, or engagement.

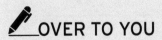 **OVER TO YOU**

Give Yourself Permission to Prioritize

Prioritization in academic work asks us deep and difficult questions. It is important to intellectually, emotionally, and ethically come to terms with the necessity of prioritization in academic work.

(Continued)

Think of instances in your own academic work in which you defined yourself based on your hours worked, inputs, or work volume. List these here.

What immediate feelings and thoughts does overtly working on far fewer dimensions of your academic work bring (that is, making choices and accepting trade-offs)?

1.   My immediate feelings are:

2.   My immediate thoughts are:

Think of your personality and of your past and current experiences: what are your three main barriers to setting priorities? List these here.

Be brutally honest about what furthers success indicators

If not's not a 'Hell, yeah!' then it should be a clear 'No.' Thus, McKeown (2014) conveys the level of attractiveness needed to elevate a possible action to being a priority. Setting this brutally high bar on what becomes a priority is important and requires deliberate thought about what is *most important* in terms of success indicators. Priorities are seldom about simply doing more or doing the simply obvious.

Prioritization is about focusing down. For Steve Jobs, in order to increase profits, it meant reducing Apple's dozens of product lines to four key products and making these the best products possible, even if competitors already had market share advantage in these areas. For Sony, almost half of their workforce was disenchanted or disengaged with their work (Schwartz, 2010). Income was down by a third. In response, Sony encouraged their staff to actually *take* more time to renew their energy between intensive projects and to address their personal needs for physical health, emotional well-being, mental focus, and spiritual significance. The working day began to incorporate shutting down email for two hours in order to tackle important projects or taking a daily walk. More than 80 per cent of workers reported being more engaged, focused and productive; 90 per cent reported more energy. Profits rose accordingly (ibid.). Working more, longer, and harder proved to be exactly the opposite of what was needed to actually affect their success indicators.

Prioritization is about allowing ourselves to focus on what most contributes to success. Game theory indicates that chess players, chief executives, and academic workers can benefit from thinking forward and then reasoning backward (Clark and Thompson, 2014) in order to base their priorities on the ends that they want to achieve. Therefore, taking the time to do this thinking is key. For Beethoven, this meant displacing himself from the piano to take long country walks to improve his creativity. Accordingly, walking, sleeping, and taking time to muse can all improve academic work (Schell, 2014).

Workplace expectations and your own success indicators do not necessarily have to be zero-sum games. Indeed, the depreciating returns from working longer hours are well established. Organisation for Economic Co-operation Development (OECD) data covering 22 years has shown that working a moderate number of hours is associated with higher national productivity and markedly lower returns evident in working weeks over 50 hours (Pencavel, 2014). Elizabeth Reid (2015) interviewed over 100 staff and identified a working culture in which work hours lasted from 60 to 80 hours per week, punctuated with low levels of perceived control over travel and communication after hours. Both men and women reported that their family and home lives substantially suffered. Asking for time off was considered 'weak'. But, interestingly, managers could not identify which staff worked longer hours in terms of their productivity unless they self-identified as such.

Given the distinctive demands of academic work as extreme knowledge work, we have to be particularly attuned to what the right balance of working hours is for ourselves. This work requires judgement, creativity, sound technical, and astute people skills, and involves many interactions both face-to-face and online, each working day. It is particularly at risk when sleep, health, and happiness are threatened by excessive working hours.

Doing the right things in academic work is not merely about mirroring workplace pressures and cultures, doing more or doing the obvious; it often requires courage and discipline. It entails a combination of sound judgement, calmness, wisdom, and determination in the face of others' advice, scepticism, and criticism. People whom we count as mentors or trusted colleagues can give us great advice on what the right thing is to do, but can also offer advice that does not fully take account of our success indicators, circumstances, or interests.

We have heard too many younger academics get bad advice on the right things from more senior academics – advice that does not put their interests first, is based on limited insight into external realities, or is self-serving. It is important to develop your own independence in judging what the right things are for you to prioritize and to develop good processes and practises to consult, listen, and triangulate but, ultimately, set your own priorities.

Be strategic

From your success indicators, strategy can help you make the choices necessary to set the right priorities – to then formulate appropriate goals and do the right tasks. In modern organizations – including academic workplaces – the word 'strategy' is used both frequently and mostly incorrectly (Malham, 2013). While *'Everyone needs a Strategy'* (Freedman, 2013: ix), most proponents have no strategy at all and fewer still good strategies (Malham, 2013).

Likewise, strategy is everywhere and nowhere in academic workplaces: across central, departmental, and individual levels. The need for strategy is loudly and widely voiced: workplaces develop 'Strategic Plans', academic workers counsel each other on the necessity of 'being strategic', strategic planning retreats involving dozens of people are convened and shiny documents produced for shelves. Yet, despite all this hallowed talk of strategy, there's a pervading lack of clarity about what strategy actually is in academic work. What does really good strategy look like? Why is it so necessary? Strategy is presented as a universal saviour but one that is simultaneously ill-defined and poorly enacted.

WHAT IS STRATEGY?

> Despite the problems of finding ways through the uncertainty and confusion of human affairs, a strategic approach is still considered to be preferable to one that is merely tactical let alone random. Having a strategy suggests an ability to look up from the short term and the trivial to view the long term and the essential, to address causes rather than symptoms, to see the woods rather than the trees. (Freedman, 2013: ix)

While the term 'strategy' dates from classical Greek, the concept is as old as humanity itself (Freedman, 2013) – evident in early humans, the Old Testament and across early Eastern and Western civilizations. Good strategy addresses the underlying factors that are most critical to success (ibid.). *Strategy isn't about success indicators or goals: it is not the success that we want to achieve but how best to achieve it.*

History documents numerous examples of good strategy. David's famous defeat of Goliath reflected a cunning underdog strategy which focused on playing to strengths, perceptions, and surprise. David made a clear decision not to try to compete against his ostensibly superior opponent on the giant's strengths but to specifically target his weakness. Accordingly, David rejected the social convention of accepting armour from Saul – leaving himself even more vulnerable to blows arising from traditional combat. By doing this, David acted to further reduce the perceived threat he posed in the giant's eyes. More capable of moving quickly, David drew on the strength he had with his sling, striking the giant dead with his vital second blow – thereby ensuring no recovery was possible (Freedman, 2013). Likewise, history is replete with stories of strategy focused on attrition, defending, distraction, incentives, and surprise (Freedman, 2013).

STRATEGY ISN'T WHAT SUCCESS WE WANT TO ACHIEVE BUT HOW BEST TO ACHIEVE THIS

What is good strategy?

Good strategy allows our strengths to be *'applied to the most promising opportunity'* (Rumelt, 2011: 9). In this way, good strategy is expressed in our success indicators, goals, and tasks but is not evident merely in their existence. Rather, good strategy refers to the coherent alignment of success indicators, goals, and tasks in ways that not only draw on existing strengths but also creates additional strength through the coherence provided by the strategy (ibid.). Good strategy entails making clear choices about what will be done to further your success indicators and should result in tasks and goals that add value to each other's contributions, this is called leveraging. Good strategy also gets to *what matters most* in a situation, irrespective of whether this is obvious or obscure. Good strategy has a number of key facets (Table 4.2). It addresses the most influential barriers or facilitators of success and helps us devise approaches to overcome these. It should be responsive to context in terms of what actions are acceptable, ethical, or doable. It should be honest in candidly addressing what really is most influential, rather than addressing what we would like to be at play. Related to this, good strategy always starts with an accurate diagnosis of 'What is going on here?': What factors in a situation really stand to inhibit or foster success?

Good strategy is about recognizing your own strengths and weaknesses, the opportunities and risks around the actions that you could take and how you can best harness your strengths to address these. In this way, good strategy is also about what you are good at.

Good strategy compels us to make the hard choices needed to concentrate our efforts on addressing the smaller number of factors that stand to make the biggest contributions to our success. It usually suggests various courses of action that are not only coherent but also leverage and amplify each other and anticipate potential barriers. This can involve single actions that have multiple useful effects that further success.

Good strategy is not then about identifying worthy success indicators, such as being 'excellent at research' or 'a first-class educator'. These noble aims may be expressed (in many forms) in The Success Pyramid but do not provide any coherent coordinated means to identify *how* to be successful. Nor is strategy just about setting simple goals, such as publishing more, teaching better or attaining funding. Also, good strategy isn't just about tasks: the litany or laundry list of different things we could do. Mostly, these actions will fall into the trap of being *the wrong things, done right*: tasks done perfectly competently that contribute little or nothing to our success indicators. As Drucker pointed out with searing clarity: 'There is nothing so useless as doing efficiently that which should not be done at all' (1963: 59–60).

Table 4.2   Characteristics of Good Strategy around Priorities

Facet of strategy	Key questions
Success indicator	What does success look like for me? What is crucial?
Responsive to context	What is tenable or viable?
Candid and honest	What factors most likely stand to help or hinder success?
Diagnosis	What is going on here that may affect success?
Strengths and weaknesses	What can I do best? In what am I less or least able?
Coherence	Do my priorities make sense when viewed together?
Concentration	Are my efforts focused as much as possible on that which will most affect success?
Leverage	How can my priorities build on each other?
Amplification	How can my priorities add value to each other?
Anticipation	Do my priorities take account of what is most likely to change?

Case study: Struggling student seeks strategy

Let's consider these concepts in a real-world situation, involving an emerging academic worker currently completing his doctoral degree (Table 4.3). Our student has been experiencing reduced performance on his doctoral courses despite working harder and relying on his usual study skills.

He knows that unless he attains a passing average, he will be removed from the doctoral programme. Accordingly, his success indicator is attaining his doctoral degree in a reasonable five-year time period. He is also aware that in order to be successful when applying for postdoctoral awards after his completion, he will need to have published at least a couple of papers. Ideally, this pressure would 'go away' but he has talked to numerous established salaried academic workers and it is the normal expectation in his discipline. What could he do in this situation? There are a myriad of different options.

Common responses would be to panic more, work harder, increase time spent studying, and writing by sleeping less and/or cutting back on social time. Taking time to reflect on his

Table 4.3   Struggling Student Seeking Strategy

Person/Situation	Doctoral researcher with decreasing performance and outputs
Problem	Improve academic performance and outputs during programme
Success indicator	Complete doctoral degree in five years
Obvious actions	Work harder to revise Write more Sleep less Seek help for study skills from student services
Diagnosis	Student has never learned how to learn
Strategy	Develop mind-mapping skills
Priority	Invest time to read books and develop skills on mind-mapping

predicament, luckily our student steps back to consider: 'What is going on here?' What is stopping him from getting the results he needs despite the considerable hours he spends revising and writing? He comes to the candid and difficult realization that he has never 'learned how to learn' – to quickly understand key concepts – and that he will get minimal returns from working, reading, and writing for more hours compared to working differently. His inadequacies in learning are now having a real impact on his success indicators. How can he learn how to learn better?

He journeys to the bookshop and comes across a great book on 'mind-mapping' from the BBC by Tony and Barry Buzan (1995). He has never come across this book or concept before, and can immediately see that it has potential to help him to synthesize large volumes of information on single sheets of papers in ways that he finds easy to organize and then remember. He can immediately see that learning this new skill is realistic, coherent, and responds to his context, strengths, and weaknesses. It is something that he can learn and also respond to in the more visual ways he has found helped his learning in the past. Learning mind-mapping will help him study but also help with his writing in organizing his reading and draft manuscripts. He can leverage his emerging mind-mapping skills to improve both types of work with the hope that increasing skill in one area will amplify benefits for the other.

He has a busy week ahead, full of course and writing demands, but then makes the decision to focus his strategy on becoming proficient in mind-mapping. This means that he prioritizes reading the mind-mapping book instead of spending more time writing or studying, and develops his skills as he works through the book.

The student knows that not all such actions strike gold. He spends a week learning to mind-map and then assesses how it helps his learning but, more pointedly, whether it improves his success indicators: does it increase his grades to help complete his doctoral studies? Encouragingly, he experiences a 10 per cent increase in his marks for the following two years and increases his writing productivity. In time, he also finds that he can use mind-mapping to organize the content of the qualitative interviews for his research, keep on top of his increasing workload, condense his conference presentations to a single sheet and organize chapters in a book on being successful, happy, and effective in academic work. We will pre-serve that student's anonymity, but it suffices to say that the few hours he spent learning to mind-map proved to be a supremely useful, even life-changing strategy.

COMMON CHALLENGES WITH GOOD STRATEGY

This situation includes many of the key concepts of good strategy but it also helps illustrate some of the key challenges.

Not specifying success indicators

In his analysis of the most successful people in politics, sport, and business, Campbell (2015) shows how they consistently devoted substantial attention to first pinpoint what specific 'success' they wanted to achieve. Nothing can be done strategically without first establish-ing what your success will be. As we approach the occluded games and genres of academic work, thinking how and where we can best be successful is important, but can only occur if we are very clear on what our success indicators are. 'What's the point?' we might very well ask ourselves. Without establishing your success indicators, you cannot begin the move to designing effective strategy, to then inform prioritization, goal setting, and undertaking tasks. Furthermore, none of these can be evaluated unless this is done against a success indicator.

Yet, much effort in academic workplaces is devoted to personal tasks, goals, and priorities that meet no discernable success indicator. Tasks that do not contribute to success indicators, however competently done, represent the archetypal 'wrong things, done right'.

Confusing 'a' strategy with 'good' strategy

Developing good strategy is tricky because the main barriers to your success can be subtle, hidden and complex. Effective strategy requires a rich mix of insight into the nature of your problems and perceptive self-knowledge. Becoming a better writer may actually involve spending less time writing and more time reading, mind-mapping and thinking on long walks. Like this, strategy often involves candid consideration of what really matters in a situation and then demands that you keep focused on doing the right things. Don't confuse having 'a' strategy with having a 'good' strategy.

Good strategy shares at least some common characteristics that imbue its actions with additional powers to affect success indicators. It has particular facets that raise it above being a mere collection of responses to a problem. Assessing your strategy for its responsiveness to your success indicators and aspects such as coherence, leverage, and amplification is important. Single actions with multiple favourable benefits almost always trump multiple actions with single benefits. It's important to assess any strategy for the hallmarks of good strategy and monitor whether your strategy is actually having its desired effects on your success indicators. Always assess your strategy about the hallmarks of good strategy. Rumelt (2011) provides exceptionally useful criteria.

STRIVE FOR SINGLE ACTIONS WITH MULTIPLE FAVOURABLE BENEFITS OVER MULTIPLE ACTIONS WITH SINGLE BENEFITS

Falling into the 'trouble-to-task trap'

Time and again, in virtually all spheres of workplace activity, academic workers shift immediately and seamlessly from confronting a particular personal or institutional problem to the tasks that should be done.

The supervisory team of a PhD student are frustrated with her lack of publishing. They arrange a meeting with her to give her their ideas on what manuscripts she should be publishing. Discussion continues apace on which journals she should target and how they could each help with the articles. At a departmental meeting, a group of 30 academic workers discuss a national recommendation that the principle of ethnic diversity should be incorporated throughout teaching, across all such departments. Immediately, discussion moves to how to tweak content of specific courses: which courses and how they should be modified. Discussion continues on the relative merits and demerits of changing particular courses in particular ways. An executive panel of national research leaders in chronic disease are concerned that a national charity in chronic disease has a vision and mission that excludes most of the research work and patient needs in their diseases. Immediately, the group moves to suggestions of how to get the Board to be more effective in fundraising, media campaigns, and advocacy. Discussion continues apace of how dysfunctional the Board is. In each scenario, this is as likely to solve the problem at hand as a blindfolded archer is likely to hit a moving target with a blunt arrow. Virtually any success is attributable to good luck.

Each of these scenarios shares the same 'play': a rapid move that we call the 'trouble-to-task trap', defined as leaping from an important problem or challenge directly to what tasks should be done to address it, without giving a careful consideration of success indicators, strategy or priorities. This means that the actions suggested are not based on:

- A stated overt conception(s) of what success will look like. (Success indicators)
- A sense of 'what's going on here' around the factors contributing to the problem. (Strategy)
- Agreement on what should be done first. (Priorities)

All of these situations involve smart, educated, creative, and well-intentioned, motivated people (they are academic knowledge workers, after all!) who care about their roles deeply and who want to help with the issues before them. Why is the 'trouble-to-task trap' so common in academic workplaces? It perhaps gives assurance of interest, action, and responsiveness. There is an alluring reassurance that something meaningful is being 'done', that a matter is being taken seriously and that the organization and/or those individuals in it care about the problem at hand.

J. Keith Murnighan (2012) addresses this paradox at length in his book *Doing Nothing*. Resisting moving to rapid solutions remains difficult but also incredibly important for knowledge workers when working with others around problems. In contemporary times, defined by action and political correctness, not rushing to do something remains difficult for the knowledge worker, and often requires a higher degree of insight, self-knowledge and confidence (even courage) than doing something. Suggesting a laundry list of things to do is a lot easier than a careful and rounded consideration of the nature of the problem, what contributes to it and the best short-, medium-, and long-term strategy to make hard choices to address what matters most in the problem. Next time you feel drawn into the 'trouble-to-task trap' (or see those around you fall into it), hold back in order to first consider success, strategy, and priorities.

Thinking 'good strategy' always feels good

While we know that 'good strategy' can benefit us, like running on the treadmill, it involves a marked degree of discipline and necessary pain. Done well, it means making hard choices, living by them and sometimes taking flak from others for what you are and are not prioritizing.

It could involve concentrating your research efforts on an emerging topic or population to the neglect of an area in which you are more expert, raising your profile on social media to the conscious neglect of supervising more students or developing new skills in teamwork when others want you just to submit more grants.

We can each recall instances in which we have been subject to negative comments from senior colleagues around the choices we have strategically made: that we should not be travelling to lead workshops on academic skills, be on social media or write creative articles in blogs and journals. Such comments are particularly disappointing when they come from senior colleagues in our organization because of the abject lack of insight that they show into the need for strategy in academic work and workplaces.ss

Strategy is corporate

Many of us are concerned about increasing academic workloads and expectations that academic workplaces march too much to the tune of governments and corporations. These are worrying trends but they are not about strategy. Effective career strategy cannot only help you to meet workplace expectations but it can also ensure a better-balanced life because it compels us to concentrate more deliberately on what matters most. With good strategy, worklife does not have to be a zero-sum game.

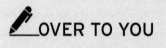 OVER TO YOU

Setting Your Priorities

Using the three Success Pyramids provided below (Figure 4.1), restate the success indicators that you worked on in the last chapter and specify three priorities for each.

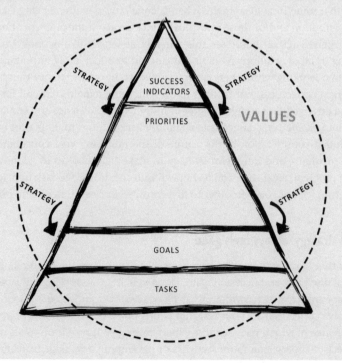

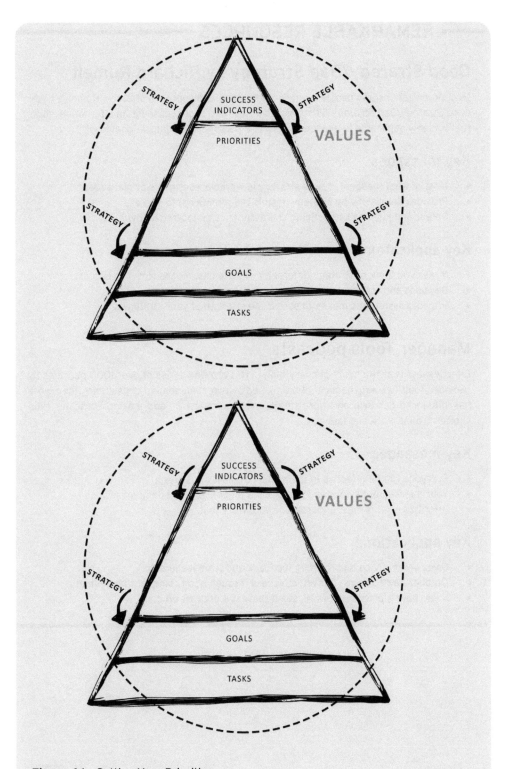

Figure 4.1 Setting Your Priorities

———— **REMARKABLE RESOURCES** ————

Good Strategy/Bad Strategy by Richard Rumelt

Most organizations and people wrongly understand and approach strategy. Rumelt's book, *Good Strategy/Bad Strategy* (2011), makes a clear and cogent case for an alternative model that is highly applicable to academic work at a personal or organizational level.

Key messages

- Most of what masquerades as strategy in workplaces is goals or platitudes.
- Provides details of why strategy itself is the pathway(s) to success.
- Details and justifies key defining characteristics of good strategy.

Key applications

- Makes you think of strategy differently – as the best means to get to success.
- Develops and refines your own good academic career strategy.
- Provides systematic means to assess the strength of your strategies.

Manager Tools podcasts

Effectiveness is at the heart of everything in this growing series of over 1000 podcasts by Manager Tools (www.manager-tools.com). Led by two management consultants, their work has influenced our own on prioritization, avoiding overwork and making conscious time choices around work and family.

Key messages

- Everyone can be effective in their role, but most of us aren't.
- Your mindset, behaviour and interactions influence your effectiveness.
- Prioritize what is most important to you. Work to it.

Key applications

- Gives great advice on providing feedback and team leadership.
- Outlines how to drive your effectiveness through good calendar management.
- If you have a problem at work, see if there is a podcast on it.

5

DOING THE RIGHT THINGS II
GOALS, TASKS, AND TIME

Turns out, life's a little bit more complicated than a slogan on a bumper sticker.

(Judy Hopps, 2016)

Success in academic work depends on great ideas, great plans, and great visions. Reality quickly catches up in our attempts to make the most of such inspiration. For, while knowing that our success indicators and priorities are essential, it provides only part of what is needed to be effective in academic work. If we can't turn these higher-end considerations into a practical set of daily focused actions, done in the right order and time, the potential of our work almost immediately suffers – even dies. Working to the right goals and tasks in the right time is the underappreciated, yet imperative, Cinderella to her more obvious and flashy sisters. Accordingly, this chapter addresses why it is so important to be deliberate about the ends our work seeks: goals, what is then done, tasks and, most importantly, the time in which these occur.

TIME IN ACADEMIC WORK

Time has a challenging relationship with academic work and academic workers. The pace of academic life can be fearsome: 'haste, hurry, and rush' seem to dominate in our academic fast lane, heading toward some vague workplace mantra of excellence (Vostal, 2014; Moore et al., 2016). Reading, writing, thinking, discussing, even doing research or preparing for teaching often seem at peril in our daily lives. The hopelessness and tension created by this are very real.

Every person reading this book has likely lamented a lack of time at least once in his or her career. Indeed, it is concerning that large surveys show that more academic work is being taken home, while levels of well-being amongst thousands of academic workers, their families and their workplaces get lower (Kinman, 2014; Greco et al., 2015). The pressures on academic workers and the upstream factors (for example, around gender and race) that contribute to unfairness of opportunity and progressing are both very real.

In conversations and experiences of everyday work, many academic workers are extremely conscious of time and its passing. Perhaps the most enduring strain of academic work is the tension between what first attracted us to this work and the subsequent seeming lack of time we now seem to get to do this.

We're quite familiar with different concepts of time. We look at our watch to get an objective sense of what the time is or how long we have to work on a particular task. Yet, time has an important subjective element, seeming to pass quicker or slower experientially, depending on the type of tasks that we are doing. This can seriously undermine our ability to accurately judge time spent on a task. The nature of some tasks we do and how they interact with us veritably swallow up copious amounts of time, while other tasks make time go by unfathomably slowly.

Time and task have an unusual symbiotic relationship, one that if not understood can have disastrous consequences. In his book on performance, Matthew Syed (2015) dissects the investigation of the crash in 1978 of United Airlines Flight 173. Two hours after leaving JFK Airport in New York City, the two pilots became aware of a problem with the plane's landing gear.

As they approached their destination, Portland, Oregon, despite their seemingly lowering the landing gear, a loud vibration was felt and the cockpit light indicated that the gear had not been lowered. With over 32,000 flight hours between them, supported by an engineer with almost 4000 hours flight time and a combined experience of 51 years, they aborted the landing and entered a holding pattern to assess whether the gear had been lowered. Landing without the gear down, while unlikely to end in a severe accident, would cause considerable damage to the aircraft. Their attention switched to work out whether the gear had been lowered: check after check was made, including contacting on-the-ground observers. With flaps down, circling around Portland Airport, check after check was made to ascertain the state of the gear. But the captain could not be sure.

Suddenly, the engineer had a horrific realization. Fuel was too low. He alerted the captain, who parried his initial cautions. Shortly afterwards, they found themselves and their 189 passengers, eight miles short of the airport on a clear night without enough fuel to make it. The plane descended and crashed into a wood, six miles short of the runway. Eight passengers, the plane's engineer and a flight attendant all died, with a further 21 people being seriously injured.

The National Transportation Safety Board Investigation indicated that the landing gear had been operational throughout. The probable cause of the crash was the failure of the captain to monitor and respond to the dangerously low-fuel state and to the engineer's warnings to take action: inattention and preoccupation led the captain to miss and dismiss, with fatal consequences. Second, the other crew members failed to fully comprehend the criticality of the fuel situation.

It's tempting to dismiss this as a tragic one-off accident based on human error despite the crew's wealth of experience and otherwise optimal conditions. Yet, similar crashes occurred resulting from pilot preoccupation with faulty landing lights in 1963 (Aeroflot), 1969 (Scandinavian Airlines), 1972 (Eastern Airlines) and LOT (1980). In each instance, the sense of time and priorities of the multiple experienced senior people flying the planes became lost because they became immersed in an important, although not vital, immediate problem. Despite decades of experience, otherwise favourable conditions and the patently severe consequences of running out of fuel, humans' awareness of time and priorities is extremely fragile and fallible.

Indeed, while focus, flow, and immersion in some of the tasks of academic work are very helpful, they also seem to have strange effects on time, with hours seeming to disappear in a few minutes. In the face of high workplace expectations for work volume and quality, and this sense of time and its pressure (Tight, 2009), academic workers:

- Spend more hours doing academic work (Kinman, 2014).
- Take more academic work home from the workplace (Gornall and Salisbury, 2012).
- Bemoan their lack of autonomy (Nadolny and Ryan, 2013).
- Set up dedicated workplace retreats to blitz read, think, and write academic work (Moore, 2003).
- Consciously do academic work more slowly (Berg and Seeber, 2016).
- Attribute challenges to underlying and complex inequities (Knights and Richards, 2003).
- Take jobs outside academic workplaces (Levine et al., 2011).

These solutions have too much 'trouble-to-task' in them than we would like. Academic workers who experience these challenges occurring in workplaces also lack:

- Consistently good established role models for integrating academic work and life (Levine et al., 2011).
- Support on how to do academic work (Chai, 2015; Gentry and Stokes, 2015).
- A clear sense of what excellence in academic work entails (Kyvik, 2012; Vostal, 2014; Moore et al., 2016).

Such deficits and ambiguities in processes, skills and outcomes are a recipe for challenges to working patterns and hours. A first step is to conceptualize time and how it connects to academic work.

Time in academic work refers to the distinct periods (years, weeks, hours and minutes) that we allocate in our daily calendars to our work. A useful schema for thinking about this is the concept of '100 Blocks a Day' (Urban, 2016) – the approximately 1000 minutes of our total 1440 minutes of time in each day that you do not spend sleeping – broken up into 100 blocks of 10 minutes each. It's important to think of your priorities, goals and tasks in relation to this representation of time. This visualization helps us counteract losing track of the vital time currency of the calendar. Time is viewed in an applied sense as being strongly linked to the priorities, goals, and tasks being enacted during any one set period or unit. We will cover time more in relation to calendars and their management in a later chapter, but for now it's vital to remember that goals and tasks must always take account of the time that we allocate to them.

GOALS IN ACADEMIC WORK

If only I had enough time … but I just don't get enough time to: _____.
(Insert: write/think/prepare/read/think/research/relax/parent/other here.)

Doing the right things in academic work is far from easy. Goals form the vital bridge from priorities (what is most important) to tasks (what is done) in The Success Pyramid, ultimately to achieve your success indicators. Formulating the right goals to express and further your work priorities is vital and allows you to do the right tasks. Based on your priorities, setting goals helps you make choices, and specific goals can be developed for the most cerebral to practical parts of academic work:

- Taking no student marking home on a Friday.
- Having a daily writing target of 500 words on a key 'tricky' article.
- Publishing four peer-reviewed papers during your doctorate.
- Setting a 5 p.m. deadline to stop answering emails each day.
- Reviewing six journal articles each year in prestigious journals.

Setting goals in academic work

Goals are needed in academic work because this work is extreme knowledge work: so much could be done to fulfil priorities, but what will make the biggest difference to furthering a priority? During a particular period of time, what is going to be realistic and right? What goals are so important that these must be fulfilled?

Merciless diligence and ongoing attention in working to goals in academic work is needed because the links between the priorities that we hold and the tasks that we do is vulnerable and prone to breaking down. Distractions come from many directions: other people, context, and our own moods, inclinations, and energy. Each of these takes more from your 1440 daily minutes and make it difficult to focus on goals.

Setting and keeping to the right goals requires pointed initial effort and ongoing discipline but makes possible the tracking and psychological rewards of progress. Merely setting goals however, is not enough. Rather, *good* goals must be set. Good goals are appropriate. Good goals map directly from your priorities. Good goals also have particular characteristics. Drucker (2006) saw good goals as sharing common SMART characteristics (Table 5.1).

Table 5.1   SMART Goals

Goals should be:	Key questions
Specific	Is your goal sufficiently precise?
Measurable	Can your goal be measured?
Achievable	Will your goal stretch you but also be attainable?
Relevant	Does your goal map from your priority?
Time-bound	Is your goal appropriate in terms of projected time?

GOOD GOALS MAP DIRECTLY FROM YOUR PRIORITIES

Some considerations are especially important in academic work, notably whether goals are achievable and relevant. Extreme knowledge work is prone to goals that are unrealistically lofty given the possible complexity and unpredictability of the work, such as setting overly optimistic project timelines or marking deadlines, as well as goals that don't readily map to stated priorities. For example, when we have stated that writing is a priority but we instead have a goal to end each day with an empty email inbox and set no goals around writing. Make sure that your goals are good.

Good strategy creates good goals

Selecting the right goals is not easy (at least, not if the full power of strategy is sought). As addressed in the previous chapter, for good strategy to be employed, single priorities should subsume multiple goals that support, leverage, and amplify each other. If being credible at research is prioritized by a senior academic worker holding a heavy administrative position, then this priority should be expressed in a number of coherent and strategically selected goals. While some of these goals may be focused on ends (such as applying for external research funds each year or publishing four peer-reviewed papers annually), others should be focused on means. In this instance, goals could be retaining a competent research assistant to manage their research and attracting talented students. If successful, meeting these goals should create powerful synergistic effects: generating new research funding to keep the research assistant employed *and* attract students *and* treat others well, thereby increasing the likelihood of good recruitment and retention. All of these leverage to free up the academic worker so as to be able to focus more on publishing and attaining additional funds to further this priority.

COMMON CHALLENGES WHEN GOAL-SETTING

Setting the right goals is not easy, and a number of common challenges arise in doing so.

Worrying about time itself

While we need goals, it's more tempting to worry about time, especially because we feel its scarcity so intensely. It's hard to come to terms with the physical sensation of not having enough time, but it's key to recognize in extreme knowledge work that we can't get more time and there will never be enough. Yes, that's right – just accept it – there will never be enough time to fully develop all your ideas, to take all the opportunities that will come your way. Now and ever, you are never going to have enough time to do all that you could in your academic work. This requires us to focus far more on what we deliberately choose to do with the 1440 minutes of time that we have each day. This is why goals are necessary.

Not setting goals

It's tempting to focus on that which is most tangible: getting stuck into work by doing tasks right. However, the wrong task can be done right. Not setting goals risks falling into the 'trouble-to-task' trap: rushing into the urgency of the 'to-do' task list before a crystal-clear consideration of what priorities are actually furthered by these tasks. Goals are vital to determining the relative value of a particular task and how much time we should justifiably devote to it. Without readily clear and verifiable goals, it is hard to monitor progress against your priorities.

Not linking goals to priorities

Some goals seem to fit with academic work but are not deliberately linked to priorities. We do them, but we are not really sure why. This is common for attractive innovations, such as creating a blog or a social media platform, around which there is enthusiasm of the new as well as consternation and discussion of their place in academic work. It's alluring to engage in such activities – they feel fresh and contemporary. However, the link(s) to priorities needs to be deliberate and calculated – a vital step in really making them add value. How, for example, does the presence of social media leverage with other goals that are important? When posting on social media, what other priorities can also be furthered via that work? All goals should be linked to priorities. For example, an academic worker's success indicator is to become internationally known in their research area, and they have set the priority to maximize their writing time, consequently their goal could be to block every Friday in their schedule for writing. If you are confused about whether your goal is actually a priority, consider whether it is overarching or specific. If it is the former, you need to translate this priority into a set of more specific goals.

Not setting measurable goals

If your goals are not measurable, then you can't monitor progress or assess with confidence whether goals have really been achieved. Use a dedicated rubric (like SMART) to ascertain if you have good goals. Whenever you can, develop measurable goals: taking zero work home on weeknights, publishing 'x' number of articles in target journals, attaining 'y' amount of research funding, or completing or marking students' assessments in 'z' hours.

Goals are not strategic

The real and true power of good strategy lies in setting and meeting the right goals. This occurs when coherent and compatible goals interact and leverage with each other to have emergent and powerful additive effects on a priority (Rumelt, 2011). Good goals enact and embody good strategy. Where you can, avoid setting single goals that map to single priorities. Instead, consider how you can select goals that have multiple synergistic benefits in furthering a stated priority. Moreover, consider, too, how single goals can further multiple priorities; for example, if we set a goal to keep one day per week free from email and meetings, then this can serve priorities around writing, reading, or current projects.

Not setting the right goals

We leave the trickiest issue last: how to identify the right goals. Due to the diversity of academic work as extreme knowledge work, we cannot prescribe or state what the right goals for academic work are. But the right work should lead directly from your success indicators and priorities. Tuning into and responding to the semi-occluded games and genres of academia is a vital skill here in determining what is most likely to help you to be successful in attaining progression. We will address this challenge more in the second part of this book in The Core.

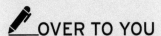OVER TO YOU

Setting Goals

Goals are vital to academic work but developing the right goals is not easy. Using The Success Pyramids (Figure 5.1) , choose three priorities from your work in the previous chapter and state three goals for each. Ensure that they are SMART goals.

1. Now, reflect on your goals: Do these goals need to be refined in order to be appropriate and good? How do they make you feel?

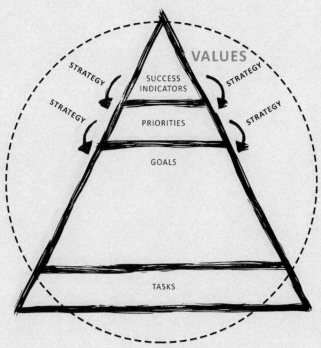

(Continued)

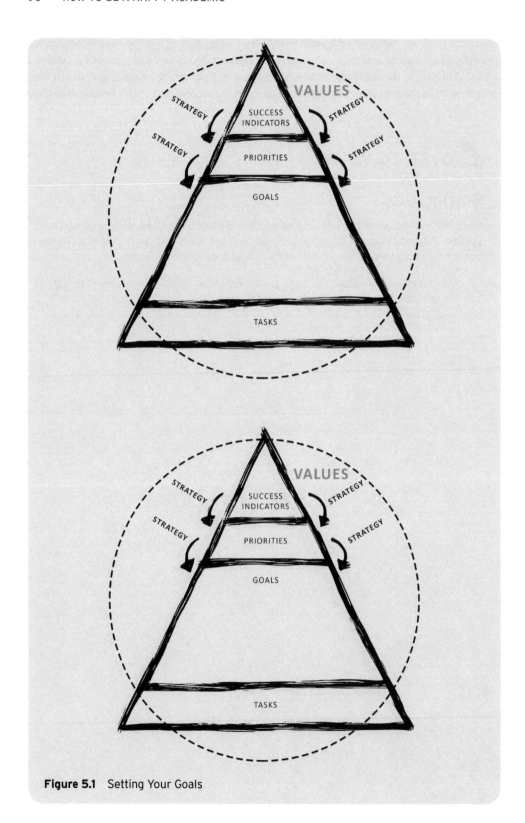

Figure 5.1   Setting Your Goals

TASKS IN ACADEMIC WORK

Tasks in academic work are the actions needed to meet your goals. The tasks of academic work can be exciting, and sometimes (often!) more pedestrian. Reducing academic work to mere tasks does little to make our pulses rise or hearts sing. It's like reducing music or poetry to black marks on white paper. However, this risks underplaying the key role that doing the right things right has in making success happen. Tasks in academic work include everything from emails done privately in the dead of night to presenting high-profile lectures done in the glare of publicity. Some tasks arise from unexpected problems or challenges: giving support to the student who is struggling, providing writing feedback to your co-authors' disastrous first manuscript draft, helping a tearful research assistant. Some tasks are more important historically or institutionally in the occluded games of academia, such as those associated with teaching or writing for publication in peer-reviewed journals or attaining grant-funding. Some tasks expected of us are newer and cause excitement or concerns: doing a media interview, tweeting or writing a blog. There is really no end to the tasks that one could do in our 1440 daily minutes.

Managing tasks can be challenging in academic work because it is varied and extreme knowledge work: the volume of tasks needing completion can be overwhelming. The importance of tasks in academia is receiving new attention in the context of the high demands on academic workers. Tricks and tips are common: social media proliferates with them. A recent guide from the UK's *Times Higher Education Supplement* recommended that workers create and stick to daily to-do lists, block off dedicated days for research, and do more of what makes them happy (2016). Such advice is welcome and useful but should always be integrated into a bigger picture, such as that provided by The Success Pyramid. It matters much less what tasks look like or are than that the tasks should always serve one or more dedicated *goals*. In this way, tasks are planned and deliberate, and we should never catch ourselves doing tasks for the sake of it.

Tasks, time, and goals

Tasks should always serve a goal and take the *right time*. Indeed, an individual task should always be considered alongside the time it will likely take to complete it. This is why *prioritization* of the right goals and tasks is necessary. Ideally, tasks should be 'checkable' – have a clear beginning and end that can be verified and checked off. Even the most large-scale projects or initiatives can and should be broken down to their discrete tasks.

What is the right time for a particular task? How many tasks should one do? These are important but tricky questions. As extreme knowledge work, there is simply never going to be enough time to do all the academic work that one could do. Allocating units of time to tasks, either in a formal calendar or regularly during your day, week, and month is important because mapping your tasks to your time is a living demonstration that these tasks are important for you. It also helps make sure that you get the task done. We have to come to terms with leaving or stopping work with tasks still to do. Consequently, choosing the right tasks to meet goals and also setting broader time boundaries around getting tasks done is key. Maintaining a calendar that includes your tasks and a system for remembering tasks can do this (more on this later in The Core). The relationship between tasks and value in contributing to goals relative to time is not straightforward. Two compatible principles convey the complex relationship between tasks and time: Parkinson's Law and Horstman's Corollary.

Parkinson's Law, mentioned first in *The Economist* magazine (1955), famously refers to the tendency for tasks to stretch to fill time or the time we allocate to them. Rapid progress can be made around tasks in the presence of pressing deadlines.

Perhaps this reflects a conception of working to goals in academic work as being more a marathon than a sprint; there are, or rather there have to be, times of slower pace, steady grind-it-down progress and painful sprinting at different times for tasks. Speed cannot be uniform in this work, nor should we expect it to be. Rather, like the competitive swimmer, we have to find our own rhythms, know what works best for us, and carefully navigate our reactions to the temptations from those swimming faster in other lanes. While this may be right for them, this does not make this right for us.

In contrast to Parkinson's Law, Horstman's Corollary, of manager-tools.com co-founder Mark Horstman, refers to the tendency for tasks to contract to fit into the time allocated. Setting ambitious times to do tasks can then contribute to the tasks getting done in a shorter period of time. Consequently, if you don't schedule and allocate clear and specific time for each task that you do, you can expect it not to be done at any particular time, take longer or to bleed out into other parts of your life.

Time and tasks have to go together, but what tasks should we allocate time to? The short answer: all. All tasks should be allocated a set time. If your priorities reflect your time and time is bound to tasks, it is important to schedule your tasks to time in your calendar. This can be done in reality in an electronic calendar/diary or less formally at the start of each working day.

ALL TASKS SHOULD BE ALLOCATED A SET TIME

HANDLING TASKS

Should we do each and every task that we could to further a goal? Instead of rushing in 'to do', tasks have to be actively deliberated before it is decided if these should be done. But where are the *real* choices? Some tasks are organizational expectations – we get into trouble if we don't do them. Such expectations commonly involve tasks such as replying to emails, teaching classes and writing manuscripts for publications. Even if choices don't exist about whether these tasks are done, academic workers usually get reasonably high levels of autonomy in choosing how to do them (Kinman, 2014). Moreover, just as strategic goals can be set to further priorities, so, too, can tasks be prioritized for action because they contribute disproportionately to goals. The key to identify from all that we could do is to do only all that we must and should do.

List possible tasks

Working from a stated goal, consider what you could do, should do, and must do. This step is akin to tasks-brainstorming. For example, the task of managing emails during your working week can be done in a variety of ways. Emails can be managed by various means that do or do not take account of the relationship between time and the task at hand, including:

- Responding to each email as it arrives even when you are doing another task (focusing on the task but not the time).
- Responding only to priority email(s) as these arrive and as other tasks allow (focusing on the task but not the time).
- Allocating three 30-minute periods during the day to sort emails into priority and non-priority, and answer only priority emails (focusing on the time and the task).
- Answering non-priority emails during a set hour once per week (focusing on the time and the task).

There could be many more ways to manage emails around time and tasks, but what matters most is allocating a particular time to tasks, and having a particular approach that both allocates time as well as contains these tasks.

When you have judged that you must do a particular task, you can commit to doing it by writing it down on a task or to-do list. David Allen (2015) documents the value of such lists in his book *Getting Things Done*. He argues that knowing that all our tasks are listed gives us reassurance and allows us to free up our brains to be more creative when doing tasks because we are not worried that we have forgotten any of them. His approach argues that *everything* you want to do, both at work and at home, should be listed. Developing master task lists is now much easier because of apps that can run on phones, tablets, and computers, which means that whatever you are doing, new tasks can be added to your list fairly easily.

Reflect and select the most important tasks to do

Just as the right priorities and goals can be difficult to identify, specifying the right tasks is also hard. This is because academic workplaces, as we noted, involve manifold semi-occluded games and genres. We usually know more about what our ideal goal is, but how to get there task-wise is a lot more challenging because the games and genres of publishing, grants, teaching, and workplace processes around employment are more opaque than we would like. As Semenza (2014) reminds us, it is useful to assume that being intelligent will only get you so far – you have to make good choices about the tasks that you do in order to be successful.

How then can we work out which tasks to do in order to achieve our set goal? As with goals, understanding as much about the processes, genres, and games involved is key. We will address this later in The Core. It suffices to say here that selecting the right tasks requires careful preparatory work, sense-making, and judgement. These are more about good habits than natural talents. Developing them is, nevertheless, vital to doing the right task.

Put tasks or chunks of tasks in your calendar

The best means to ensuring that you do a task is to allocate time to it in your calendar and then work to this scheduling. It is a matter of luck to get a task done if you do not schedule time for it. If you don't schedule a task that is important to you, assume it will not be done. This is no bad reflection on you, your skills, or diligence but reflects the nature of academic work as extreme knowledge work. If a task is important enough for you to do it, schedule time for it and then work on it during that time. This means that you are unavailable to do other tasks (including being available to others) but it is essential for doing that task. If it's important, put it in your calendar and do your very best to work to that time.

It's important to do this for all tasks that are important to achieving your goals, including (especially!): writing, reading, and thinking – even going home. Steve Jobs famously allocated three hours of every working week to tasks intended to solve a single troublesome problem. While these problems no doubt varied a lot in his time at Apple, his prioritization of them did not waiver. In preference to catching up on his emails, more meetings or doing the mammoth amount of other tasks that he could do, he protected and prioritized time to *focus* and to focus on how he could contribute most. We will discuss this more as part of The Core.

Do nothing now, soon, or ever

Chances are, many of the tasks that you could do should not be done – or at least not right away and not by you. The paradoxical power of doing nothing is explored in whole in a book by Murnighan (2012). Working to priorities requires that you reflect and think mercilessly on whether tasks should be done at all. Will it *really* further your goal or are you doing it for other reasons that don't fit with your priorities? To foster our sense of perfection or competency, to give a favourable impression or attain a sense of reward? Remember, while you do that work task, you cannot easily do another, and that time is irreplaceable.

Delegate or pass on tasks

There are persuasive arguments that effectiveness in knowledge work depends on doing only those tasks that you can contribute to. If someone else who you manage or supervise, such as a research or teaching assistant, can undertake a task, then it should be delegated to them. What stops people delegating tasks to others more often? Worry that they won't do these as well as you? A fear of letting go or losing control? Nervousness over giving negative performance feedback? Indeed, when work is delegated to students and research assistants, this may result in lower-quality work. However, vitally, this allows you to allocate more of your time to the tasks that only you can do. This is usually an acceptable trade-off.

Do the most important task next

Not all tasks are equally important. Tasks can and should be prioritized. Consider which tasks stand to contribute most to the goal, taking account of the amounts of time, energy, and other costs of doing that task. Remember: each task that one could do consumes never-to-be-returned time and also your own precious focus and energy. Its nature and need should be considered before action. It is important to get comfortable with doing tasks later.

Include home time, family, and social activities

Manager Tools (2016b) has a great piece of advice on how to ensure that you prioritize family and other important 'life' tasks in your week: allocate time for these in your schedule first and work your other tasks around them. One principle reason that any knowledge worker stays late at work is not scheduling when they will actually stop work and go home. As well as making choices about tasks, it is also important to set reasonable boundaries. If you do not, you can fully expect tasks to seep out across your work, home, and life.

COMMON CHALLENGES WITH TASKS

Time does not tally with priorities

It may be easier to identify when tasks don't need to be done because they don't align with your priorities. However, it can be harder to allocate the right time to the right tasks *relative* to your priorities. Few academic workers can avoid spending time on emails and meetings but our concern is more that we spend too much time on these low-priority tasks relative to other tasks which stand to further our goals to meet priorities. These types of tasks are necessary but mischievous; they need to be tamed and to fit into the time we choose to allocate to them, not how long they can take to do.

Always be conscious of what your main priorities and goals are. Take time to list these, know them and ensure your time maps to them. When you start to feel that your priorities or goals do not reflect your tasks or time, assess in your calendar what you are actually spending your time doing.

I feel uncomfortable

Working consciously about what tasks you choose to do always means making choices and often leads to feelings of discomfort. We are wary of leaving even the least important tasks incomplete, we worry over how people will view us when we do not return their call/email, or request 'quickly', we fear saying 'no' to work requests. These are understandable but necessary feelings. In their book *The Time Trap*, Mackenzie and Nickerson (2009) suggest many useful strategies about how to address the inherent but necessary challenges of making such choices. Other academic workers can be far more understanding than we expect because they also feel these pressures.

Looking too much to others

Other academic workers can be a source of insight around tasks but also of distraction. Others may seem like they are streaking ahead with their academic work tasks, and we choose to do more of what they do without considering and assessing whether tasks are right for our own goals. Like tennis, golf and all manner of other competitive sports, a large proportion of the battle of academic work is with yourself. Never lose sight of whether your tasks are right for your goals, priorities, and success indicators. Brown (2012) addresses the danger of such ill-informed comparisons: when you feel yourself emotionally or intellectually making favourable or harsh comparisons with others, reflect on what you are really, deeply concerned or vulnerable about. Almost always, these comparisons are about our own fears – not others.

Not seeing obligations as tasks

Different academic workers in different organizations and countries have markedly different levels of autonomy and job security. Yet, all of us have to meet at least some basic workplace expectations. From maintaining an ethical conduct and interactions with others to answering emails competently to turning up for the classes that we teach, some aspects of our work are non-negotiable. Should such fixed matters be expressed in priorities, goals, and tasks? We think so. However, the degree to which any type of task is prioritized relative to others is important. We all know some colleagues who prioritize replying to emails at all times, day or night. How such rapid responsiveness fits with their success indicators is less clear, even though they appear to be prioritizing emails beyond other types of work they could be doing. Obligations of your workplace and role should be reflected in your priorities and included in the tasks that you do, but should be considered relative to your other priorities and time allocated.

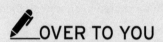OVER TO YOU

Setting Tasks

Use The Success Pyramids (Figure 5.2), provided below. Choose three goals from your work earlier in the chapter and state three tasks for each.

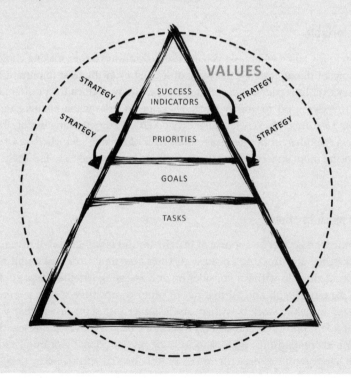

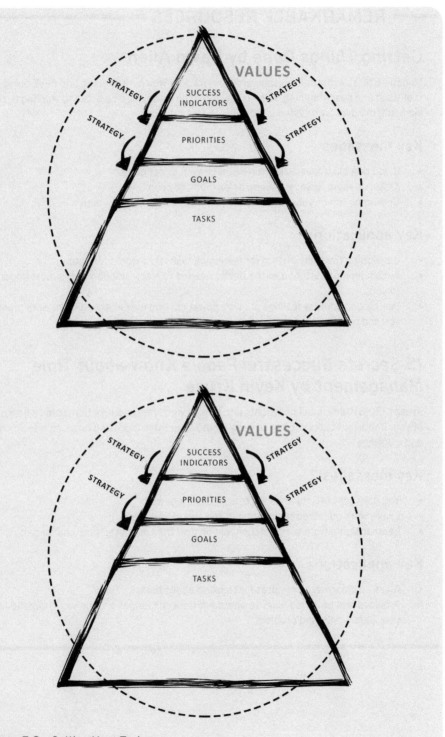

Figure 5.2 Setting Your Tasks

━━━ REMARKABLE RESOURCES ━━━

Getting Things Done by David Allen

Managing tasks without forgetting or losing track of which need doing and need doing next is difficult and overwhelming. Allen is the authority on developing lists and working to these via habit, mindset, and systems (2015).

Key messages

- If you don't list your tasks, don't expect each to get done.
- Tasks: do them, delegate them, defer them, or drop them.
- Getting on top of your tasks makes you work better and feel better.

Key applications

- Developing the right system for managing tasks that works for you.
- Becoming more attuned to the habits needed to track and do what is most important to you.
- Learning to address feelings of being powerless and overwhelmed when work manages you and not the other way around.

15 Secrets Successful People Know about Time Management by Kevin Kruse

Kruse's (2015) book is full of insights into how to view time and how to maximize how many of your important tasks you can fit in by focusing on them more and focusing less on emails and meetings.

Key messages

- You only get 1440 minutes each day - use them well.
- Leave work guilt-free to go home at the end of your day.
- Learn insights from successful people on how they mastered time challenges.

Key applications

- Gives an empowered mindset for thinking about time.
- Provides lots of varied ways to approach time challenges around work, depending on your personality and problem.

SECTION 2

DEVELOPING THE CORE

Nurturing and improving The Core (see figure on the following page) is integral to being an effective, successful, and happy academic. The Core is a set of related and cohesive domains of development that separately and together provide the foundation for the tasks of academic work. While The Success Pyramid helps us to focus on what academic work should be done, The Core helps us to develop the insights, abilities, and skills to do this work. In this section, a chapter will be devoted to each of The Core's elements: Creativity, Human Work, Learning, Influence, Writing and, finally, Habits and Systems.

Strengthening The Core means that you do not have to approach and improve the tasks of academic work separately and discretely. Our approach is different to that which dominates. The bookshelves of academic workers creak with ever more specialized books on writing research proposals, writing publications, skills in social media, better student supervision, etc. Academic workers encounter worries and problems around such tasks during their daily work and reach out for resources to help with these. We see this approach as wasteful because it treats these undoubtedly challenging academic work tasks as if nothing in common unites them. Like the novice exerciser whose efforts to develop their core muscles to prevent injury, reduce lower backache and increase balance, stability, and respiratory function and improve posture, efforts to develop The Core yield multiple benefits for academic work. We don't approach academic work in such a task-specific or oriented way by focusing on the 'how to' of grant-writing, teaching, tweeting, etc. Instead, like our bodies' core muscles, improving The Core helps us across the variety of tasks and situations within academic work.

While the domains of The Core are discussed separately, its elements are linked. The Core is best developed when its domains leverage and amplify each other. For example, 'creativity' (although a domain on its own) is part of a 'learning'-focused response to failure (another part of The Core), which also likely necessitates a degree of 'human work and self-work' (themselves part of a dedicated domain of The Core). It is through such synergistic benefits that the true power of The Core can be unleashed to provide a powerful driver for successful academic work.

Success in academic work derives from your ongoing efforts and ability to direct efforts and learning to improve facets of The Core. Focusing deliberately on developing The Core is unnerving because academic workplaces and socialization in education (from the age of about five years) provides the foundation for how we view academic work and ourselves. Our abilities are the seat of whether we succeed or fail in the various tasks and tribulations that come

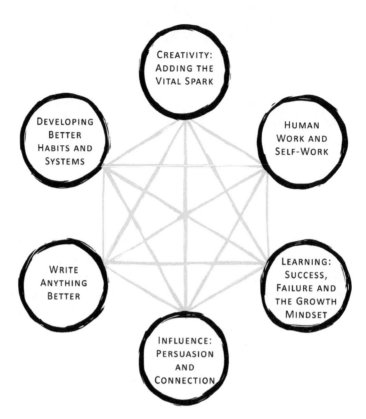

Figure S2.1   The Core

our way. To get better results, we reassure ourselves that as well-qualified, smart people, we have the skills, education, and record of accomplishment needed to be successful in the tasks of academic work or focus on developing around discrete work tasks, such as grant-writing or teaching techniques. Almost all of this reasoning is arbitrary and, ironically, likely to be wasteful or even counter-productive.

Instead, success can be seen as lying in whether and how we develop aspects of The Core on what is a lifelong journey of improvement. While academic work will, indeed, in most cases, be overtly focused on research, teaching, and engagement, we believe that focusing on developing The Core is the most efficient and effective means to foster success in academic work and to ultimately be happy while doing it. This approach contravenes decades worth of messages and reassurances that we, as 'smart people', are there already: experts, emerging, or established, with the building blocks needed for academic work. In practical terms, developing facets of The Core in this deliberate fashion entails prioritizing your focus, time, and energy *beyond* the specifics of the *academic* work to an underlying, more transcendent realm. Focusing precious resources on its development can therefore seem to be luxurious and indulgent. It is incongruous in academic workplaces so preoccupied with task outputs and 'success'-related talk and action that exist around such tasks. As with our earliest memories from school as children, this colours how we view ourselves, think and see, and what we strive for and focus our efforts on.

While we don't focus primarily on the The Core simply to produce more academic work, there are decades worth of research and historical examples to indicate that it will provide a deeper, more useful, and more sustainable means to do academic work. Our abilities around The Core are not fixed but can be improved as long as we are open and able to devote efforts to prioritize this.

6

CREATIVITY

ADDING THE VITAL SPARK

Creativity enhances life. It enables the great thinkers, artists, and leaders of our world to continually push forward new concepts, new forms of expression and new ways to improve every facet of our existence.

(Southwick, 2012)

Writing is easy: all you do is sit staring at a blank sheet of paper until the drops of blood form on your forehead.

(Gene Fowler, quoted by Bayles and Orland, 1993)

Creativity in academic work is necessary but challenging. Creativity is associated with the production of ideas that are novel, useful, or practical and is influenced by aptitude, process, and context (Zampetakis et al., 2010: 24). As extreme knowledge work, academic work addresses the most complex, uncontrollable, uncertain, ambiguous, and problematic in and during work. In short, academic work needs and demands creativity. Having good ideas and doing the right thing in this extreme knowledge work requires an ongoing ability to produce great ideas, think, write, draw on your values, communicate, solve problems, make arguments, persuade, interact with other people, work with difficult colleagues, raise the performance of ourselves and others … and in all such things (and many others), do what is not necessarily easiest, most obvious or conventional, but what is right. This, once more, is a reminder that academic work is extreme knowledge work. Doing it well requires doing the right things, and this, in turn, often requires us to be creative. This is why creativity has its place in The Core: it is integral to meeting the challenges of academic work across its many facets. Moreover, creativity helps not only to define what the right things are to do but also how to do these things well. This is why nurturing creativity is so strategic.

More than this, creativity in academic work can express something 'bigger', more primordial or different in us and about us. Instead of being focused on 'solving problems' via tasks, work becomes a more profound or personal outlet for an expression of our values, talents, and experiences. Situations can become seen in entirely new and different ways, and both individual and collaborative creative work can sustain and uplift us during some of our most difficult or challenging times.

Yet, in academic and other workplaces, creativity seems threatened. High demands and stakes, the negative consequences of seeming to fail, the apparent volume and complexity of all that can be done, and all manner of apparent uncertainties and ambiguities squeeze creativity (Catmull, 2014). In the face of this, it's tempting to work longer and harder, and to cut ourselves up for not being able to do or achieve all that we want. While academic work and workplaces are often centrally operationally labelled as being 'creative' places, our identification with and nurturing of creativity stands in bipolar contrast:

> The creative impulse is of particular importance to scientific research ... Unfortunately, in the academic world - where much of today's scientific innovation takes place - researchers are encouraged to maintain the status quo and not 'rock the boat'. This mentality is pervasive, affecting all aspects of scientific research from idea generation to funding to the training of the next generation of scientists. (Southwick, 2012)

It's easy and tempting to blame governments, funding bodies, students and society for a seeming lack of creativity in academic work or workplaces. High, diverse, and complex expectations have reduced academic workers to task 'do-ers', output agents, zombies, and workhorses. Yet, the culture of academic workers themselves also serves to further the creativity taboo. Peer-review processes in publishing and grants overseen by established academic workers tend to breed conservatism, risk-aversion, and laissez-faire. Condescension and nervousness about creativity comes to all too readily. In such cultures, it is hard to conceive how we can truly be creative. Accordingly, in this chapter, we address the point that no matter how busy or how much pressure you feel, creativity is an integral dimension of being successful, effective, and happy in academic work.

BEING AND STAYING CREATIVE OR 'THE BATTLE FOR CREATIVITY'

If you want to deliver the right idea at the right moment, you must begin the process far upstream from when you need that idea.

(Henry, 2011: 3)

Beethoven walked, Drucker studied Japanese painting, and David Bowie played chess. Ed Catmull, the head of Pixar, does different kinds of work tasks. Many activities help us to be more creative in work: we call these behaviours 'creativity replenishers'. When we accept creativity as integral to and in academic work, it's important to consider how we can foster this important part of academic workplaces and ourselves through engaging in behaviours that can replenish our creativity for when we need it most.

Academic workers, to coin Todd Henry's phrase, are 'accidental creatives' (2011: 2): while being 'creative' was not necessarily something that was specifically signed up for or identified with as much as workers in advertising or architecture, being creative is a vital part of academic work. While sometimes this does not seem to be the case, the overriding feature of recent work on creativity is that, like many other aspects of workplace effectiveness, there is lots that can be done to protect and nurture this important facet of work (Henry, 2011; Catmull, 2014).

The converse of this is that creativity does not just happen. Too much time just 'doing tasks' without being attuned to our creativity will inevitably lead to its decline.

Recognize different paths to creativity

Nurturing creativity involves what we do both beyond and during our work. It most definitely is not about being a talented or committed artist (although engaging with the arts may help); it is about doing that which brings better balance in and across work and life. However, as Catmull writes, while the idea of balance seems a hollow universal good, merely wanting balance does not make it happen but depends on what we see 'balance' as being. He rejects concepts of balance solely based on achieving a Zen-like stillness, but sees creativity as being fostered by work priorities and goals that reflect 'all the seasons', thereby fostering an equilibrium of priorities, goals, and tasks in work:

> Imagine a balance board - one of those planks of wood that rests, at its midsection, on a cylinder. The trick is to place one foot on each end of the board, then shift your weight in order to achieve equilibrium as the cylinder rolls beneath you. If there's a better example ... of the ability to manage two competing forces (the left and the right) I can't think of one. (Catmull, 2014: 140)

To approach creativity in academic work, it's important not only to recognize the value of this to our work but also to recognize the diversity of the ways in which creativity can be fostered outside and inside work. Further, as creativity is similar to effectiveness (Drucker, 1967), while it may not come naturally to us, it can be learned and fostered through good habits, irrespective of natural talent, personality, or proclivity (Zampetakis et al., 2010; Catmull, 2014).

Schedule regular time

Taking a more deliberate approach to creativity in academic work by scheduling time to foster our creativity is vital. Seldom does this creativity come when, after struggling to write, we then sit at the laptop, valiantly trying to write for another four hours. As with any other kinds of tasks, 'creative time' (or, rather, time intended to serve creativity) can and should be scheduled in our weekly calendars. Research on time planning and creativity shows that planning your days more and thereby exercising more thoughtful influence over what we do dramatically helps our creativity (Zampetakis et al., 2010). This scheduling fosters a higher sense of perceived control over time and a higher confidence in longer-term plans: both seeming antidotes to the stricken panic of time shortness that often squeezes out creativity in our schedules.

As with any other priority, if it is important to you, it is not going to happen by magic and no one is likely to schedule it *for* you. Creativity needs our time and attention. It's up to us to prioritize it in our schedule. Make the choice to schedule creativity in your calendar, no matter what that looks like.

Stick to your scheduling

When there is so much that could be done, creativity can feel very squeezed in favour of more time spent on tasks that ease our immediate pressures to get things done. Ensuring that you guard your creativity is actually one of the most disciplined acts you can do as an academic because creativity is less about inspiration and more about dedication and discipline to scheduling. Even though 'discipline' may appear ostensibly to be opposed to creativity, the two are, in fact, well linked, as Pressfield explains: 'Someone once asked Somerset Maugham if he wrote on a schedule or only when struck by inspiration. "I write only when inspiration strikes," he replied "Fortunately, it strikes every morning at nine o'clock sharp"' (2002: 64).

Misunderstanding the strong links between creativity and discipline has contributed to creativity being perpetually threatened at the organizational and personal level: perceived expectations from workplaces to produce particular kinds or great volumes of research, to chase short-term favourable student-teaching evaluations or to prioritize what others seemingly expect in our academic work. Creativity is about becoming more aware of your own creative rhythms: when, where, and how you can do particularly creative work in your work day and even when you don't necessarily 'feel' an inclination to be creative, putting in place the necessary building blocks for your own creativity to happen and getting down to the work. These building blocks could be about the time(s) during the day or week when we are most creative, the place (whether office or home) where this happens, the physical spaces where we work, how much time, and with how much work we can expect to be creative.

Discipline is needed to ensure that we respect our own needs to schedule time for tasks that serve our creativity. Unlike missing teaching a class or meeting our boss, there will be few immediate negative sanctions if we schedule creative time but choose to work on other tasks instead.

Effectiveness over hours and efficiency

Worrying too much about the clock, your inputs and efficiency can harm creativity because this is focused on the wrong 'input' side of knowledge work. When we view academic work success as being determined principally by doing the right things, this gives permission to recognize the sound investment that creativity is: to understand that creativity can yield better results, given our finite time and energy. Conversely, working more hours, particularly on the same task, usually harms our creativity. It may make us feel committed but is counter-productive to what we are trying to do.

When our schedules are cluttered up with too many tasks or we spend too much time on any one task, this usually diminishes our capacity to be creative because it robs us of the energy, focus, and diversity that creativity needs (Henry, 2011). We live with this challenge every day as we write this book: while we would love to crank out great words every minute of the working day, our primary aim is to write the right words – not just those words that come quickly or easily. Giving ourselves time to engage in other aspects of our lives and work during our day improves our capacity to be creative: to find the right words during the three or four hours each day spent on it. To do otherwise is likely counter-productive because we have quickly realized that it actually takes longer to edit and re-edit badly written words. Ironically, even the seemingly simpler insights and contributions require creativity to truly see, visualize, and give words to our ideas. Doing too much of the same work, working longer hours or working on the same task too long diminishes our creativity. To evaluate your academic work creatively, focus more on what you produce; learn your rhythms and what helps you do work that demands more creativity. While everyone's balance is different, think first of what kind of creative balance is needed for your best work.

Finding what works for your creativity and self-care

Creativity enhances many aspects of our lives, including our health, relationships, energy, and degree of focus (Henry, 2011). As we navigate (and sometimes endure) the academic journeys we are on each day, our academic work suffers because we think better work will result when we work harder, longer, and more intensely. While many of us have experienced some success doing so in the past in short bursts, as a longer-term strategy, this is a recipe for difficulties for our longer-term physical and mental health, and work. These manifest in academic workplaces in many different ways: from absenteeism and seeking jobs outside academia to passive aggression, disengagement, presenteeism, and overt aggression in our workplaces.

No single activity is guaranteed to help creativity in everyone. Some elements do, however, seem to help us invigorate our creativity. Creativity expert Henry in particular targets focus, energy, and inputs (ibid.): that we take dedicated and regular time out to focus away from our normal work to focus *on* creativity. While there are well-established and research-based creativity enhancers, newer strategies also have potential. For example, improvisation, via acting classes or as part of groups, can help listening, thinking, and relaxation (Poynton, 2013). Additional strategies include:

- Participating in a physical activity (Colzato et al., 2013).
- Reading widely. (Hegarty, 2014, recommends a quick way to do this is to read *The Economist*).
- Listening to music (Lesiuk, 2005).
- Doodling (drawing imaginatively and freely; Brown, 2015).
- Engaging in 'Flash Fiction' (join one of the many online writing groups to write 100 words of fiction on a prescribed topic).
- Playing more (ideas from Tim Brown's TED Talk 'Tales of Creativity and Play', 2008).
- Asking more (and better) questions (strategies from Sawyer, 2013).

Getting to know what really works for helping our personal creativity is important. Self-knowledge and awareness are critical, staying mindful and responsive to when we feel creatively low and doing something about this.

Using foils for creative work

Scheduling tasks that further Catmull's work balance (2014) overtly helps us to get away from our immediate tasks. In this way, all manner of other essential academic work tasks can also be a foil for our creative work. Doing tasks that require low creativity such as mundane emails, routine meetings, student marking, or reading can all be done when we feel our creative energy is lower but provide sufficient change that replenishes creativity, allowing a return of this energy to then restart the more creative work again. Understanding what makes you more or less creative is important, but so is understanding which foils can help you most as your creative energy waxes and wanes.

Working in creative collaboration

Whereas most doctoral academic work is done alone, salaried academic workers work extensively with others. These people can influence our own creativity substantially. In fact, the collaborative nature of academic work is one of the greatest gifts that we can give to creativity and happiness in academic work. We are not compelled to work alone on projects or goals, and can consciously choose to work with others, from working on research projects and manuscript-writing to teaching or chairing conferences. Working with other people involves both personal costs and benefits; you are no longer simply accountable to yourself but share both the responsibility and work around goals and tasks. If you have never experienced the 'click' that can come from working with people who not only complement but also add to your abilities to particular undertaken tasks, it is something to behold. This reflects what sociologists call 'emergent properties': whereby the power of the collaboration is greater than that which could be achieved by the individuals separately (think Lennon and McCartney!).

This is not to say that every collaboration has to reach an epoch of creative spark; work with others can be more perfunctory, practical, and 'alongside'. However, real power for creativity can accrue to academic work when these interactions move to a deeper and stronger plane. Vera John-Steiner, in her history book *Creative Collaboration* (2000), documents the range of powers that creative partnerships have had in dozens of historical figures from academia, science, literature, and the arts, including the pioneers of the DNA structure (Watson and Crick), quantum mechanics (Bohr and Heisenberg), existentialism (de Beauvoir and Sartre) and the arts (Picasso and Braque, Stravinsky and Balanchine, Plath and Hughes, and many others). John-Steiner's highly detailed analysis spans centuries of endeavour at the cutting-edge of all manner of academic work and gives convincing weight to her claim that: 'the construction of a new mode of thought relies on and thrives with collaboration' (2000: 7).

Time of day

THE POWER OF THE COLLABORATION IS GREATER THAN THAT WHICH COULD BE ACHIEVED BY THE INDIVIDUALS SEPARATELY

Generative ideas emerge from joint thinking, from significant conversations, and from sustained, shared struggles to achieve new insights by partners in thought.

(John-Steiner, 2000: 3)

The kind of magic that can come from this collaboration partly requires an understanding of your own 'incompletion': that one's own efforts, talents, insights, and contributions alone are inferior to those that can arise when we openly, generously, and whole-heartedly work creatively with others. We have to risk stepping outside of ourselves. Conversely, if we believe and feel that we, alone, are always 'correct', sufficiently talented or well-rounded to do all the work, being truly open to the collaborative contributions of others is much more difficult. While we will address the added benefits of this open mindset further in the next chapter, it's more important here to recognize the breadth of benefits that can come not only to the work but also to ourselves and others from creative collaboration. This follows because, in such collaborative endeavours:

> we learn from each other. By teaching what we know, we engage in mutual appropriation. In partnerships we see ourselves through the eyes of others, and through their support we dare to explore new parts of ourselves. We can live better with temporary failures as we rely on our partners' strengths. By joining with others we accept their gift of confidence, and through interdependence, we achieve competence and connection. Together we create our futures. (John-Steiner, 2000: 204)

Collaborations do not need to be based on sameness. Indeed, collaborative spark is more about a rich mix of similarity and difference. In the sciences, John-Steiner (ibid.) surmises that key factors supporting creative collaborations are complementarity training, discipline, analyses, and working styles, yet often opposing perspectives and a healthy degree of disagreement. In the arts, shared communities and supportive partnerships were especially key and often fostered a shared sense of creative growth and mutual appropriation – what John-Steiner (ibid.) calls 'integrative collaborations'. Across these realms, the emotional dynamics of collaboration remains strong, with evidence of some complementariness of temperament and belief in the partner's capabilities but often varying levels of external credit. Quoting Howard Gardner, she conveys the momentum to work that such emotional dimensions of collaboration bring:

> the time of creative breakthrough is highly charged, both affectively and cognitively ... The kind of communication that takes place is unique and uniquely important, bearing closer resemblance to the introduction of a new language early in life, than to the routine conversations between individuals who already share the same language. (Ibid.: 12)

How then to find other academic workers to collaborate creatively with? Is this easy, hard, or a one-in-a-million chance? The process could even be likened to dating: your first attempt to collaborate might not turn out to be 'the one' or even of benefit, reciprocally or individually. Nevertheless, it is important to be open and reflective about each creative collaboration. It may take multiple attempts of working collaboratively with others to find the right fit (and even then the right process) to create a true collaborative spark. However, it is worthwhile to persevere and be open to the thought that the right collaborative spark may come at times or from people we don't expect.

THREATS TO CREATIVITY

Many of the threats to creativity that we face as academic workers are reflected on the other sides of the many coins that this chapter covers: not valuing creativity enough to schedule time for it, working more hours or focusing only on the work alone. Creativity can be harmed by all manner of elements, including:

- Aspects of workplace culture (notably, short-termism, leadership, and what is rewarded) (Andriopoulos, 2001).
- Physical dimensions of buildings and space (Hegarty, 2014)
- Inner thoughts and feelings of being a fraud (Pressfield, 2002).
- Fear of the work (Catmull, 2014).
- Fear of failure (ibid.).
- Dismissing uncertainty or ambiguity in the work (ibid.).
- Thinking too much (Hegarty, 2014).
- Cynicism about others or the work (ibid.).

It's easy to be cynical and continue to bemoan any talk of prioritizing creativity in academic work as luxurious, naive or otherwise soft. What are the deeper places that such criticisms come from?

Fear and doubt

Creativity is often stifled due to fear in the face of academic work that intimidates in almost every way. To have to respond to the seemingly large, competitive, and concrete challenges of academic work with creativity seems like a colossal mismatch. It is tense to face an expectant class, hard to reach the community or a blank sheet of paper or screen. Are we truly good enough to meet the challenges of this academic work? It can feel more controllable and even comfortable to work longer and harder, while burying the fear that we feel. The book *Art & Fear* is solely focused on the pains and perils of creativity in work (Bayles and Orland, 1993). These fears come from both inside and outside: 'fears about yourself prevent you from doing your *best* work, while fears about your reception by others prevent you from doing your *own* work' (ibid.: 23).

Consciously engaging in academic work at the edge of boundaries, conventions, or our comfort requires courage and authentic openness. While comfort may, indeed, be the enemy of creative work (Henry, 2013), this can be a place filled with doubt and fear that can harm our creativity. It's important to acknowledge that these feelings (and others, such as being overwhelmed, paralysed, or highly anxious) are not unusual in creative work. Many of the fears in us around creativity come because we don't feel good enough or worthy enough to meet the immense challenges set by our academic work. These doubts are normal: 'Self-doubt can be an ally. This is because it serves as an indicator or aspiration ... The counterfeit innovator is wildly self-confident. The real one is scared to death' (Pressfield, 2002: 39).

Over-trying

Sometimes, we want something so badly and we think about it so much and so hard that our performance is actually harmed. Thus, runners, swimmers and artists alike seek to retain a crystal-clear focus on the task at hand, while keeping negative thinking, preoccupation with others, or self-doubt away (Goleman, 2013). In the next chapter, we will address some of the self-work that can be done to address these thoughts. Over-trying is a positive indicator of passion and care for your academic work but, unless channelled in the right direction, it can harm performance.

Accept and celebrate constraints

Most academic workers are all too aware of the factors that constrain this work. Structures and requirements abound around casual contracts, lowered autonomy, teaching, journal interests, national research performance assessment exercises, metrics-based cultures, promotion criteria, idiosyncratic funding body priorities, and many more. We yearn for simpler times without such constraints. Constraints are everywhere and surround us at every turn; they cause us pain, frustration, and paralysis. It has, however, also always been thus in creative work. For centuries, artists have been all too aware of the inherent constraints of the medium through which they work – what it can and cannot do in terms of their vision and expression (Bayles and Orland, 1993). Constraints can be lamented but can also be a source of inspiration and determination to do the best work possible within them. As Orson Welles observed, 'the enemy of art is the absence of limitations' (quoted by Henry, 2011: 15).

It is because the world is so replete with knowledge work with such constraints that our academic work and the talents that we bring are so important – not to write out the constraints or ignore them, but to actively know their precise nature and implications and, nevertheless, do successful academic work. While it would seem so much easier to have endless time and resources for our research or control over our class sizes, it is actually these constraints that push us further and push us to ask questions that we may not have otherwise asked of ourselves in order to be more creative and innovative.

Approached creatively, these constraints, despite their prevalence and seeming permanence, can actually become part of what inspires academic work: to work around, to work within, and to work despite the constraints; and, moreover, to bring the best of ourselves to this inevitably compromised and compromising extreme knowledge work.

It remains an ongoing challenge in academia that systems of reward and recognition (from promotion to Nobel Prizes) are at the individual level. This devalues and dissolves the value of creativity to academic work. It also downplays the importance that other collaborators have in creative academic work. Identifying ways and people to work with in order to increase your creativity remains one of the most rewarding and important facets of academic work. We ignore the importance of our own creativity at our peril. Making choices, spaces, and collaborations to grow our creativity benefits ourselves, those we work with and the work that we do.

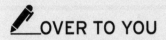

OVER TO YOU

Exploring Your Creativity

1. Think of what tasks within your current academic work demand the most creativity. List the tasks below and state in what ways or why they require or demand your creativity.

(Continued)

2. What activities or behaviours are your 'creative replenishers'? List them below along with what they tend to do to help your creativity.

3. When are you at most risk of failing to prioritize creativity in your schedule? What can you do to better ensure that you devote time to replenishing your creativity?

4. Thinking back to The Success Pyramid, which tasks or goals in your academic work would you most benefit from working with another particular person on? With whom would you want to work? Think why this is the case and why that person, in particular. Do your values align? What steps will you take to involve this person in your work in the future?

─── REMARKABLE RESOURCES ───

Creative Collaboration by Vera John-Steiner

Creativity often comes or is increased because creative people work together. This takes many forms and increases creativity in many ways across the sciences and the arts. John-Steiner's history of creative partnerships explores the common facets that these diverse relationships brought to the process and outputs of those involved (2000).

Key messages

- Creative collaborations are defined by overlapping values, a common vision and large amounts of trust, even during arguments and disagreements.
- The creative partnerships frequently used the relationship as a basis for taking emotional and intellectual risks, achieving a productive interdependence in their work.
- Relationships were not defined by consistent harmony, constancy of role or contribution or clear boundaries.

Key applications

- Conveys the power and diversity of collaboration, providing reassurance from prominently successful partnerships that collaboration comes in many forms and was often not easy for either party.
- Illustrates the importance of relationships, respect, and commitment in productive collaborative partnerships. Seldom was the need for the work not pressing or the process of collaboration intense or easy.

Creativity, Inc. by Ed Catmull

This biography of the animation studio Pixar is told by its president, Ed Catmull (2014). Charting the growth of Pixar from an idea, a failure, and an opportunity, the book provides a manifesto for individuals and organizations seeking to be highly creative in their work.

Key messages

- Creativity often needs high degrees of honesty and candour in order to succeed, which itself necessitates safety and mutual self-regard in relationships.
- Fear and failure frequently accompany creative work – even in those who have been very successful in the past. Taking risks is inherent in creative work.
- Creativity is more than being open: it is the dynamic engagement of ideas in an ongoing process.

Key applications

- Gives a positive approach to failing for those engaged in creative work.
- Exemplifies the intense doubts, tribulations, and strains that creative work often has even when ostensibly the results appear critically and commercially extremely successful.
- Provides administrators with ideas for making their organization more nurturing of creativity.

The Accidental Creative by Todd Henry

Many jobs require seemingly spontaneous creativity to address particular tasks or problems. In this book, Henry provides for the full range of knowledge workers a frame of reference and strategies to maintain and grow their creativity in the midst of busy, demanding, and high-stakes work environments (2011).

Key messages

- Many types of workers do creative work under pressure. Anyone and everyone can be creative.
- To be creative in your work, you have to allocate time to behaviours that help creativity.
- Everything is connected. Energy, exercising, and sleep do not detract from creativity but are essential to creativity.

(Continued)

Key applications

- To grow your creativity, focus on the tasks requiring creativity but also maintain your energy and sleep. Invest time in key relationships or collaborations with others and actually getting away from the tasks at hand.
- Provides tools and resources to increase your ability to focus deeply and maintain space for nurturing your creativity – not only during creative work but also in how you manage your other work, including emails and meetings.
- Practical advice on how to deliberatively build and sustain your relationships, clarity of focus, and allocation of time to priorities and stimuli.

7

HUMAN WORK AND SELF-WORK

The PhD is the monarch of the academic community ... the very highest accomplishment that can be sought by students ... Its recipient is now ready, eligible and indeed obligated, to make the most dramatic shift in roles: from student to teacher, from apprentice to master, from novice or intern to independent scholar and leader.

(Walker et al., 2008: x)

Knowing that what really matters starts from the quality of the relationships we have with those around us, both in our personal and professional lives, allows us to see the people around us not as enemies or as mere instruments to our own success, but as allies in our journey.

(Gallo, 2016)

It was all supposed to be about eureka moments and ever longer individual résumés (Walker et al., 2008). Yet, in contrast to the first quote above, after taking our first paid position, working alone becomes far less the norm and much less influential in determining the success of academic work. Conversely, working well with others quickly becomes a daily inevitability and a sometimes complex challenge. This is why human work is part of The Core. This human work actually represents some of the most challenging facets of academic work because it asks such deep questions of ourselves. Can we, for example:

- Be truly non-judgemental and supportive to a person we work with who lives by markedly different values to our own? (Brown, 2012).
- Put ourselves 'out there' to come alongside a student we teach – to be vulnerable and authentically open in their presence? (Palmer, 2007).
- Listen with true respect to the perspectives not only of those people with whom we identify but also of those with whom we have had past disagreements? (Stone et al., 2010).
- Feel and convey to others our own lack of confidence in our skills and expertise? (Kegan and Lahey, 2016).

How well we meet such challenges is pivotal to our individual success, effectiveness, and happiness.

The centrality of working well with other people in academic work – what we will call *human work* – justifies its place in The Core. While it's alluring to think that each of us can fully realize the potential for our work and contributions by working on our own, this neither recognizes the reality of modern academic workplaces nor the full scale of the challenges of academic work.

Accordingly, human work can be done with those whom we call peers or colleagues, the students whom we teach or supervise, mentors and mentees, or the collaborators and others whom, in diverse ways, have a role in our academic work and workplaces. Despite, or even because of, the need of human work within all of these various forms of relationships, the interpersonal dimensions of academic work can be some of the most rewarding and meaningful aspects of our work. Just as deep rewards can result from counselling and supporting a struggling student to eventual success in their degree, so, too, can working to make decisions, resolving conflicts, and building trust with others have its own challenges and benefits. Beyond this, the influence and imprints that our personal influence can have on others is an impact that can last long after retirement.

While the focus of this human work appears predominantly to be externally focused *on* others (*inter*personal), the role of ourselves in this work is pivotal. Because of this, the human work of academic work also involves *self-work*. Indeed, the centrality of self-work is what makes human work one of the most rewarding, challenging, and important parts of The Core.

THE SCOPE AND NATURE OF HUMAN WORK

Academic workers do not have a reputation for being effective or successful in human work. Kellaway (2006) memorably characterized academic workers as being 'employees from hell': unsuited by education, training, and volition to modern organizations. Are they, as Sparks and Bradley (1991) summarized many years ago, too conscious of their cleverness, overly critical, questioning, and resentful of new initiatives; poor team players who see their colleagues mainly as rivals, or as complacent, inert and insecure, wilfully resistant to authority, and satisfied with status quo and disagreement, lacking in emotional intelligence and ... (wait for it): introverted? (Ouch!)?

These challenges emanate from human work also being self-work – work that is not merely technical and procedural, but encompasses interpersonal interactions (both face-to-face and virtually), trust, relationships, emotional intelligence, teamwork, building relational networks, mentorship, conflict resolution, difficult conversations, making connections, persuasion, influence, presence, and feedback. These not only cross teaching, research, and engagement but also run deep in and through these areas. We could spend a whole chapter on each of these dimensions.

We don't take such a jaundiced and uniform view, but aim to recognize the distinctive sophistication and challenges of human work. Most academic workers care a lot about their personal academic work (expressed in values), which can contribute to challenges in working with others. It may be the centrality of 'cleverness' to the academic workers' identity (Goffee and Jones, 2009), which makes human work challenging across multiple dimensions (Table 7.1). All too often, academic workplaces feature some of the less desired behaviours and practices that are indicative of not doing human work well.

Table 7.1   Aspects of Human Work in Academic Work

Less desired	Human work with others	More desired
Fractious, wary, status-oriented	**Approach**	Open, generous, relational, supportive
Judgemental, cynical, contrary, argumentative	**Understanding**	Empathetic, patient, affirming
Judgement-focused	**Receptivity**	Listening-focused, encouraging
Prone to favouritism	**Balance**	Separates people from issues
Holding, guarding	**Information-handling**	Sharing, open
Impulsive and closed	**Decision-making**	Collaborative, yet decisive
Focused on expressing self	**Conflict**	Focused on understanding others

When human work in academic work is not done well, this may be evident in discussions around these specific difficulties, but more often manifests in other ways. These symptoms include:

- Avoiding making decisions or always seeking total consensus.
- Not broaching conflict, feedback, or other 'difficult' conversations.
- Overly associating status, rank, or role with worth, contribution, or ability.
- Disengagement and under-performance.
- Passive–aggressive behaviours.
- Selectivity in praising others.

In more prevalent and worse forms, challenges around human work contribute to toxic work environments and cultures, which feature: workplace bullying and harassment (horizontally and vertically) as well as mobbing, during which groups focus inappropriate conduct on one person.

These are not just words. These negative repercussions can come to dominate lives during and after work, and harm mental, spiritual, and physical health. They result in workplace cultures of drift, low morale, disengagement, and low retention. This is the antithesis of what makes for success, effectiveness, and happiness.

WHAT AFFECTS HUMAN WORK?

Where to begin in the manifest and manifold challenges of human work? To avoid moving from 'trouble-to-task' in our goals around human work, it is important to first understand what is going on in the human work of academic workplaces.

It is easy to be anxious, avoid human work and want to plod on alone. The human work of academic work is extremely hard to face and do well: it is not sufficiently recognized, rewarded or done well in most academic workplaces. Combined with a lack of focus on developing skills in human work, this stacks the odds of doing human work well against most academic workers who arrive in this work after individual success in work done mostly alone. How then can we break these barriers and move to doing human work well?

The prospects of such human work – having difficult conversations, giving negative feedback, working collaboratively with various personalities – can cause shuddering and recoil.

Not only do these situations churn in our minds and affect our emotions but they can also strike us physically. We may feel powerful physical sensations and emotional urgency to close ourselves up, shut things out, get our points across, 'show them!', shut down, strike back, or otherwise get away or make 'their' life difficult in other ways.

Faced with these feelings, often our reactions understandably are frequently avoidance-based. The symptom of not addressing human work and self-work well is less a conflict over decisions than avoidance of communication and decisions. We choose not to broach matters with others in the hopes that they will go away, avoid having the difficult conversation or fill up our time and heads with other less troublesome issues, like email. Usually, this means that matters don't move forward, decisions are not made, and the next thing comes along to relieve our fears. When involved in the imbroglio and minutiae of human work, the focus, by nature, tends to be on others. We wish that the world could suddenly be devoid of people who are difficult, don't get us, or have it 'in' for us. We bemoan others' weaknesses, values, foibles, or seeming disrespect: 'Why can't they change?' We feel angry about what people are doing or thinking about us, so we choose to get angry with other people or other things, sometimes with those who are closer to us, who we know will stick with us. In short, we do almost anything to remove the focus from ourselves.

HUMAN WORK DONE WELL: FIRST STEPS

Stronger and more influential than in any other sphere of the work, the lens or frame through which one approaches human work in academic work is transformative. When the role and nature of human work in academic work is truly appreciated, this allows a focus on what matters most when working with others. This not only increases the effectiveness and success of academic work, but also allows one to see all manner of difficult problems, situations, and people whom you navigate helping you to learn, grow, and improve (Dweck, 2006). It can then help happiness: each of us can be more open to, and then let go of, long-held and often intense apprehensions, avoidance, and fear over human work (Brown, 2012). This enables progress in its most powerful forms: even the seemingly most perilous problems, situations, and people can be seen, approached and transformed into elements that actively help us reach our goals and priorities (Holiday, 2014). The obstacles, indeed, become the way (ibid.).

Firstly, it *is* all about you

One single insight forms the element in human work of which we can truly be certain. One sure bet is that human work does and always should start with self-work. This recognizes the immutable fact that we can only ever directly control one person: ourselves. Authentic understanding of this truth is a realization that we often battle with, but is both profound and essential for effective human work.

The recognition that self-work is at the core of all human work guides most approaches to conflict resolution (Stone et al., 2010), stress reduction (Lazarus and Folkman, 1984) and performance psychology (Peters, 2013). Yet, focusing first on our self takes courage and strength. It requires you to open yourself to the challenge that beyond high credentials, social status or a CV as long as a novel, you are a colossal and all-too-often imperfect work in progress.

It can be hard to see ourselves in this way, particularly while simultaneously preserving our sense of personal competency. This competency is broadcast sometimes in how academic workers are encouraged to 'sell' themselves and their work as constantly successful and distinctive. More than this, some academic workers confuse this narrative with reality in itself, appearing grandiose, high-handed, and superior. Unsurprisingly, this is not a good foundation for self-work. While almost all of us have seen these tendencies in others, do we have the courage to recognize them in ourselves? Ironically, academic workers who need to do self-work the most are often the least likely to perceive it to be important. This shutting down is itself a sign that self-work is necessary and needed (Brown, 2012).

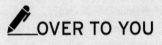

OVER TO YOU

Human Work and Self-Work

Think of a stressful or challenging situation involving your work with another academic worker(s).

1. Describe the situation from your perspective.

2. Describe the situation, as much as you can, from the perspective of the other person (people) involved. How was their perspective similar *and* different to yours?

3. Think about *why* you found the situation challenging. What questions or issues did the situation raise for you in terms of yourself? Think of similar situations that elicited similar responses.

You are enough

Once we recognize that we can only control our own behaviour, we can move to begin to accept the real uncertainty involved in facing others' behaviours and reactions without seeking to impose our control or seeking the path of least resistance. We cannot control others' behaviours – nor should we try (Stone et al., 2010).

This brings us back to ourselves and our own foibles around self-work. A range of different recent approaches to well-being have recognised the paradoxical importance of self-acceptance. This recognition is best exemplified in Brené Brown's 'you are enough already' *ethos* (2012), but is also found in performance models based on psychology (Peters, 2013) and productivity (Catto, 2016). The next vital step in self-work is to closely evaluate your own intensions and contributions to any interaction. If you concluded your approach reflected good intentions, be fair to yourself as you tackle the complexities of human work, which does not always progress or result in what we want or need. When, for example, a difficult conversation goes badly, such as a student being upset at feedback you gave, while we can regret the student's reaction and feel less inclined to give feedback again in the future, we should honour the sincerity that guided our feedback and reflect candidly on what you could do differently and better next time.

We have probably all come across academic workers who appear as the very last people who need to be accepting of themselves in this way: they can appear brusque, vain, rabidly overconfident, intimidating, and entirely self-assured. It's easy to judge harshly. Nevertheless, such bravado is more likely a constructed front and the best means to approach such conduct is non-judgementally, with empathy, and assuming positive intention. This, in itself, is self-work, and this is some of the hardest self-work to do in practise. Often, hostile behaviours relate to the 'success' or 'perfection' narratives that we choose to project to peers and even ourselves, because it's difficult to truly face our weaknesses and imperfections or exist outside of the status security that our academic worlds provide. Preserving your intentions is important not because everything you do will work but because you are a values-driven person and most-often do what you can to be successful in human work. Filtering your self-talk to recognize such merits is the foundation of effective human work.

RELATIONSHIPS IN ACADEMIC WORK

This foundation in self-work allows for a relational approach to academic work: a basis that sees all the human work academic workers do as based in relationships. This can range from relationships yet to be formed within relational networks, collegial relationships with peers and co-workers to mentorship relationships. All human work has a relational basis.

Formal relationships in academic workplaces are those to which organizations accord some degree of formalization, expectations and outputs: supervisory relationships with students as part of teaching or research, line-manager relationships with team members and other staff members, or with a mentor, mentee, or collaborator. These relationships usually have some kind of perceived or actual power differential. This can raise many challenges pertaining to openness and candour, and can ultimately make raising issues difficult, contributing to a lack of communication within these workplaces.

Collegial relationships may have similar such power differentials but these are far less formalized and more often absent because these relationships have a horizontal rather than vertical orientation in academic workplaces. An academic worker's relationships with peers or colleagues both within the workplace and outside of it are the most common collegial relationships.

Why are relationships so important?

Relationships are not important in academic work because they are fun, people are interesting, or we should be respectful. Of course, relationships can be rewarding, hugely mutually beneficial and reflect our shared humanity, but they are also pivotal to getting academic work done effectively.

Developing relationships means taking time to build trust with the people whom you have formal or collegial relationships. As award-winning effectiveness writer Stephen M.R. Covey observes that trust is about others having confidence – not suspicion – in you, your intentions or actions (2006). Trust is not 'soft' but a real, quantifiable factor that can be transformative, created, destroyed, restored, and harnessed (ibid.); in relationships, trust can make or break others' reactions, interactions, and approaches to you.

There is a risk that relationships (along with trust and other associated positive dimensions) are mistakenly seen as self-evidently right to prioritize when discussed in this way. But, often in academic workplaces, this does not happen. Instead, human work is focused around roles, authority, and the inevitable power differentials that these lead to. Instead of relying on relationships to get things done, reliance is based on authority, seniority, or status. The underlying assumption can be that there will be hidden consequences to not complying. An alternative view is that relationships should always come before roles. The rationale for this is that, of course, other people are very much aware of the various role powers in an organization but will find a deeper, more trusting basis for the work if their relationship with you is good. While people may 'do as they are told' based on role reasons, a relational focus provides a deeper, more sustained foundation for human work. There is a strong responsibility on everyone to invest time and effort in maintaining good relationships with others in our academic workplaces. This can mean knowing more about the lives of the people you work with outside of work, spending some time outside of work together, or more formally engaging in workplace team-building initiatives.

BUILDING RELATIONAL NETWORKS

Like conflict, 'networking' is a divisive concept for academic workers, and the mere mention of the word creates a visceral reaction for many. For those with personality traits associated with 'introversion', the prospect of 'working the room', making small talk with strangers and expanding one's network is understandably anxiety-laden (Cain, 2013). Conversely, those with fewer reservations may determinedly sift through their countless interactions with other people to ruthlessly find the movers and shakers who can be used to get to the next step. While clearly characterizations, these opposites are just some of the baggage that 'networking' has. As with conflict, the frame of reference is key and determines a lot in approaches and reactions to this human work. This is why we advocate for 'building relational networks'.

In essence, building a relational network is about developing and sustaining new and existing relationships. As with creative collaborations (discussed in the previous chapter), these relationships can be immensely meaningful and helpful across many aspects of academic work. While we often feel 'busy' with all manner of pressing tasks, your network provides valuable insurance for rainy days, when you might need someone's help. Inside and outside of your academic workplace, this network can be drawn upon on an ongoing basis for all manner of insight, help, support, and practical assistance. While time needs to be devoted to this network, it provides value and opportunity and, as such, is an important asset that warrants prioritization in your time schedule. Moreover, unlike your physical office, your network is your *own* personal asset. It moves with you from job to job, much like your reputation or résumé does, continuing to provide value, irrespective of your physical location.

YOUR NETWORK IS YOUR OWN PERSONAL ASSET

Developing a relational network will, in most cases, not happen by magic and it requires some deliberate actions in terms of tasks, either by attending functions with the goal of building your network and/or devoting time in your schedule to meeting new people (Farrazzi, 2005) and building relationships. As with all priorities, if developing your network is important, you need to allocate time to it in your schedule. Just one hour per week devoted to building your relational network will extensively expand and deepen your relationships. This could include taking someone new for coffee to know more about their work, attending a specific event or joining a committee addressing work that aligns with your own academic work interests. Over a sustained period, this small amount of your time can markedly develop and widen your relational network.

In the past, taking opportunities to build your relational network was associated mostly with taking place in physical spaces, such as conferences, social functions, and similar meetings. However, the advent of social media, in particular, allows us to develop our network and sustain it electronically. This can be especially useful for those less predisposed to old-school 'networking' (Cain, 2013). Striking up conversations, sharing content and contributing to debates on social media are all new and acceptable ways of not only becoming more known in your field but also of developing relationships with others in your field. The use of social media in this way has added benefits of targeting your connection with academic workers who share your interests. By doing this, your relational network is also likely to expand internationally and can be done so conveniently and at a low cost compared to attending conferences and events in person.

FEEDBACK

The role of feedback in contributing to high human performance in teams is increasingly being recognized but is also usually done poorly in terms of frequency, focus, tone, and emotionality. While the importance of feedback could be a chapter in itself, it is important here to understand the foundational concepts of feedback and how it contributes to effectiveness through human work.

Most simply, 'feedback' is 'communication about performance' (Horstman, 2015: 103) and can be given in formal relationships (for example, to students or research assistants) and in collegial relationships (to peers or even your 'boss'). Feedback is focused, 'first and foremost ... on learning, developing and changing' (Harvard Business Press, 2006: ix), but how this is achieved is open to question.

Feedback in academic workplaces is most often absent or given only during annual formal performance reviews or student progress assessments. When talking to others about performance in feedback discussions, the focus is often only on the negative ('what went wrong'), the past and/or how the conduct of the recipient of the feedback was deficient. This tends to lead to shame on behalf of the recipient, who then also struggles to really hear and be receptive to the substance of the feedback because of being 'called out' in this way.

However, as Mark Horstman (2015) concludes, none of these practices is likely to actually change future behaviour, and instead he advocates that feedback:

- Happens frequently as part of regular conversation (that is, almost daily).
- Focuses on both the positive and the negative.
- Is future- and change-focused, not past- and blame-focused.
- Identifies specifically how future preferred actions will contribute to better outcomes.
- Is neutral in emotional tone and never given in anger.
- Is relationship-based – not role-based.

Providing feedback in this way normalizes performance conversations in the workplace and helps to neutralize common, yet understandable, negative reactions to feedback. While this feedback model is more often used in relationships with power differentials, it can also be used in collegial relationships, in which the desired outcome of the feedback focuses solely on better meeting a desired goal. As discussed earlier in this chapter, relationships are an essential part of the human work within our academic work. Trust developed within these relationships can form the basis from which feedback can be both given and received, and is essential to truly harnessing the value of feedback.

Finally, a more neglected aspect of feedback relates to the importance of receiving feedback well. This recognizes that feedback is always relational and, as such, involves at least two parties – in this instance, the provider and the receiver of the feedback. While the onus is on the provider of the feedback to do this effectively, for feedback to work optimally the receiver shares part of the responsibility as well. This entails openness to the message, preserving the intention with which the feedback was given and, ultimately, valuing the relationship. Further to this, the most adept receiver of feedback is actually able to compensate for weakness in feedback that has been provided. For example, the provider of the feedback may have competently conveyed the action that needs to be changed in future but may have done so in an angry tone. Instead of the receiver then reacting angrily, they can see beyond the inadequacies of the feedback delivery to focus on the underlying message. Like the skilled receiver in American football who can catch a badly thrown pass but actually make it look like the pass was well done, the skilled receiver of feedback can render even clumsy feedback effective.

TEAMS AND WORKING GROUPS

Sometimes, academic workers function in *teams* – groups with shared leadership roles, and mutual and individual accountability that have a specific purpose and remit to produce collective works (Katzenbach and Smith, 2003). Research project teams, teaching teams, or academic leadership teams overseeing departments are common examples. Such teams need trust, commitment, and collaboration in order to be effective. Alternatively, academic workers can function together in working groups – in which leadership is focused on a clear leader and group members work more alongside each other rather than together (ibid.). Common examples of working groups in academic workplaces include departmental committees, supervisory committees, and small project working groups. Other times, people working on a shared project – even if they are labelled as 'teams' – do little more than exist as a list of people on paper. Seldom meeting, sharing, or collaborating, this anti-model is all too common in academic workplaces.

If teams and working groups were broadly the same, contributing to them, establishing, leading, and sustaining them would be much easier. However, these teams can vary in size, diversity, values, formality, and composition, and increasingly include non-academics, such as members of communities/the public, workers from government or external organizations and project managers.

Note here that commonality of values, compatibility or similarity of personalities or the exclusion of those people who are difficult, different to you or otherwise non-threatening, does not come into it. As discussed in Chapter 2, it is important not only to accept real and deep differences in people but also to embrace these. While we can hanker after team members who are just like us, as Alex Ferguson, one of the world's most successful sports coaches reminds us, teams cannot win if they play 11 goalkeepers (Ferguson and Moritz, 2015). Diversity, difference, and differentiation are assets and should be seen as such, but to be truly open to this is very challenging as this necessitates working with difference in terms of values, backgrounds, disciplines, personality traits, and a myriad of other characteristics.

Prioritizing your efforts and skills in establishing and sustaining high-performing teams and groups is one of the most important skills that an academic worker can have because such teams, as also with creative collaborations, generate benefit: that is, they can contribute to effectiveness, vibrancy, and quality of work more than an individual can separately. Being part of such an effective collection of people can be inspiring, discomforting, and invigorating at the same time.

CONFLICT

Few things make our blood run colder than the thought of conflict. Yet, as soon as we recognize that people in our workplaces have different priorities, passions, responsibilities and skills, and personalities, disagreement and conflict are inevitable.

Firstly, it is important to distinguish these cousins. Disagreement is *not* conflict (Manager Tools, 2006). Disagreement is an integral, healthy, and positive part of self-expression, openness and relationships. It has contributed to some of history's most successful groups in science and art (John-Steiner, 2000). Some even argue that instead of fleeing from disagreements, we should orchestrate them (Heifetz et al., 2009). This discipline requires seeing disagreement as being necessary to better futures, being comfortable with some degree of tension and discomfort, and realizing that this process actually strengthens relationships and trust rather than weakening it.

DISAGREEMENT IS *NOT* CONFLICT

In contrast, conflict is characterized by some of the less desirable behaviours noted earlier in Table 7.1. While these behaviours are not desirable, conflict is often stigmatized as being symptomatic of the failure of other people, our workplaces, or ourselves. This can lead us to focus on the demerits of the other people involved, making conflict personal, and striking back at others (Manager Tools, 2006). These not only heighten emotions but also focus the conflict on other people as opposed to their behaviours and ourself. This is understandable because addressing conflict, especially in some cultures, is difficult. As Brown notes, as humans, we would often rather do anything rather than face and deal with conflict: 'to control a situation, backing out of it, pretending it's not happening or maybe even pretending that we don't care. We ... dodge conflict, discomfort, possible confrontation, the potential for shame or hurt and/or criticism' (2012: 165).

How conflict is framed informs our feelings about it and our ability to address it, either when we are directly involved in conflict or when we are responsible for addressing conflict between others.

The research-based approach detailed in *Difficult Conversations* (Stone et al., 2010) is particularly useful for working through conflict situations. Building on this self-work, the approach is founded on the realization that you can only control your own behaviour and should stop trying to control other people's behaviour. This approach addresses the strong urgency that we have in conflict situations to forcefully focus most on what 'I' have or want to say and convey to the others involved. Yet, paradoxically, it is far more important in conflict situations to be open to and understand your own reactions better and then use these self-insights to truly listen and understand the perspective of the others involved.

This approach asks each party in a difficult conversation over a conflict situation to:

- Be open to *feeling* your own feelings without shutting them down.
- Understand what facets of the situation have triggered your feelings.
- Focus on listening and understanding the perspective of the other parties involved.
- Be empathetic and non-judgemental – avoid attributing negative intentions or personal characteristics to behaviours.
- Articulate only what you yourself contributed to the conflict happening.
- Support others to share how they contributed to the conflict.

Understanding your own reactions better requires not shutting down or trying to 'numb' your personal feelings or discomfort in conflict situations. Rather, recognize that disagreements and strong feelings about them make us what we are as humans. Use this state of acceptance to reflect on the specific triggers for your own emotions in the situation (Stone et al., 2010; Brown, 2012). What is it about conflict situations (whether specific topics, tones, or people) that cause your own intense and sometimes difficult feelings and sensations? This again draws attention to the importance of self-work as the basis for human work.

Taking this approach further, conflict can be seen to be *the* problem rather than a lack of communication or poor relationships with others (Manager Tools, 2006). Further, in the face of conflict, we avoid communicating around disagreements or dwelling on others' differences or deficiencies. As academic workers, we can find all manner of criteria in which others are different and usually inferior to ourselves! While conflict is seen as the source of our workplace problems, it is actually reflective of how effectively disagreements are handled. Mistakenly, personal and workplace capacity to deal with conflict is weakened precisely because communication is reduced and our relationships become weakened in its face. This explains why so many academic workplaces are characterized by ongoing and divisive conflict. Fostering workplace cultures that centre on mutual acceptance and openness to sharing personal vulnerabilities, weaknesses, and disagreements not only render conflict more normalized and less stigmatized but also provide the best way to avoid the less desirable behaviours associated with the poor handling of conflict. This approach is exemplified by Kegan and Lahey (2016) in their articulation of the Deliberately Developmental Organization.

HUMAN WORK, SELF-WORK: A JOURNEY WITHOUT END

This chapter brings out the centrality and the paradoxes of human work in academic work. While our focus in academic work is often on work 'ends', human work is everywhere, yet nowhere. While our focus in our work with others is often on those others, the seat upon which almost all human work is done is yourself. This is at once both profoundly and breathlessly challenging, yet also liberating and empowering: it yields a focus that is truly and absolutely under our influence or control. This is why human work is part of The Core and, as we will see in the next chapter, we are all always learning and growing.

━━━ REMARKABLE RESOURCES ━━━

Daring Greatly by Brené Brown

In her book *Daring Greatly*, Brown (2012) discusses the questions from what or where do many of our biggest challenges and fears around ourselves and other people emanate? How can we best develop our own capacity to communicate, work through, and be with other people in work and life?

Key messages

- The shame we feel about ourselves forms the basis of our reactions to many difficult or threatening situations. This leads to emotional reactions and powerful physical sensations.
- This arises from our own unfair and unrealistic expectations of, and on, ourselves, which often disregard our talents and positive intentions.
- We have to recognize that 'we are enough' before we can then move to be vulnerable with and toward other people, and be more empathetic to others and ourselves. This self-work is key to healthy, positive, and growth-focused interactions with others in human work.

Key applications

- Helps to generate 'literacy' in understanding our own feelings and emotions, particularly in difficult situations with others.
- Reframes what are seen to be negative and/or weakness reactions (such as shame and vulnerability) into essential elements of humanity and personal growth.
- Can be used in workplaces to foster greater insight into the need for self-work and to foster cultures that promote openness, empathy, and empowerment of self and others.

An Everyone Culture by Robert Kegan and Lisa L. Lahey

Kegan and Lahey (2016) ask in their book, while we can do human work well, individual to individual, what kind of workplace cultures, structures and practices are needed to foster workplaces that are built on effective self- and human work?

Key messages

- Most workers in workplaces are focused on masking and defending their fears and weaknesses about themselves and their workplaces.
- This contributes to wasted energy, lack of creativity, and a poor growth mindset in individuals and groups in our workplaces.
- An alternative model, built on deliberate development, recognizes that we can always grow, that weaknesses and errors are opportunities for growth, and that we need workplace practices and leadership that build the best platform to facilitate self- and group-development.

(Continued)

Key applications

- Helps conceptualize and delineate the influence of self-work on human work.
- Integrates the role of self- and human- work within learning and workplace culture.
- Provides leaders and managers with suggestions on the building blocks needed to foster more open and growth-focused working cultures.

Quiet by Susan Cain

Success in human work is often seen to be incompatible with introversion. Cain's (2013) book addresses the nature of introversion and how, in relation to self- and human- work, introversion can form the basis for success, effectiveness, and happiness.

Key messages

- Being an introvert can make for fears, feelings of inferiority and loneliness in a world that seems to value extroversion and charisma far more.
- Research and history consistently shows that introverts often make extremely successful leaders, team members, and creative forces.
- The place and power of people who are introverts needs to be recognized and rewarded more.

Key applications

- Details how introverts can recognize how their personality and talents can be used more effectively and positively to fully realize their contributions to human work.
- Can be used in workplaces to foster greater insight into the need to support introverts, harness their contributions in teams and working groups, and promote their leadership and progress in the workplace.

The Obstacle is the Way by Ryan Holiday

Anyone who seeks to be influential, innovative, or otherwise get things done in the world has to navigate all manner of obstacles or barriers to their goals. Holiday's remarkable book draws on the life and examples of Marcus Aurelius, the first Emperor of Rome, and other notable figures to show why and how these obstacles should and can become the means to meet goals and do tasks successfully (2014).

Key messages

- Obstacles, difficult situations, people, and issues have always been, and will always be, with you. Accept this now.
- The key to not only neutralizing but also to utilizing these obstacles is in your frame, your will and, in doing the right things, in your actions.
- The foundation for rendering obstacles to become 'the way' is in yourself and in human work, and in maintaining strength, clarity, and endurance even when obstacles seem insurmountable or surround you.

Key applications

- Build a strong foundation for seeing obstacles as a means in your human work via addressing aspects of the self, including: your energy, creativity, proactivity, and resilience.
- Helps view your own situation around academic work, no matter how perilous, in a historical context in which conflict, politics, and disagreements resulted in all manner of gruesome torture and death. Perspective is everything.
- Learn the framing and flexibility needed not only to tolerate the obstacles but also to build strategies and goals that ensure that you can be grateful for the new opportunities that they yield so as to meet these goals.

8

LEARNING

SUCCESS, FAILURE, AND THE GROWTH MINDSET

I don't divide the world into the weak and the strong, or the successes and failures ... I divide the world into the learning and non-learners.

(Benjamin Barber, quoted by Dweck, 2006: 16)

It's comforting that our talents, abilities, and past achievements equip each of us for the many challenges of academic work – comforting but also arbitrary, risky, and likely counter-productive. Instead, we can view ourselves as ongoing 'works in progress', defined principally by our ongoing discipline and ability to bring our best efforts to focus on the right priorities and always, always, always seeking to learn to get better at tasks. This learning-orientation has come to be known as the 'growth mindset' (Dweck, 2006).

In this chapter, we discuss the nature and implications of a learning-focused or 'growth mindset' around the successes and failures of academic work. Contrasting this with the alternative, the so-called 'fixed mindset', the learning-centred 'growth mindset' approach not only reframes how we can view ourselves, academic work, and its processes, but also what success and failure in this academic work are and can be used for. Ultimately, we argue that mindsets associated with learning are at the centre of sustained success, effectiveness, and happiness in academic work, which is why these mindsets along with how we learn from success and failure are key components of The Core.

MINDSETS IN ACADEMIC WORK

What is success in your academic work: a growing résumé or a growing person? How much do the entries on your résumé reflect your personal talent, brains, and skills? Successes, from outstanding high school exam results to Nobel Prizes, can be attributed to the personal abilities and aptitudes of the individual involved. Those academic workers most prominent or revered in their fields, whether dead or alive, can look superhuman; intimidatingly productive, they shift from success to higher success. We are likely to see such 'academic stars' in our workplaces or disciplines. We may feel admiration, jealously and fear. How can we ever be as talented or successful as them?

These academic workers appear blessed with abilities akin to those of Michael Jordan or Cristiano Ronaldo, attract acclamation like Meryl Streep, and produce hit after hit with the consistency and creativity of U2 or Pixar (Catmull, 2014). Yet, in the most competitive of fields, each of these outstanding individuals, groups, and organizations share one vital dimension beyond sustained success: the ability to see yourself not as an endlessly progressing work colossus but as a colossal work of endless progress. Each may well have been blessed with ability, but what has made them stand out in terms of continued world-class outstanding performance and results is an ongoing readiness to devote deliberative efforts to learning to improve. Their peers were undoubtedly as, or even more, talented, passionate, and effortful in their respective crafts, working long hours with passion and commitment. However, what makes them outstanding and collectively reach the highest levels of sustained performance is what psychologist Carol S. Dweck (2006, table 1) terms a 'growth mindset'.

SEE YOURSELF NOT AS AN ENDLESSLY PROGRESSING WORK COLOSSUS BUT AS A COLOSSAL WORK OF ENDLESS PROGRESS

Growth mindsets in academic work

People with growth mindsets (Dweck, 2006) tend to focus far less on their past successes or current talents or abilities than on four main facets, which, like self-work, are all directly amenable to their control:

1. Bringing one's best efforts to furthering priorities, goals, and tasks, no matter what.
2. Prioritizing some goals and tasks for higher efforts (that is, doing the right things).
3. Learning from *whatever* transpires.
4. Repeating steps 1-3 ad infinitum.

Adopting a growth mindset in relation to your academic work has implications for how you see yourself and this work (Table 8.1). Adopting a growth mindset is desirable because it has been associated in many research studies with contributing to:

- Sustained meeting of higher success indicators (ibid.).
- Greater comfort and ability to meet 'stretch' goals and priorities (ibid.).
- Higher motivation for, and aptitude in, work tasks (ibid.).
- Enhanced and distinctive brain development to increase abilities across wider ranges of tasks (ibid.).
- Lower rates of distress, anxiety, and depression (ibid.).
- More positive, supportive, and effective workplaces (Kegan and Lahey, 2016).

Yet, adopting this growth mindset in relation to your academic work is destabilizing because it:

- Conflicts with comforting reassurances that you are an expert, clever, well-qualified or otherwise 'correct' (Dweck, 2006).
- Is incongruent with the many messages received since childhood about your relative 'smartness' (now also physically embodied in your ever-lengthening résumé) (ibid.).
- Goes against the dominant currency of success 'narratives' and talk that surround us in academic workplaces and careers (Kegan and Lahey, 2016).
- Leads to feelings of vulnerability and physical discomfort (Brown, 2012; Henry, 2013).

Indeed, although attractive in terms of work outcomes, work process, and personal well-being (particularly taking account of the complexity of academic work as extreme knowledge work), growth mindsets are not as common in academic workplaces as would be expected.

Table 8.1   The Academic Worker: Fixed vs. Growth Mindset Perspectives

Domain of Academic Work	Growth mindset	Fixed mindset
Intelligence, abilities, and skills	Variable personal facets that can be improved over time	Fixed personal facets that underpin work
Intelligence and learning	Learning from all situations as the primary goal, intelligence varies and can be developed	One can learn new things but intelligence is fixed
Goals and tasks	Seeks always to primarily embrace opportunities to learn from efforts and results	Focused on outcomes, provides evidence, verifies intelligence and abilities
Career successes	Reflects learning, openness, and effort in the right directions	Reflects ability, existing skills, and intelligence

Fixed mindsets in academic work

In contrast to the growth mindset, a 'fixed mindset' is more common. The fixed mindset dwells more on one's perceived talents, credibility and record of accomplishment and attributes successes to aspects of the self. Success in meeting a work task, goal, or priority provides sustaining self-verification and vindication of these foundations: success in the present is linked to being smart and successful in the past. As such, fixed mindsets immediately make us feel good, especially as we navigate the immense complexity and range of academic work. Despite all the mess, at the centre, we have our ability as the rock upon which to found our teaching, research, and engagement performance (Table 8.2).

Table 8.2 Fixed vs. Growth Mindsets in Relation to Academic Work

Facet of academic work	Fixed mindset	Growth mindset
Approach to tasks	Dwells on track record, personal credibility, qualifications, and past successes to date	Focus on investing current efforts strategically on right goals and tasks, learning from whatever transpires for the future
Approach to challenges, high risk, and high aspiration	Fear and threat: Failure brings threat to self-identity as talented, able, and successful academic worker	Openness: Failure brings opportunity to learn about self and process and an opportunity to learn to be better
Manuscript accepted for publication	Affirmation of personal reputation and talent. Reinforcement of talent and credibility	Confirmation of match between results of effort invested and journal requirements, learning opportunity for future for repetition
Manuscript rejected for publication	Personal talent and abilities cast in doubt, reputation doubted/on the line, possible defensiveness	Indication of mismatch between results of effort invested and journal requirements, learning opportunity for future for improvement
Negative feedback from student	Closed: Difficulty accepting veracity of student feedback, tendency to cast doubt on student motivation, fairness, and integrity. Dismissive	Open to opportunity to learn how to improve teaching further. Focus on listening, being open and developing as needed
Colleague gets major prize for work	Fear: Success of other threatens personal credibility and status	Continued focus on efforts towards self-improvement

Excessive identification with being 'intelligent', successful, or accomplished in terms of a 'fixed mindset' means that 'our success is a function of some innate quality or talent we possess, rather than a function of one's determined efforts in the face of expected stumbles' (Kegan and Lahey, 2016: 92).

Growth and fixed mindsets considered together

While growth mindsets may appear immediately to be 'softer' and less success-oriented approaches to work, actually, the converse is the case because fixed mindsets are more likely to reduce the likelihood of sustained success and harm both individuals and their work-places. Extrapolating from the tendencies noted by Dweck (2006) in fail situations, academic workers with fixed mindsets are less likely to seek work opportunities that they associate with high degrees of uncertainty, aspiration, or challenge. Instead, work tends to gravitate to more certain, safer wins. Dissatisfaction with work results tends to be attributed to self-failure or matters beyond personal control (Syed, 2016), because truly assimilating failure strikes to the core of self-confidence (Brown, 2012; Syed, 2016). Failure in a particular task or initiative is extrapolated into deeper failure in one's ability, talent, or aptitude: 'I succeed because I am talented' becomes 'I failed because I am a failure', or, more likely, the failure is attributed externally to something other than one's talents, abilities or aptitudes: '*They* just don't *get* my work', 'The student that gave me that feedback is just hostile', and 'My colleague is just vengeful'. In such instances, opportunities to become better are lost because of the failure.

Finally, Dweck (2006) notes that failing while having a fixed mindset results in holding a more negative and disparaging stance toward others. This happens when the integrity of our sense of personal success becomes buttressed by feeling better about ourselves by putting others down relative to our more successful selves. Might it be that the wide prevalence and high likelihood of personal 'failure' in academic work, such as negative student feedback, rejected grant applications, and manuscripts actually contribute to workplace conflict, condescension, and bullying because fixed mindsets are so prevalent? Indeed, there is good evidence that workplaces in which employees are more open to and about personal growth, are more harmonious, dynamic, and risk-taking (Kegan and Lahey, 2016).

Even when we cannot help or feel compelled to be focused on 'hard' success, growth mindsets are more likely to achieve this over the long term. For example, it was a fixed mindset that led employees at Pixar to dwell on the international acclaim for *Toy Story* and put the success of the film *Toy Story 2* in jeopardy via their reliance on their past success even when they believed that the early edits of the movie were weak. Complacency, over-confidence, poor prioritization, and a reluctance to admit failure in their new work led the development team ever deeper into basking in their identity of 'successful' filmmakers. They reasoned that their touch and talent would be enough to ensure that the movie was successful (Catmull, 2014).

However, a shift to a growth mindset made it possible for Pixar's staff to do the courageous: to recognize the brute inadequacies of their failing sequel even though this was during the later stages of its first edit. This led to the hard decision to cancel a very firm release date, rip the movie to pieces and start again pretty much from the beginning, with a commitment to learn from what had gone wrong. The human and corporate risks of moving from fixed to growth mindsets that Catmull (2014) describes were profound and deeply challenging to how workers saw themselves. Yet, to ensure that the final product was successful required a mindset and action plan that put the failure front and centre with candour, and focused all efforts from learning what had gone wrong in order to put it right. The resultant movie went on to become one of the most commercially and critically successful of all time. The lessons to Pixar from this challenging experience have extended to the present day (ibid.).

Exploring your mindset

How do you know if you have a fixed or growth mindset? Likely, there are elements of growth and fixed mindset in us at the same time. However, irrespective of your own 'mindset balance', being aware of the nature of each in yourself and understanding the ramifications remains key.

Although usually presented as a neat dichotomy (Dweck, 2006), more likely 'growth' and 'fixed' lie on a continuum, with each of us having different mindsets for different parts of our life and academic work. While we may readily see ourselves as growth-focused in relation to academic work, in other roles as parents or partners we may see ourselves as more fixed.

In relation to academic work, many successes are likely to elicit positive feelings and thoughts:

- Not making mistakes in tasks.
- Lengthy résumé or framed degrees on your wall.
- Compliments received from others.
- Positive annual performance review.
- Favourable student feedback.
- Personal award or grant recognizing your work.
- Doing academic work well that you perceive others to find challenging.
- Submitting manuscripts that are often accepted for publication the first time.

However, when these successes are attributed clearly and decisively to your own inherent talents and abilities, this demonstrates having a fixed mindset. Conversely, someone with a growth mindset is more likely to attribute these positive occurrences to the process of ongoing learning, openness and effort in the right directions. Other expressions of a growth mindset are when you:

- Find academic work tough but try hard and do something better than you could before.
- Can see how your behaviour contributed to a negative situation with a colleague and are motivated to behave differently in the future.
- Eventually complete a difficult task successfully by trying different things.
- Develop the quality of your ideas after five journal rejections of your manuscript and then resubmit it.
- Always seek improvement, irrespective of results or outcomes.
- Realize that you missed an opportunity for your dream job because you missed something glaringly obvious in the interview but work to never repeat this mistake.

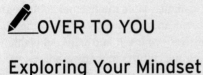

OVER TO YOU

Exploring Your Mindset

Think back over academic work in your career to date or alternatively, over your life more broadly.

1. Identify your top three achievements, contributions, or accomplishments. Force yourself to select only three that are the most meaningful or important to you.

(Continued)

2.   To the best of your ability try to pinpoint the reasons for why you chose these three – what about each of these stands out and makes you feel most proud/satisfied?

3.   Do your answers to question number 2 focus on the process and pathway to achieving these accomplishments or on the outcome itself? Do they focus on the effort, strategy, and learning required or your natural ability, talent, or qualifications?

Taking account of your answers, on the continuum below, place your mindset around academic work:

Fixed mindset _____ Growth mindset

Our own mindsets can be inferred from candour in answering these questions. How do we feel when we confront the reality of our mindset around success? For some, a fixed mindset is a state of affairs that is self-evident: Does anyone *not think like this*?! It reassures us that our successes are based on our high qualifications, commendable intellectual abilities and finely honed knowledge and skills. However, a growth mindset focuses on focusing your efforts to learn, work hard and strategically, and cultivate your self and skills deliberately.

Fixed responses may appear alluring and align with the cultures in many academic workplaces, these are 'hard', 'outcome-focused' and broadcast our success. Yet, all manner of historical counterexamples and research suggest that it is the latter growth responses that actually help you to achieve real and sustained success (Dweck, 2006; Tavris and Aronson 2015; Syed, 2016). Paradoxically, to be really successful, our focus needs to be on learning rather than on the success itself.

LEARNING FOR GROWING: WHAT AND WHY

Learning comes in many different forms in academic work, both intellectual and practised. Most obviously, learning occurs in relation to the acquisition of new knowledge and skills associated with teaching, engagement, and research. For example, as careers progress from doctoral work, academic workers are expected to become more adept at managing their own priorities, budgets, and staff, and to write successfully in different ways and for different purposes, such as publications, research grants, or accessible course material for teaching. Such skills are important; job progress depends on them but these aptitudes don't magically accrue on attainment of a doctorate. In this way, learning can be defined as: 'a process of enhancing learners' capacity, individually and collectively, to produce results they truly want to produce ... the building of capacity for effective action as opposed to intellectual understanding only' (Senge, 2006: 364).

Hence, learning to do academic work concurs with what Schon famously termed 'knowledge in action' (1984: 59): a more complex tacit knowing used in practise that moves beyond following rules and procedures. This type of learning goes far beyond didactic knowledge as reflected in developing aptitudes in how all manner of situations, issues, and problems within academic work are perceived, broached, and addressed: academic workers' learning involves 'sensing and acting locally' (Senge, 2006: 365). There are many opportunities to learn in academic work. However, we focus here on issues around learning from success and failure.

Success in academic work

When we do academic work successfully and effectively, all seems well with our world. Another publication attained, positive student feedback, accepted grants in competitive places, compliments from colleagues and bosses. All affirm and testify to our choices, abilities, skills, and talent. Memorably, Dweck characterizes this kind of movement from activity to attribute as 'somebody-nobody' syndrome (2006: 105): with success, we readily move from work results to ourselves in broad, personal, and very reassuring ways. What's not to like?

Indeed, as well-qualified people with years of experience, high perceived intelligence and knowledge, high social and occupational status and expertise, academic workers are *primed* to see success in their work even in extreme instances when this is highly dubious or even damaging (Syed, 2016). Even when a particular success is but a small proportion of what could have potentially achieved, we tend not to recognize these alternative 'more successful paths'. We are also more likely to attribute successes to ourselves. This follows because our minds are primed not only to be more open to that which we perceive as being successful but also to readily overstate our contributions to these successes (ibid.).

Our preponderance toward success is a very human reaction, yet also highly likely to be selective because these success attributions are replete with all manner of cognitive biases: the 'stories we like to tell ourselves' about who we are and what we stand for. Michael Syed (2016) analysed decades of research into medical errors, politics, economics, history, business, law, and the airline industry. Time and time again, 'expert' characteristics are associated with remarkable and dogged psychological preponderance toward perceiving success. Despite people wrongly going to prison for decades, suffering serious injury, or even dying avoidably – despite all evidence to the contrary – it's very hard not to see yourself as being and acting successfully' (ibid.).

Even when a lack of success is recognized, strong tendencies exist toward minimizing our complicity in such failures. When dealing with the manifold ways in which our work does not fully realize our intended successes, we reassure ourselves that, nevertheless, we are still successful people because:

- Nothing different could have been done.
- These things happen.
- It was going to happen anyway.
- It's actually X's (insert: the students', reviewers', colleagues', partner's, etc.) fault.
- We can't be sure, we don't really know why it happened.
- Everyone has the same problem anyway.

These attributions and difficulties in being able to truly judge success are less a result of the state of the world than a result of:

1. *Cognitive Dissonance*: Selective perception and processing of current and new information and situations.
2. *Narrative Fallacies*: Simplistic anecdotal post hoc rationalizations, including philosophical centralism, the tendency to erroneously attribute lack of success to single, isolated factors.
3. *Ignoring Counter-Factuals*: Failing to take account of alternative courses that could have happened (but likely did not).

FAILURE: NECESSARY AND USEFUL

The path of least resistance is a terrible teacher.

(Holiday, 2014: 138)

Despite the seeming dominance of success in our horizons around academic work and workplaces, centuries of intellectual endeavour, ongoing effort and contributions from generations of the best and brightest indicate that most things don't realize their full potential or fail (Omerod, 2007). Without failure, almost every aspect of our lives and science would be weaker (Firestein, 2016). Failure remains the impetus for some of society's most creative and innovative solutions, such as James Dyson's paradigm-shifting vortex vacuum cleaners. Failure can be deliberately built into design processes: one detergent manufacturer contrived 450 failed attempts to perfect a single nozzle design (Syed, 2016). Failure is also a matter of perspective. Thus, a medication that failed in its desired goal of reducing blood pressure had a notable, sustained and popular side effect: Pfizer stumbled across Viagara, one of the most famous, impactful, and profitable medications in recent history.

While evidence suggests that it is hard not to see things as successful, it is also difficult to truly face and embrace failure. Academic work asks the hardest questions of us professionally and personally. How can we really make our mark? Ongoing and seemingly endless struggles in our academic work hurt (Clark and Thompson, 2013). Recognizing failures may lead us to anger, doubt or defensiveness – are we really good enough? Why are other people so successful? And why does the system put so many impediments in *our* path? We may even lose confidence in our decisions, our abilities, and even our values.

A major obstacle to learning from failure is simply not being open to acknowledge that the failure occurred and we contributed to it. This represents a loss of opportunity for learning but is understandable when failure is wrongly stigmatized in us and our academic workplaces (ibid.). We erroneously believe that failure is far less common, necessary, and helpful than it actually is.

Further, over time, the deeper and more entrenched you are in your success, the harder it is psychologically to come to terms with being unsuccessful and to state failures openly to others. In dealing with the layers of intellectual and ethical justification at play here (both conscious and otherwise), this is less about spinning failure and more about not really seeing it in the first place. As Syed memorably characterizes: 'the most effective cover-ups are perpetrated not by those who are covering their backs, but by those who don't even realize that they have anything to hide' (2016: 96).

Building your foundation to learn from failure

From a growth mindset, failure is not reflective of the inherent or damaging limitations of the self or anyone else involved but is reflective of the reality that 'failure is inevitable in a complex world' (ibid.: 58). In the face of failure, rather than dwell on how failure casts doubts on us, the focus should be on being open to learning what contributed to outcomes and focusing efforts accordingly for improvements. Growth mindsets encourage reclaiming 'failure', calling it that and owning it, thinking about what we contributed and seeking improvements next time. "Failure is inevitable in academic life, but wasting it is not" (Clark and Sousa, 2015).

FAILURE IS INEVITABLE IN ACADEMIC LIFE, BUT WASTING IT IS NOT

As with human work, undertaking self-work is the vital first step in learning from failure. Understanding our own emotions and vulnerabilities around failing and failures is key because our reactions to failure and success have their basis in understandable but damaging self-protection (Brown, 2012; Syed, 2016). We choose the comfort of success and denial over the discomfort of failure and shame (ibid.) If failure is so common and useful, why do we feel so vulnerable about it in academic work? What is it about failure or particular kinds of failures that makes us especially likely to feel tense, push back or otherwise struggle with recognizing and responding to the failure? Though diverse, the work of Bréné Brown (2012), Steve Peters (2013), and Jamie Catto (2016) each explore the links between our thoughts, reasoning, emotions, and internal shame dialogues. Their work draws attention to the disparity between these reactions to failure and what we can *actually* directly control. Ironically, our most common reactions stand to render us less prone to truly acknowledge the existence of failure and far less capable of perfoming better in future to reduce the likelihood of further failures. Truly being more open and authentically honest about ourselves, our contributions, and the failure, allows for openness to learning from failure.

Recognizing and being open to our feelings around failure, allows us to then better separate our personal sense of competency, our intentions, and the results from any situation. Adopting a growth over a fixed mindset is a vital means to do this (Dweck, 2006). A growth mindset around failure not only recognizes that successful people fail but more deeply reframes what success actually is and places it more directly under our control. Success via growth mindset is dependent not on outcomes or events that we cannot control but on whether we can be, and stay open, to learning to do better whatever happens, and continue to put our best and most strategic efforts into maximizing success over failure in the future. This we can control.

SUCCESSFUL PEOPLE FAIL

Deeper still, this growth mindset breaks the fixed mindset bond between our self-worth and the results of our academic work efforts. From this growth mindset, you can better celebrate your intentions and also accept your fallibility in order to recognize the contributions that you made to the failure. These cease to be about personal limitations or 'failings' that undermine your identity, but from a learning perspective are 'your growing edge' (Kegan and Lahey, 2016: 92). You remain valuable as you fail. This makes it far easier to apologize to others if need be for your contributions to failure, but you also feel excited (yes, excited!) about learning to do better next time. 'Sorry' ceases to be the hardest word when you focus on learning and doing better next time.

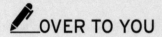 OVER TO YOU

Exploring Your Failures

Think of a particular tangible failure or mistake that you regret. If you can, pick one that you *really feel sensitive about.*

1.   How would you explain to a person who does not know you what contributed to this failure?

2.   How much would you attribute this failure to:

- Fate or other uncontrollable or unknown factors?
- Other people?
- Your approach or actions?

3.   Understanding the difference between a growth and fixed mindset, how would you feel, see, and act in relation to this failure differently in future (if at all)?

SUCCESSFUL FAILURE: A SIX-STEP APPROACH

How, then, can we take this further to really and deeply use failure for our learning? Drawing on a wealth of recent writing around successful failure (Clark and Thompson, 2013), and the latest research around failure (Stone et al., 2010; McArdle, 2014; Firestein, 2016; Kegan and Lahey, 2016; Syed, 2016;) we developed a six-step process for failing better (Clark and Sousa, 2015). It echoes other elements of The Core, especially around self-work, and was developed following reading and responses we both felt after we had contributed to a failure in our own work. Ironically, a manuscript that we had submitted on this process was rejected from at least five journals before finding a prominent place in the world's most read, serious newspaper, *The Guardian*. This is itself, we might say, the embodiment of a successful failure.

1. Be open

After a failure, recognize that the failure happened and specify as much as you can what the failure actually was. Be conscious of the cognitive and attitudinal biases that can act to dismiss the existence of the failure and consciously seek to be open, humble, and proactive in recognizing the failure. Call it out as such. Be aware that intense feelings, hurt, and physical sensations are a natural part of this stage of openness and vulnerability (Brown, 2012). Rather than suppress or numb these feelings, be open to fully feeling them. This is a hard but necessary first step because being open to the fact of the failure is about talk, action, and living this process of recognition.

2. Express gratitude

That's right: don't just acknowledge the failure and feel its impact, but seek to be consciously grateful for that failure. It is a gift (Clark, 2014), an opportunity, a glimpse of what can be.

In *The Up Side of Down*, Megan McArdle (2014) details all the many ways in which failure is the foundation for success; that's why when failure happens, it's important to be thankful that it occurred, that it was not bigger, or had worse consequences. The vast majority of failures in our academic work can be much worse and usually don't have disastrous consequences.

3. Crystallize *your* contribution(s)

Even when failure is acknowledged, one of the most common cognitive biases around failure is blaming other people (Syed, 2016). This helps us feel better about our involvement in the failure because we perceive the failure to be more about the deficiencies of other people (ibid.). In this complex world, seldom are failures caused by single factors acting singularly. The reasoning that leads us to such attributions is the favourite of armchair sports fans. Games are lost based on the poor performance of a single player's ability or the tactical blunder of an inept manager. Reality, however, is a lot more complex (Clark et al., 2012). So much more is going on and not everything that matters is necessarily measurable. We also tend to attribute situational failures to person-based or personal failures, focusing less on behaviour or actions than on people and their limitations.

It can be easy to cut yourself up over the failure at this stage. Conclusions from a fixed mindset dominate: we are 'incompetent', we let others down, we are failures as academic workers. This ignores the role that failure has in most personal and academic work successes and the degree and frequency at which successful academics and other knowledge workers fail (Firestein, 2016). Preserve and reflect the positive aspirations and intentions you had in relation to your priorities, goals and tasks. If you feel ashamed about the failure, reflect on and work out why before coming back to the positive intentions that you had in the situation. In preference to pointing the finger at others involved, think carefully and reflectively on how you specifically contributed to the failure. That's all you can ultimately influence next time: how did your own actions interact with other elements of what was going on to contribute to the failure?

4. Share and support others

As failure is so chronically stigmatized in our workplace, we all tend to pretend that it does not exist (Kegan and Lahey, 2016). As with conflict, we 'handle' such difficult conversations mostly by avoiding them altogether. When others talk to us about how *they* contributed to failures, it is important to be empathetic, supportive, and alongside each other. It can be easy to get angry or frustrated with others, but it's also important to remember that very few people come to work intending or thinking of doing a 'bad job' – a recurrent theme from Manager Tools. Preserving or attributing positive intention to behaviours is important.

Sharing your failures openly is important because this also culturally establishes failure-talk as a more normalized part of our workplaces (Kegan and Lahey, 2016). Sharing failure can be easier when we have developed a strong relational network (as discussed in the previous chapter). Especially when those talking openly of failures are established academic workers, this makes overt the nature, degree and commonality of failure in successful academic work and successful academic workers.

5. Learn and grow

With contributions shared, clues may be evident as to what can be done differently to ensure that next time the failure is less likely to occur. Notice here that, like feedback, the focus is only on the future. This stage is the antithesis of a discussion that is about attributing blame for past occurrences. This future focus recognizes that the past cannot be changed. Instead, the focus should be on what each party themselves could do differently next time to increase the likelihood of success and lessen the likelihood of failure. Ongoing trial and error is needed (Syed, 2016). Some workplaces, however, actively build failure into their work development processes (Kegan and Lahey, 2016) by creating opportunities for academic workers, particularly established academics, to openly and candidly share their own career failures so the others can learn and grow from these experiences.

6. Move on

Given that failing is inherent in doing aspirational academic work – failure will happen often. For failure to be truly normalized and better utilized, ongoing 'scores' or other resentment from the failure should not be carried forward. However, these experiences must not be forgotten in order to ensure ongoing learning. Keeping a journal to reflect on your main lessons and insights for the future may be helpful. Ultimately, having moved through this process, give yourself permission to move on optimistically and with a future-focus.

━━━ REMARKABLE RESOURCES ━━━

The Up side of Down by Megan McArdle

Why do we shy away so much from failure? McArdle's (2014) book provides a positive, affirmative and scientifically well-informed foundation for seeing and handling failure differently.

Key messages

- Failure is common, misunderstood, and a necessary part of complexity.
- It's important not only to accept the existence or a high probability of failure, but also to see it as an opportunity for which one should be grateful.
- Documents different kinds of failures: accidents, mistakes, failures, and disasters.

Key applications

- Breaks down failure and targets those parts that you have most difficulty with, including crisis management, admitting error, blaming, punishing, and moving forward.
- Provides robust scientific evidence supporting the value of using failure well.
- Can be used to understand your own approaches to failure and puts into perspective the relative 'low' harms of most failures in academic work.

(Continued)

Black Box Thinking by Matthew Syed

Syed (2016) discusses the question: How can we put performance improvement first in work and attain higher levels of performance even when our brains, cultures, and societies function to consistently emphasize success over failure?

Key messages

- Over the last century, highly educated professionals across many spheres have caused the most serious damage to others, both knowingly and unknowingly, by failing to recognize and state when they have failed.
- This lack of recognition is caused by well-established cognitive biases, narrative fallacies, and counterfactual reasoning.
- Uses historical examples from science, law, and society to show how huge numbers of smart people are equally or more prone to cognitive biases as novice undergraduates.

Key applications

- Provides a systematic means to consider the various ways in which academic workers can fail to recognize and harness failures.
- Focus on being open to learn, using data if possible, break down problems to focus on their incremental parts, use trial-and-error strategies supplemented with data for incremental performance improvement.

Mindset by Carol S. Dweck

What is a growth mindset and why does it have so much potential to help you to be more successful, more open to learning and less anxious about what you cannot control? Dweck's (2006) book is the definitive text detailing the cadre of research, theory and reasoning into this emerging facet of learning.

Key messages

- Provides research evidence for the presence of growth and fixed mindsets from school-age onwards, from scientific research, sport, and society.
- Documents research into the negative effects on learning, self-esteem, and standards of behavioural conduct of fixed mindsets.
- Illustrates the protective effects for learning, self-esteem, and high standards of behavioural conduct of growth mindsets.

Key applications

- Can be used to better understand your own mindsets around aspects of your work and personal life.
- Provides robust scientific evidence supporting the presence and influence of different mindsets.
- Can help better ensure that you bring a growth mindset to all your academic work.

9

INFLUENCE
PERSUASION AND CONNECTION

All the great speakers were bad speakers at first.

(Ralph W. Emerson)

People don't want to hear, read or otherwise engage with your ideas, contributions, or words (Pressfield, 2016). They are not immediately persuaded by your intellectual arguments, credibility or personality, nor excited at the prospect of your presentation, your new manuscript or contribution to 'the meeting'.

It is difficult to view ourselves as lacking influence. Yet, interest, openness, and expectancy from others are best seen as bonuses. We should expect to have to proactively work hard for these rather than assume that they will readily come or happen irrespectively. Adopting this more sceptical (or some would say, realistic) approach to others' receptivity to ourselves and our work is the first and necessary step toward doing something about engagement. As we shall see, this entails becoming more self-aware as a basis for then working to actively ensure that our words, interactions, and actions are influential, which is a fundamental point for development within The Core. Accordingly, in this chapter, we address how to create interest, intrigue and (if nothing more) attention to your contributions: in short, to become attuned to and increase the *influence* of yourself and your work.

This 'influence' play is one that many of us would like to pretend that we don't engage in or need to pull off. We may have had varying experiences and approaches to this, sometimes contentious, aspect of academic work. It's 'crass' or 'sales-like'. We assume that the 'facts and evidence' implicit within our arguments or our perceived credibility will be enough to sufficiently engage and persuade. Attempts to influence others' receptivity to our work and ourselves can be cast as manipulative, contrived, or superficial, and as a symptom of the ills of modern-day academic work and workplaces.

However, the art and science of influencing others is no modern invention of the age of 'spin', post-truth or advertising: it dates back to ancient Greece and the finest of classical intellectual traditions of Plato and Aristotle (Leith, 2012a). Indeed, if you enjoy interacting with other people and being thoughtful, careful, and creative with expressing ideas in words, developing your ability to influence others is useful for many varied areas of academic work.

RHETORIC: THE BASIS FOR BETTER INFLUENCE

Although rhetoric was developed in ancient Greece, rhetoric remains all around us, not only in advertisements, television infomercials or political campaigns and debates, but also whenever colleagues, speakers, or writers are charged with moving people to action or emotion. The historical and intellectual basis for influencing others has its roots and many of its techniques in rhetoric: the art to inform, persuade, or motivate others in specific situations (Leith, 2012a). Rhetoric encompasses a wide variety of different techniques – a whole handbook describes the full gamut of these different rhetorical techniques in 161 pages from Abbaser to Zeuxis (Lanham, 1991). While this material is somewhat dry when presented as a list, in practice, these techniques can help your work and contributions to fully realize their potential. The techniques have also been brought alive in a number of immensely readable books (Heinrichs, 2007; Leith, 2012 a, b) on the uses of rhetoric in everyday situations.

The place of rhetoric in academic work

Being influential is an important part of academic work. Done ethically and thoughtfully, rhetoric provides a means of ensuring your ideas or perspectives are better set up to be well received and connecting with others. This could occur in your contributions to departmental meetings, for conference presentations, your writing in emails, manuscripts and grants, social media postings, formal speeches or, indeed, any time when you aim to persuade or influence another person of the merits of your work, ideas, or perspective.

BEING INFLUENTIAL IS AN IMPORTANT PART OF ACADEMIC WORK

While the techniques are certainly not a replacement for devoting time and effort toward human work (for example, via maintaining good relationships with your colleagues), rhetoric is important and useful but increasingly neglected. How then can we work to foster rhetorical skill in our academic work?

INVENTION: ARGUMENTS, AUDIENCE, AND SUCCESS

All effective attempts to influence commence with a careful consideration of what you want to say, your perceptions of those whom you are addressing (referred to here as your 'audience') and what success in the situation will be. This is what Leith (2012b) terms to be the *invention* stage of rhetoric.

Many questions can be asked about audiences. What do they need? What are their likely values, interests, and composition? Are they likely to be friendly, neutral, or hostile to you or potentially to your messages (Lehrman, 2010)? In virtually all of our interactions with audiences, knowing the mix of your audience in terms of career stage, disciplinary background, occupation, and dominant country of residence will affect how much information is shared and whether topics should be avoided or addressed. For example, your conference talk on using social media in academic workplaces will be pitched markedly differently if most of your audience are relatively inexperienced technophobic users compared to seasoned technophiles who are highly enthused about the latest platforms.

With a clear sense of your audience, you can then consider which arguments are likely to be most appropriate to make. These fall into three classical categories or proofs: *logos*, *ethos*, and *pathos*. *Logos* refers to arguments using facts, reason, and evidence. *Ethos* pertains to elements that are more ethical: what 'should' happen or be the case, including elements of your own character and reputation. Finally, *pathos* refers to feelings and emotions (Lanham, 1991). So, just as a particular brand of car can be marketed using data on its fuel efficiency (*logos*), the importance of buying it for its reputation of environmental sustainability (*ethos*) or the brand's association with being 'green', cool, and effortlessly sexy (*pathos*), so, too, can different levers be used with audiences. Of course, as academic workers, we are often predisposed to value data or theory-driven *logos* and, to a lesser degree, principled *ethos*. Our presentations, imbued with all manner of scholarly or scientific conventions that build the credibility narrative of what we have to say, often rely more on claims to knowledge informed by data, theory, method, and reason. Nevertheless, *pathos* has its place, too, and should not be underestimated as emotions are integral to how we understand, often through feeling – even for us academic workers!

Different situations have different ends and means. A plenary keynote address likely seeks not only to inform intellectually but also to inspire its audience emotionally; a departmental meeting may involve trying to convey your ideas well, but also in ways that will elicit support from hesitant and even critical others. If you know ahead of time that others are likely to be hostile to your ideas, your approach is likely to be very different. Take, for example, the departmental head who enthusiastically presents a new workplace mentorship programme to colleagues who are so demoralized and tired that any new initiative (especially containing 'buzzwords') causes immediate weary groans and resistance, irrespective of the merit of the suggestions. A concurrent research paper at a conference seeks to describe your study technically, but it is also important to make the findings interesting and relevant for the group. In each scenario, you have to pointedly consider what constitutes success and how you can best go about contributing to this likelihood. This, in itself, needs a broader understanding of the likely impediments in the audience or situation to being successful, and the possible levers that you can pull to increase the likelihood of success. What are others' expectations, fears, or hopes in the situation? What are the most intractable, immediate, or heavy barriers you will face to influence? How are they likely to see and immediately react to you? What image or relational challenges might you have with them that you are either aware of or don't want to admit to?

This sense of audience requires the ability to ask the right questions of others and yourself. Failing to do so can result in spectacular and crashing failure to influence. We don't want to be the after-dinner conference speaker whose presentation contains all manner of risqué and misogynous material, charged with making a room full of fairly old-fashioned nurse academics laugh. Alex was there, and it was not pretty! Similarly, we don't want to be the conference speaker who assumes far too much background knowledge of his increasingly mystified audience. Everything in rhetoric serves the end you desire but has at its start your audience and where they are coming from.

ARRANGEMENT, STYLE, AND DELIVERY: CONNECTION AND IDENTIFICATION

Next, we seek to unite the two previous steps by bringing you and your audience together as one, using aspects of arrangement, style, and delivery (Leith, 2012b; Table 9.1). 'Arrangement' addresses how best to organize and frame what you want to say in ways that will foster connection, empathy, and broadly get people onside, while 'style' encapsulates how best to present this in ways that will maximize its influence. This is the fertile ground upon which much can be grown. Accordingly, how you start to get people engaged (known as 'exordium') is very important. You might choose to use 'narration', a framing of the history of the issue that you

Table 9.1 Stages of Rhetoric

Stage of rhetoric	Description	Key concerns	Techniques
Invention	Thinking of what arguments will most persuade your audience and the likely counter-points or barriers	Knowing your audience in advance and their likely response to you	*Logos, ethos, pathos*
Arrangement	How to best frame, sequence, and organize your contribution	Identifying the best means to appeal to audiences, harnessing what is in your favour and pre-empting barriers to persuasion. Ensuring this is in the most persuasive order and form (rhetorical moves)	*Exordium;* narration, jokes
Style	How you can best connect to your audience	Considering which language, gestures, tone, and attitude to use	Decorum
Delivery	How to deliver all the elements of your contribution	Control of voice, tone and, where appropriate, gesture	Decorum
Memory	How to achieve quality and seeming spontaneity in speech	How to convey your messages without notes by relying on memory	*Sprezzatura*

want to address, a well-calculated 'joke' that lightens the mood but fits with the decorum of the situation, or a clear focus on the contested issue at hand ('division'). Finally, it's important to deliver this well in the moment, using elements of voice, control, and gesture.

The ability to readily connect with others using these combinations of rhetorical techniques across seemingly futile chasms of irreconcilable difference was most famously exemplified in Mark Antony's funeral oration in William Shakespeare's play *Julius Caesar*. His speech followed that of Brutus, who provided a detailed, fact-laced, *logos*-based treatise to the crowd, first as 'Romans' – reflecting his priority on preserving the country. Brutus's speech was immediately effective in moving the crowd away from protest to feeling peace about Caesar's death. Following this, Mark Antony could have the last word but he started with an opening intended not only to surprise, but also to grab the attention of the large, desperate crowd: 'Friends, Romans, Countrymen, lend me your ears.' He draws his audience gently toward him as humans – one in united, collective connection. In contrast to Brutus, Caesar's *ethos* and *pathos*-based implore engaged the audience as 'friends'. This immediately appealed to their collective kinship, not only with each other but especially with him, despite their vast and obvious differences in rank, status, and wealth. Rather than demanding their attention in a grandiose, authoritarian, or role-conscious manner, he uses the gentlest of phrases, choosing a framing to ask humbly if they will just listen to what he has to say. Having done the early work, he then employs all manner of techniques so effectively that consequently the crowd turns on Brutus, burning his house down and chasing him out of Rome.

These techniques are very much alive today. Both Donald Trump and Hilary Clinton employed rhetorical techniques to attain more votes in the 2016 American Presidential election. Whereas Clinton focused more on the substance of her fact-based arguments and track record, many bemoaned the lack of warmth and connection they felt with her *logos*-based approach. Conversely, despite his sizeable personal wealth, Trump all but abandoned *logos* to adopt the decorum of being 'one of us' to his core voters – the antithesis of the 'insider' establishment Washington politician. He created a strong sense of identity and connection with his audience via both *ethos* and *pathos*. His speeches, gestures, tone, image, and attitudes screamed from every orifice that he was not a politician who would be beholden to the rules that normally apply to politicians seeking this office. Bemused journalists attempting to hold his public utterances to conventional account, likewise could not fathom the degree to which he seemingly did not care about *logos* or following the conventional rules of the campaign game. Rather than pretend to be something he was not, he played to his strengths as an outsider and reframed his limited political experience or track record in politics as a strength. This helped create a strong and, ultimately, effective personal connection and identification with voters even though they were so markedly different to him in terms of wealth.

MEMORY: PRACTISED, EFFORTLESS SPONTANEITY

Finally, providing your contributions from memory is important (Leith, 2012b) in situations in which rhetoric is used in interpersonal situations: presentations, meetings, and other exchanges. While having notes to help you speak or provide prompts has its place, it can also undermine your audience's confidence in your messages. Particularly, avoid obviously reading or, in presentations, using slides as a way to display every detail of your message. While this might immediately smack us as inauthentic, done well it can demonstrate preparation and mastery, as well as allowing you to focus more on aspects of eye contact, gesture, and tone. Presenting without notes is a step not embraced by many academic workers, but is one, we think, worth taking, providing sufficient preparation and practise is made.

Sprezzatura refers to 'well-practised naturalness' or 'rehearsed spontaneity' that often accompanies decorum (Lanham, 1991: 143). This can be particularly useful in handling questions, such as might be asked after a presentation. Even if you have practised an answer a thousand times, making it appear like you are thinking about it and answering it for the first time is a useful rhetorical device.

ABOVE ALL: BE SELF-AWARE, BUT BE YOURSELF

An awareness of *logos, ethos,* and *pathos* as a lens for approaching influence and becoming more deliberate (even creative) in how you present your contributions has important uses across all manner of academic workplace situations. However, even with supreme foreknowledge of your audience, there are no magic bullets for what makes for influence on a particular audience in a particular situation.

Rhetoric suggests that interactions that appear generic, formulaic or otherwise forced or inauthentic are actually likely to be counter-productive to attaining success. Trying too hard or making your interactions too overt, obvious or contrived, likewise, reduces its effects. We are not all orators, and nor should we try to be. Former US President Barack Obama is the politician most recently associated with the use of rhetoric, due to his tendency to make speeches that not only employ a wide variety of rhetorical techniques, but also harness a style of rhythmic speech more familiar to old-school preachers than to politicians (Leith, 2012b). That said, some found his style too much, his employment of rhetoric too conscious and deliberate. Nor is rhetoric about being verbose, forced, or consciously erudite. Indeed, some of the most effective recent proponents of rhetoric, in terms of results, have employed its devices exactly by framing their interactions in terms of absence of: being 'plain-speaking', 'straight-talking' and otherwise outside all the usual speak – think former US President George W. Bush; British Foreign Secretary Boris Johnson; former Australian Prime Minister Tony Abbott; and US President Donald Trump.

Sage advice comes from Leith (2012b), who advocates for techniques (Table 9.2) that are highly responsive to your preferred style, personality, and ultimately values. It is a mistake to try to ape others or confuse your departmental meeting with a TED Talk or the Gettysburg Address. On this basis, knowing your actual and perceived strengths, playing to your abilities and talents in your actions and using all elements of communication are key to being influential in your words and actions.

We don't advocate that academic workers employ the campaigning techniques of Trump (or any other politician) or the dramatic oration of Mark Antony. However, connecting 'who you are', as reflected through your values, to your audience is vital to create the stage for influence. What do you have in common with your audience? What could you have in common? The ability to create a sense of strong and authentic identification and connection between you and your audience is a key asset as you then try to move toward influence. Using decorum to do this is crucial. It's not just what you say that's important but also how you say it: your gestures, tone, attitude, sense of order, and image (Leith, 2012b).

Table 9.2   Rhetorical Devices

Rhetorical technique	Purpose
Exordium	Introduction to establish credibility and make connection; focuses on subject and purpose of discourse
Narration	A sequence of events, a history
Division	A framing on which points are at issue
Performative	Could include intentional hyperbole (overstatement), intentionally overstating a point, its importance or its significance; climax (ascending series): a series of clauses of increasing force
Refutation	Arguments against; counterpoints or oppositional statements
Decorum	The style in which the discourse is approached, from high and grand to low and plain: everything has style
Jokes	Arguments made with humour, often assuming a shared background understanding
Sound	Employing speech rhythms and sounds for persuasion, including *tricolons*, repetition, mixing short and long phrases

This involves a weight of establishing who you are but also requires being brutally realistic about how you are seen (fairly or unfairly) by other people. Richard Nixon's 'Checkers Speech' is a wonderful example, showing crystal-clear self-knowledge and acceptance of the plight of his predicament. Nixon, running as vice president to Dwight D. Eisenhower in 1952, stood accused of accepting illegal gifts and used the television speech not only to confront the allegations but to turn them firmly against his opponents, portraying himself as the most 'ordinary' American family man imaginable, before finally ending on his family's endearing love for their cocker spaniel dog.

Despite Nixon's future travails, the speech is a wonderful example of a speaker immensely, even brutally, perceptive of the negative way in which he was perceived and of the damaging repercussions of what he was accused. He used *logos*-based and *ethos*-based arguments to admit that he had done wrong, but that he had not become wealthy as a result and he opened all his personal accounts. He not only responded directly to the accusations that were made against him but then turned them to his advantage by creating common connections with the American families watching, via his family's affection for their dog.

Developing your personal style around these various rhetorical techniques, based firmly on who you are and what you stand for, can help you and your work be more influential. However, in our experience, the most vital motivation for becoming more influential in your writing, speaking and interactions is the ongoing desire to get and keep getting better: to keep working at finding what works best for you, pushing yourself out of your own comfort zone to try new things and enjoying doing so. In short, to consciously make being influential a sphere of academic work and development that you keep honing over time. This could involve publishing your reflections in a professional journal about what you have tried rhetorically in meetings or presentations, how it went and what you would try next time. Most crucially, by integrating rhetoric with your own sense of style and voice, along with this determination for growth, your presentations, writing, and approaches to meetings will never be the same again.

✎ OVER TO YOU

Preparing to Present

Think of your next presentation, major meeting or public talk. Based on this chapter and the Remarkable Resources section:

1.   How will you now prepare differently?

2.   How will you draw on *logos, ethos,* and *pathos*?

3.   Break down what you will do in relation to:
Invention:

Arrangement:

Style:

```

```

Delivery:

```

```

—— **REMARKABLE RESOURCES** ——

Words Like Loaded Pistols by Sam Leith

Rhetoric is all around us and can be used in a variety of situations to influence others. Leith's book (2012b) provides an accessible and historically well-informed approach to building rhetoric into your interactions.

Key messages

- To be rhetorical, follow the stages of invention, arrangement, style, and delivery.
- Many varied rhetorical devices can be used, including *logos*, *ethos*, and *pathos* proofs.
- Be creative but ultimately be yourself when using rhetoric.

Key applications

- Provides a historically informed lens that can be useful whenever you need to influence others.
- Develops and refines your own style and reliance on traditional rhetorical devices.
- Provides systematic means to consider how to influence.

10

WRITE ANYTHING BETTER

If you want to be a writer, you must do two things above all others: read a lot and write a lot.

(Stephen King, 2000: 145)

Academic work and writing are inseparable. From giving students written feedback, dashing off emails, policy changes, tweets, and text messages to crafting research manuscripts of various types, alone or in groups to writing proposals for grant-funding – academic writing functions for so many different kinds of purposes and in so many different kinds of ways. Many of these writing outputs are for others and are, accordingly, used, scrutinized, and evaluated – often critically. Consequently, few areas of academic work influence success, effectiveness, and happiness or preoccupy academic workers more than writing and, therefore, developing The Core in the area of writing is necessary. Reflecting this wide prevalence across the tasks of academic work, writing is *the* recurrent practise of academic work (Sword, 2012).

THE VULNERABILITY OF WRITING IN ACADEMIC WORK

Irrespective of their career stage, academic workers are wary and vexed by pressures to write more (Archer, 2008; Pare, 2009), write early (Pare, 2009), write quicker (ibid.; Clark and Thompson, 2015), and write better (Sword, 2012). As the means and the ends of this extreme knowledge work, writing communicates knowledge but also allows its discovery as ideas develop, formulate, and extend. Expressing ideas in words ideally just flows (Csikszentmihalyi, 2008) but more often feels effortful: we grapple, strive, and push to get the next writing task done. Academic writing is seldom only for self-expression but also helps, is scrutinized, and is criticized by others (Kamler, 2008). Jobs and career progress depend on how well academic workers meet the challenges of writing. Teaching evaluations, grant-funding success, administrative prowess and, of course, publishing success, all heavily depend on it. In modern academic workplaces, writing is simultaneously creative and pressurized. Were this not squeezed enough, the advent of social media and blogging platforms has further brought new forms of academic writing work and expectations.

Academic writing has been viewed as a problem to be solved for some decades. Conscious of battles past and ahead, many doctoral students yearn to write better, faster, more easily, and otherwise ensure that the potential of their academic work is more fully realized in the world (Kamler and Thomson, 2014). Indeed, most help on academic writing is sought by and provided to doctoral students (Sword, 2012), who can learn about writing in books (Kamler and Thomson, 2014), in writing groups (Aitchison, 2009; Aitchison and Guerin, 2014) or by attaining support via dedicated units (Aitchison and Lee, 2006).

A broader focus on writing across the academic career is now provided via new social media 'places' (like #acwri and other hashtags on Twitter), replete with information, insight and personal support around academic writing. Reflecting the centrality and stakes of writing in academic work, publishers' catalogues and conference workshops heave with writing help. Most such resources still focus on writing in general (Sword, 2012), but topics such as grant-writing and 'writing for publication' are enduringly popular.

Academic writing is seldom ever impersonal or neutral. Rather, it is central to what makes academic work wonderfully rewarding and also difficult. When your writing flows, soars, and 'speaks', there's little to beat it. Values are expressed in academic workers' writing (Hyland, 2002) but they must also then struggle with the questions that writing asks of these values (Archer, 2008). Am I a scholar of truth, honour and curiosity, or a metric-motivated word factory of ever more academic outputs? If and when you hate writing, when it's difficult or dementing: all academic work feels like a struggle, too.

For such a pivotal part of academic work, what audacity to then propose that a relatively short chapter in a relatively short book can help writing across the many academic writing tasks. Indeed. A chapter title as immodest as it is justifiable. We stand by the use and efficiencies of the genre-based approach to writing outlined *across* the many varied kinds of academic writing work. It is an approach not as well known as the 'tricks-and-tips' genre of self-help that overflows in books and social media. Writing 'tricks and tips' are alluring like fast food, but as we will discuss, the resultant transitory satisfaction or even 'buzz' should not be confused with useful sustenance. Underpinned immeasurably better by theory and research, the genre approach is preferable not despite the manifold variations in academic writing but precisely because of these many different types of writing tasks and contexts. What different forms does this academic writing then take?

DIFFERENT TYPES OF WRITING IN ACADEMIC WORK

Writing transcends almost all types of academic work and virtually any space in which academic work is communicated. Accordingly, academic work entails a diverse plethora of different *types* of writing:

- *Process writing work*: Free writing, manuscript annotations, data annotations, Post-it notes, note-taking, memoranda, journaling or diary entries, to-do lists, mind maps, analytical notes, emails, text messages …

- *Procedural writing work*: Meeting minutes, teaching notes, journal reviews, departmental evaluations, journal-review responses to reviewers, cover letters for journal submissions, grant reviews, responses to grant reviewers, promotion reports, consent forms, marketing material, personal websites, under-article comments ...
- *Product writing work*: Teaching materials, theses/dissertations, manuscripts for publication, mass media articles for public or academic worker audiences, research grants, audio-visual aids, tweets, blog entries, emails, academic workplace websites, academic promotional material ...

THE QUALITY-PREVALENCE PARADOX OF ACADEMIC WRITING

Given that writing of such types is so pervasive in, through and across academic work, why is so much of the most readily available academic writing quite so bad? The most sobering recent treatise on academic writing for publication (Sword, 2012) reviewed 1000 articles from across disciplines in the sciences and humanities. It was found that 10 articles picked at random from this set would only elicit 1 or 2 articles (actually 1.5) that are clear, concise, and engaging. It is fruitful to recognize two truths: that in various places, we have contributed to this detritus of academic writing that is unclear, bland, or clumsy. Some of it may be in this book! However, that should never deter us from our individual, life-long quest to write as well as we can and then write better. The world needs this. It's also good for academic workplaces as it makes our work more interesting, relevant, and inspiring.

So, as we strive to write well, the vast proportion of the academic writing that surrounds us is bad. What does the quality minority do that the majority does not? Academic workers from 70 disciplines identify good writing with the ability to express complex ideas clearly. Most common characteristics included: well-crafted sentences, attention-holding energetic prose without jargon, and accessible, pleasurable, imaginative, and creative text (Sword, 2012). Do these observations provide aspiration or hint of normative standardization of writing that is smart but also stylistically hollow and uniform?

THE LIMITATIONS OF TRICKS, TIPS, AND SOCIAL MEDIA

Making recommendations for academic writing, even in relation to a single type of writing, is a dangerous business then. It is, however, at least in academic spheres, as lucrative. Resources, chat, advice, and support around certain types of academic writing proliferate. Faced with a particular writing need, our reach is often for a writing book around that need or a cadre of writing 'tricks and tips': writing a proposal? There are a dozen books to help with that.

Yet, the biggest challenge around 'tricks and tips' for academic writing is how the more prescriptive approaches can help with the immense diversity of academic writing (Lee and Aitchison, 2009). Taking writing grants and manuscripts alone, writing is about communicating well but is also context specific: writing always for and to particular audiences at particular times around particular conventions (Thomson and Kamler, 2010) and in particular ways. These conventions are fused with all manner of disciplinary country- and time-specific perspectives and norms (Aitchison and Lee, 2010 Kamler and Thomson, 2014;). As Swales (2009) conveys in his qualitative study of the 'text-makers' in a single small university building, these differences do not just create different writing places, but also create different writing worlds in which very few writing norms are identical.

In the face of these variations, advice on academic writing in books tends to fall back to prescriptions for grammar and style, clarity, structure, and emotional and psychological aspects of writing, even though these elements vary markedly across books and disciplines (Sword, 2012). The 'tricks-and-tips' tendency to rely on on over-generalized advice fails to take account of these variations (Kamler and Thomson, 2008) because uniform writing prescriptions impoverish the wide tableau of possible academic writing for different audiences, purposes, disciplines, and contexts. This task-focused response to writing challenges is akin to an athlete seeking improved performance in running for international competition deciding to run up a hill in Scotland in May, seeking improvement by focusing only on that hill, at that time, in that place. A much better approach is to develop core muscles, skills, endurance, and mindset that can be applied and adapted to running in a much broader range of circumstances and instances.

'Tricks-and-tips' books sell well because, in the moment, as we are confronted with a specific challenge, they appear to offer compelling, ready solutions – there is, indeed, a hill that has to be imminently conquered, a grant to be written, and an article to be submitted. However, by often being normative and prescriptive, the advice struggles beyond the generic and risks being unresponsive to context: this particular academic writing work, at this time, in this place. Thus, reflecting The Core, we aim to use a genre-based approach to develop deeper writing skills that can help across different forms, types, and conventions of writing: different writing muscles for the different writing terrains of academic work.

GENRE: A DIFFERENT APPROACH TO ACADEMIC WRITING

Every day, usually before 10 a.m., most academic workers have already contributed writing across a number of academic writing genres. Emails with other academic workers will have been responded to; texts, tweets, or notes for the day may already have been produced. Mindful of their own writing priorities, some may have written work lists, teaching material for students, or parts of manuscripts, grants, and journal reviews: different kinds of academic writing, produced for different purposes.

The genres of academic writing has been explored in relation to graduate dissertations (Kamler and Thomson, 2014), research proposals for grants (Tardy, 2003) and abstracts for conference presentations (Halleck and Connor, 2006). All this writing, indeed all writing, is genred. A genre in this way is:

> a class of communicative events, the members of which share some set of communicative purposes (that) are recognized by the exert members of the parent discourse community, and thereby constitute the rationale for the genre. This rationale shapes the schematic structure of the discourse and influences and constrains choice of content and style. (Swales, 1990: 58)

Accordingly, writing that falls into a particular genre (such as a tweet) echoes particular facets, which give rise to a piece of writing being said to be able to fit in with that genre (Frow, 2006), including shared:

- *Formal features*: The appearance and structure of the writing.
- *Thematic structure*: The topics and foci of the writing.
- *Situation of address and tone*: The feel and formality of the writing.
- *Structure of implication*: What is presupposed by the writing.
- *Rhetorical function*: The socially agreed upon aims of the writing.
- *Frame*: The physical and social setting of the writing.

When we look at writing through a genre lens, writing choices become more manifest. Must writing within a particular academic writing genre contain all such facets? Some of such facets? And, if so, which and why? For example, must a grant proposal be persuasive in terms of rhetorical function or can it merely be descriptive? Does it need, in terms of formal features, to contain the literature review at the start of the proposal or can this be integrated with the methods section? Must it be written in situation of address in the third person or the first person? Can it be colloquial as well as formal in style? In terms of the structure of implication, how much should the proposal explore the backstory of historical disciplinary debates over the proposal's topic?

Immediately, the challenge of a 'tick-the-box' approach to genre classification is apparent. In addition to all the likely variations, this fails to recognize that as cultural artefacts as opposed to biological species, writing can evolve and grow in indeterminate open-ended ways, which may, in itself, stretch and develop the genre over time (ibid.). In relation to academic writing – occurring as it does across manifold disciplinary, geographical, and political/ideological contexts – variations in practice quickly become as troublesome as 'tricks-and-tips' approaches become less applicable.

As such, a purely definitional approach to identifying genre may appear easy, but in practice is fraught with exceptions, caveats, and grey areas. Just as fruits (Swales, 1990: 49) are difficult to box into single sets of defining characteristics (oranges, bananas, and coconuts), so, too, is developing 'all-or-none' features of academic writing across all contexts a lot more difficult in practice. Beyond focusing only on defining characteristics, Swales (1990) recommends that 'protoptypicality' be used in relation to genre. This means viewing the most socially typical members of a genre as being prototypes but that less typical members can still be recognized as falling into a genre – albeit a less typical one. Olives are a fruit but a less typical fruit in the eyes of many compared to an apple. Accordingly, writing that falls within a genre tends to share a common purpose: it can differ markedly in appearance (and many other facets) but, nevertheless, still falls into a particular genre. In this way, genre both produces and constrains writing (ibid.) and can be reflected in how writing is viewed in terms of the social conventions (ibid., 2004) of academic workers as articulated in formal guidelines (for example, instructions on the sections of a manuscript) or in 'hints of boundaries' (Frow, 2006).

Genre-based approaches to academic writing have grown since the 1980s (Swales, 2004). In research, attention to different genres of academic work has increased with proliferation of different types of academic writing genres around process, procedure or product, new media and social media technologies to support new genres like tweets, blogs, 'rapid comments', and synergies between writing and technology.

Genre and academic writing: Implications

'Success' is always specific to genre. What will make my tweet, editorial, or teaching resource successful? The strata of The Success Pyramid help us to do the right academic work but can also ensure that writing is right, too. Taking account of genre, like The Success Pyramid, all writing starts with the question: 'What does success look like?' In other words, 'What will make *this* specific piece of *my* writing successful for the likely audience?' Answers should always take account of your values about what constitutes good writing but is always also about the genre in which you seek to write and the audience with which you seek to engage. Take manuscript-writing alone: what makes a successful editorial for a journal does not make for a successful manuscript in that journal. Part of this sense of success comes from understanding the audience who reads that journal, what is important to them and how you can connect your contribution to it. By then becoming more attuned to genre, you can prioritize what you want the writing to achieve – its goals – and then bring these down to the daily writing tasks of, and in pieces of, writing to focus on.

A genre-based approach attunes us to the similarities, diversity, and distinctiveness of different writing genres in academic work. Also, it problematizes generic 'feel-good' approaches to writing that are insensitive or do not address the nuances of particular expressions of genres.

Learning to write better, smoother, and more quickly in some academic writing genres is easier because 'successful' examples of some genres are more readily available. Journal articles, while containing different types of academic writing (theory papers, qualitative or quantitative research reports, or methods papers, editorials, etc.) can all be viewed as readily available 'successful' writing examples by vent of their very publication. That is, they are examples of academic writing accessible beyond those directly contributing to them or directly involved. Likewise, tweets, blogs, and conference abstracts are types of academic writing that can be accessed fairly readily in particular academic spaces. However, other types of academic writing are 'occluded'. Only those privy to certain access privileges or directly involved are exposed to them, such as grant proposals, grant reviews, journal article reviews, responses to reviewers, teaching materials, text messages, and emails (Swales, 2004). This occlusion raises challenges for those seeking to write within these genres because of the more limited open availability and accessibility of these texts.

Recognizing the genred nature of academic writing and these variations in access, we offer the following processes for writing well across the manifold types of writing that academic workers need to do during academic work. Each consideration should be employed, taking account of the specifics of the writing to hand.

Developing your eyes and ears for genre

To write better and to write more: first read more. We agree with one of the world's most commercially successful writers, Stephen King, that the roots of good writing are in reading and writing appreciation, particularly via a genre-aware lens (2000). Accordingly, successful academic writing has its roots in developing your sense of what good academic writing in particular genres looks like, whether that writing is for theory manuscripts, tweets or even emails. This helps hone our personal vision and abilities to produce such writing in and for our own academic work.

Writing well within a particular genre therefore entails developing understanding of its nature and sensibilities: truly reading, analysing, and appreciating it at a deeper level. This involves accessing and attuning your senses to the particular type of writing, exposing yourself to typical and atypical examples of that genre and using a rhetorical lens to examine, at a deeper level, elements of content, structure, and techniques that contribute to its success or failure. Rhetorical analyses, as detailed by Faigley et al. (2006), can help this at first (Table 10.1).

Table 10.1   A Rhetorical Analysis of a Written Piece of Text

Element	Description of rhetorical dimension	Key question
Intended audience	Who the writing is explicitly for or implicitly aimed at	What are the audience's likely concerns, constraints, or parameters?
Strategies	The rhetorical techniques that are used to achieve the aims of the writing	What rhetorical techniques are used? What is the balance of *logos*, *ethos*, and *pathos*?
Rhetorical moves	The main steps the writing uses to achieve its purpose	What are the main points or rhetorical moves in the writing used to achieve its aims?
Evaluation	The degree to which the writing achieves their purpose	Your evaluation of whether the writing achieved that which the author(s) intended
Justify	What knowledge is assumed in the writing and how much does it advance?	What is the cultural or social significance of the writing?

Most texts don't come readily labelled as being good or useful examples of writing in a particular genre. As academic work involves so much writing, when academic work is done, writing is often involved as procedure, process, or product. Each piece of writing that one encounters in such work offers an opportunity for learning more about particular academic writing genres. When the genre of academic writing to be addressed is occluded and thus, examples are not readily available, colleagues, supervisors, and mentors offer a potential source of examples. Opportunities to contribute to grant or peer review, whether internally or externally, offer useful opportunities to see good, bad, and ugly examples of writing in occluded genres.

Writing examples that are especially good, bad, prototypical, or unusual, all offer insights that can be useful in improving one's own writing. Graff et al. (2009) go further, to offer a range of specific templates for academic writing that can be used to reprise others' arguments, summarize literatures, and introduce quotes. Although one's own evaluative lens will develop in time, books on writing, based on genre approaches often provide useful examples of articles using particular rhetorical techniques (ibid.; Faigley et al., 2006). Like becoming familiar with a new genre of music for the first time, at first only obvious details may be apparent. However, time and effort to develop appreciation allow new insights and understanding. Using a rhetorical analysis for a more systematic approach to view and break down writing helps discern the nuances and depth of texts and consciously develops awareness of possible variations within a particular genre of academic writing. One can better notice and understand the different techniques that writers use to achieve their ends.

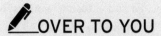OVER TO YOU

Identifying Genre

Take one research paper, one academic book in your field and one of your favourite non-academic books:

1. Break up the writing in each of these three pieces of writing into the facets of genre described above by Frow (2006).
2. Compare and contrast each of the three pieces in relation to:

    - Formal features.
    - Thematic structure and situation of address/tone.
    - Structure of implication and rhetorical function.
    - Frame.

How, then, to make the immense variety of our academic writing better, taking account of all manner of genre-based considerations and differences? Drawing on the genre approach, we suggest the following.

Contributing value to scholarly conversations

Addressing the question 'So what, who cares?' is essential as you utilize the MARKET approach (detailed later in this chapter). It adds a key consideration that is often absent in academic writing: quite simply, why should the reader care about your contribution?

This concept is challenging because too many writers – particularly academic writers – presume that readers are disposed to be interested and retain that interest in their writing: that the reader wants and needs the writing, and is inclined to work hard and dig for meaning, contribution, and profundity. Instead, write from a basis that assumes that other people actually do not want to read your writing. Indeed, it's the last thing they want (Pressfield, 2016). Like you, they have much to do, and there is already *so* much to read. Unclear and lacking concision and clarity of its own contribution, seldom does academic writing zing enough to really engage the reader.

To address this challenge, Pat Thomson and Barbara Kamler present an academic writing approach centring on the contribution of the writing. Their approach positions your writing as a form of co-construction, in which writers form their accounts of contributions to ongoing conversations taking place in specific scholarly communities. Extensively detailed in a number of books on writing teaching materials (Kamler and Thomson, 2014), manuscripts (Thomson and Kamler, 2012) and removal of bad habits (ibid., 2016), this sense of knowledge as scholarly conversation immediately resonates. The conversations are held amongst members of scholarly communities and defined by a shared interest in a scholarly topic, not a discipline, background, or career stage. For example, distinctive scholarly communities exist that focus on interventions to promote exercise in people with diabetes; the effects of T cell proteins on learning; the history of Ukrainian folk dancing; and academic workers' use of social media. The scholarly communities are engaged in ongoing conversations on social media, at conference presentations, in bars and corridors, and in the published journal and thesis literature.

Established academic workers seek to make active, ongoing, and useful contributions to these scholarly conversations. In these conversations, some voices are loud and say lots but little; other voices are quieter, saying little but lots. There are clear themes in the content of conversations (historical parameters, hot, contentious, or emerging 'sexy' topics) but the conversations are also about what is assumed, what is argued over and what goes assumed or unsaid in silences.

During and up to the doctoral level, a priority is to understand the conversations in the first place – to listen to and make sense of them. This is necessary because seldom are all facets of the conversations of a scholarly community around their core topic written down in any one place. Instead, emerging academic workers have to sense-make, sussing out as they go what is being 'said', what is being assumed, where the big disagreements are and so on. This concept of sense-making, is akin to 'forcing the octopus into the jar' (Kamler and Thomson, 2014), which captures well the challenge of imposing order, direction, and containment on the complex, amorphous, and multifaceted literatures that form the scholarly conventions of particular communities. Note here that the conversations don't just present themselves for writing, but need efforts to both listen and then make sense. Writing from this perspective becomes more strongly focused on the contribution(s) or added value of the particular type of writing to the relevant knowledge community. Reflecting the rhetorical devices discussed in Chapter 9, this means tuning into and responding to the language, concerns, and framings of the target knowledge community and connecting your contributions to and through these facets rather than focusing on what *you* have to say, on your terms and in your language.

Read widely

'Reading is the creative centre of the writer's life' (King, 2000: 147). Accordingly, writing well, demands reading widely. King (ibid.), the best-selling novelist, makes this argument at length in his memoir of his own writing growth. Reading helps build the tools of your writing, he explains, in terms of:

- *Vocabulary*: Long and short, common and unusual words (providing that your words are appropriate and colourful).
- *Grammar*: Should be known but not necessarily understood.
- *Paragraphing*: The basic unit of text (rather than words) (ibid.).

Reading widely means learning from the good, the bad, and the ugly, and channelling these insights into your inner 'writer' – the part of your brain that proffers the words you then write.

Convenient for the multimillionaire novelist, how, then, amidst the flow of tasks needing done, does the academic worker find time to read? Unsurprisingly, our immediate response to this is to prioritize reading in your weekly or even daily schedule by allocating time for it (more on this in Chapter 11). If academic work pivots around thinking and writing, reading must be a priority: 'If you don't have time to read, you don't have time (or the tools to write). Simple as that' (ibid.: 147).

There are many small life situations where you can steal back snippets of time to read, by always having reading with you (book, tablet or phone) in waiting rooms, on short and long journeys, in shopping checkout-lines, via audiobooks in the car or at singleton meals when at conferences (ibid.). Don't confine yourself to academic books either – fiction offers many insights for writing to engage, and concise writing on complex topics can be found in the mass media. *The Economist* magazine-format newspaper, for example, covers just about every topic imaginable and is written for diverse readers with very little time or attention span. It has wonderful examples of opening sentences, that are clear, creative, and enticing: content that is ever-responsive to the 'So what, who cares?' questions of their readers.

Use self-knowledge

Writing, as well as being a practical activity is an intellectual and embodied practice. As part of the extreme knowledge work of academic work, there are few tasks in which input and output are potentially more misaligned than writing. Hours of writing time can be devoted to yield but a few sentences, while, at other times, 1000 words drift effortlessly onto the page. A mere moment can provide the realization needed for the career-defining paper. Insights in The Core on creativity (Chapter 6), learning (Chapter 8) and influence (Chapter 9), can all be applied to increase the value of your success indicators of your writing time and efforts.

Because of these irksome unpredictabilities, writing tasks, more than other aspects of academic work, need to be planned using self-knowledge. When do you write best – First thing in the morning, afternoon or evening? Where do you write best – At work or home? Upstairs, downstairs? At your desk, in your armchair? In your bed? How do you write best – With time deadlines, word deadlines, pressing deadlines? Developing and drawing on self-knowledge is essential to academic writing: and is strongly associated with increased writing productivity by academic workers (Sword, 2017). Writing longer papers, theses or books or having less time to write (for example, with a busy administrative or teaching schedule) exherts particular pressure on your self-knowledge. Writing this book, for example, would be fresh for around three or four hours each day. Words and ideas flowed easily, but beyond four hours, word 'output' returns on time inputs diminished rapidly. At that point, it was better to do something else instead – and this book is better for this, too, because it then received only the 'best of attention'. Times of each day in which you tend to be tired or lacking creativity are likely the worst times to write, particularly if your writing demands creativity. Use this time for meetings or for writing that is less demanding, such as email. Whatever you do, make sure that it responds to your own rhythms and that you prioritize your 'good' times of day to do your writing.

Allocate time in your calendar for writing

Writing will only happen if and when time is allocated to it in your calendar. In our many interactions with academic workers, frustrations about not writing enough are most often linked to a lack of proactive allocation of time to writing within the schedule of their working week. Writing tasks that happen only when most or all of the other academic work tasks are done or even when there are no urgent other tasks to do, likely get little few of your 1440 minutes. Moreover, little of your best mental and physical energy either. As your academic work priorities should map to the time that you allocate to them (Drucker, 1967), everything about the nature of this extreme knowledge work suggests that, no matter your talent or tenacity, writing will only get done when it is prioritized via allocation of time in your schedule.

In practice, at the start of your allotted writing time, this means shifting completely away from any other task to what you need to write. Like turning up to teach a class of students, everything else has to be placed on hold while you prioritize writing. This psychological shift can be challenging because writing is embodied: the physical location in which we write influences how and what we write. Our mental ability to shift gears is also tested by moving from different kinds of tasks.

Your allocation of your writing time should seek to respond to your own mental rhythms and preferences, while also scheduling the right time to writing. This allocation should respond to your preferences and other commitments, for example you can set regular, shorter periods of time (one or two hours per day) for writing or blocks of time (days per week or weeks per year) (Silvia, 2007). Learning about how you write best is useful and important but takes time. Managing your writing is an ongoing work in progress, and an ongoing sense of dissatisfaction and urgency to write more, better and more quickly is an important driver to keep developing how well you can write in the time that you allocate to this priority.

Keep seeking to get better at writing

Academic workers talk of writing a lot, but how seriously do we take the lifelong project of getting better at our writing? While writing is, indeed, integral to academic work, improving at our own writing should be just as important. While more experienced writers or more established academic workers may think that they have their writing cracked, there is so much scope for clearer, more concise and more engaging academic writing (Sword, 2012). We can all play a part in improving this state of affairs.

MARKET: A TOOL FOR WRITING BETTER

Rhetorical approaches can help inform particular types of academic writing, such as journal publications. Over a number of years, we developed an approach in our workshops to focus on the contributions and writing of publications known as 'MARKET' (Table 10.2) to crystallize and frame the main contributions to scholarly conversations of any journal article. Intended to focus writers less on simply expressing what they want to say, but more on the added value and contributions of their writing to an important scholarly conversation amongst a defined knowledge community. MARKET supports academic writers to get rhetorical in how they construct their contribution to connect to targeted knowledge communities.

Once you have worked through the elements of MARKET, we challenge you to create a MARKET statement and then get feedback on your preliminary statement from a colleague, who preferably isn't familiar with your work. The MARKET statement is a short, clear, concise, and engaging 'pitch', that should be presented verbally and last no more than 1 minute. It is formulated from the components of the MARKET approach, but crucially in a different order.

Table 10.2   MARKET Approach to Writing

Element	Description	Key questions/considerations
(M)essages	Select 1-3 (maximum) main points for your paper	Think of the different messages this paper could have and why you would choose some over others. Don't think only about what you want to say, but also iteratively around the suitability of fit with the audience, value to the knowledge community and framing. What story do you want this paper to tell?
(A)udience	Your paper should be targeted to defined knowledge communities	Which knowledge communities are having scholarly conversations related to your messages? Who is the most apt audience(s) for the messages? Are the messages framed right for the target knowledge community(s)?
(R)hetorical moves	Setting the stage of the messages for your audience to explain and justify the significance of the contribution of your writing specifically for them	What rhetorical devices can be used to persuade your audience of the high importance and high significance of your paper's messages. How best can you connect to the agenda, concerns, and language used by your target knowledge community? What simple, yet persuasive, arguments render your contribution to be useful, timely and relevant to an important scholarly conversation?
(K)ey journals	The possible target journal(s) for the paper	Have you identified all of the journals that could be appropriate within your targeted knowledge community? Is there a close match between the messages, audience, and selected journals? Is there a more suitable message, audience, or journal?
(E)nveloping	Your choice of how you frame your messages to appeal to your targeted knowledge community	What possible frames could there be for your contribution? How have you chosen to frame your contribution? Are there any better alternatives?
(T)itle	Descriptive, yet attractive, title	What title is descriptive, fits in with those in your key journals, but also clearly and engagingly conveys your contribution?

My paper will be entitled _____ (Title). It is intended for _____ (Audience) in the journal(s) _____ (Key journals). This paper is useful because _____ (Rhetorical moves) and my paper will _____ _____ (Messages, taking account of Enveloping).

After you have received feedback on your preliminary MARKET statement it is important to take time to revise the statement accordingly. Common challenges we have experienced that academic workers have with developing their MARKET statement are:

- The 'Messages' and 'Rhetorical moves' are predominantly or exclusively descriptive rather than clearly persuading the intended 'Audience' of the distinctive value and contribution of the paper.
- Framing and phrasing the elements in terms of the writers language, priorities, and agenda as opposed to those of the intended 'Audience'.
- Having too many 'Messages'.
- Having no sense of the defined knowledge community or scholarly conversation that the paper will contribute to.

- The 'Rhetorical moves' justifying the paper are not clear or don't flow well together.
- The 'Title' does not sufficiently describe the paper and/or its contribution in a clear, concise, and engaging manner that grabs the 'Audience'.

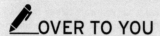

OVER TO YOU

Using the MARKET approach

After the research is done, but before you start writing your next academic paper, complete the following steps.

1. Utilize the MARKET approach, breaking the paper down into each of the elements of MARKET, as outlined in Table 10.2. Try to consider the different elements iteratively and in relation to one another.
2. 'Pitch' or deliver your MARKET statement to a fellow academic worker, whom you trust to give you good feedback in 90 seconds or less. Try not to hesitate, obfuscate, or deviate from your statement.
3. Obtain feedback regarding the strengths and weaknesses of your MARKET statement. Encourage them to consider the question: 'So what, who cares?' (Graff et al., 2009). As they feedback to you focus on listening to the feedback, do not respond, defend, or explain your statement further.
4. Modify your MARKET statement based on the feedback that you received. Consider the ways in which it has improved based on this feedback and your further reflection.

——— REMARKABLE RESOURCES ———

Helping Doctoral Students Write by Barbara Kamler and Pat Thomson

Writing approaches are too often confined to prescriptive 'trick and tips' that have limited application to different contexts, disciplines, and academic workers. Using a genre-based approach, academic workers can use Kamler and Thomson's (2014) approach to learn how to position work relative to existing scholarly conversations in ways that are more responsive to these considerations.

Key messages

- The early stages of your academic career involve becoming attuned to and being able to construct written accounts of literatures as scholarly conversations taking place in knowledge communities.
- Writing involves positioning yourself in these scholarly conversations. Be crystal clear on what you are adding to important conversations.
- To help doctoral students write, do not edit line by line as this is less likely to help them appreciate, understand, and assimilate the genere in which they are trying to write. Instead, edit alongside them and articulate your thinking and insights, in relation to the writing genere.

Key applications

- Provides a lens through which to understand all academic writing and scholarly products that focuses on rhetoric, language, and contribution. Provides deep insights.
- Offers an approach to both writing and helping others to write better.
- Reduces the wasted effort that many academic workers put into correcting the work of others, despite the limited benefits of this to their learning, via an approach that is not only informed by theory but also actually helps others write better.

On Writing by Stephen King

The world-famous novelist Stephen King (2000) shares insights into his writing challenges, breaks, and philosophy in this narrative-heavy account of how he made a stellar career from writing. The book avoids 'tricks and tips' to provide deeper insights into how to develop your ideas, voice, and structure based on reading lots of other people's work.

Key messages

- Read a lot. Read more. Try to read well-written writing, in particular. If you want to write more and better, you are not too busy to read more and better.
- Writing well is difficult. Even the best writers fear, procrastinate, and yearn to run away from the tasks of writing. Get down to work. Develop your writing space both physically (like your favourite desk or place) and organizationally (when and where in your day).
- Writing only when you feel like writing is the last thing you should do.

Key applications

- Helps dispel myths that for highly successful and productive writers, writing: comes easily, with creativity not discipline, without many rejections or by focusing only on the writing itself.

11

DEVELOPING BETTER HABITS AND SYSTEMS FOR EVERYDAY TASKS

> Every day do something that will inch you closer to a better tomorrow.
>
> (Doug Firebaugh quoted by
> McKeown, 2014: 193)

Hidden paradoxes abound in academic work: working with others is mostly about working through the self, writing is founded on reading, and worldly success indicators are built on the most personal of internal values. So, too, the work that we want to do is related symbiotically to the work that we have to do: the everyday tasks of academic work.

It's easy to be dismissive about the everyday tasks of academic work. These tasks don't look or readily appear 'academic': reading and answering emails, meeting with other people, managing reference libraries, organizing student courses, taking telephone messages. Yet, these everyday tasks can take up a lot of time. Each task consumes some of our 1440 allotted daily minutes. Inevitably, each minute that these tasks take equates to one less that we can devote to another aspect of teaching, research, and engagement more likely to contribute to a success indicator. These everyday tasks are seen as benign, but are actually a peril to our effectiveness. While they may appear alluringly simple to do well and give a sense of achievement or tasks being progressed, emails and meetings have been cited as the two single biggest reasons for academics not having enough time for their own research and teaching work(!) (Ziker, 2014). Moreover, as we now argue, doing everyday tasks well is integral to successful academic work around our most fundamental success indicators. Thus, the profound external and internal joys of progress in academic work is dependent on managing a plethora of everyday tasks well.

EVERYDAY TASKS: MARGINAL AND FUNDAMENTAL GAINS

While busy people lament not having enough time to develop systems and habits to manage their everyday tasks, effective people are far more likely to say that they are too busy *not* to have such habits. In our experience, the most effective people do not find themselves too busy, and this is precisely *because* they do have good systems in place. Like the pit stop crews in Formula One (F1) racing-car teams who change tyres and make small repairs at mesmerizing speed and high efficiency, meeting your main success indicators is built on doing the necessary very quickly and very well.

As James Vowles, Chief Strategist for Mercedes Formula One, explained to Syed: 'The secret of modern F1 is not really to do with the big ticket items; it's about the hundreds of thousands of small items, optimized to the nth degree ... success is about creating the most effective optimization' (2015: 195).

This is the science of marginal gains: small, even indiscernible, gains across smaller elements of work can aggregate, contributing to much bigger improvements and a far greater likelihood of meeting your main success indicator. Indeed, a marginal-gains approach has been used to underpin large increases in performance in competitive teams (Clear, 2014). Moreover, some of the biggest gains arise when improvements are:

- Taken seriously, especially when they involve routine 'everyday' tasks (Sower et al., 2008).
- Address facets or steps that are predominantly overlooked (Clear, 2014).
- Approached with an openness to acknowledging the need to improve (Syed, 2015).
- Practised often (Sower et al., 2008).
- Apply learning and creativity to make such improvements (Syed, 2015).

Approaching the everyday tasks of academic work with a marginal gains lens, effectiveness is less about avoiding meetings, emails and other similar everyday administrative tasks, and more about applying skills from The Core to develop consistently better routines, habits, and systems to doing these tasks well, while also reducing or even minimizing the time you chose to allocate for these tasks. While everyday tasks in academic work may appear mundane and less relevant to our more glamorous success indicators, finding the marginal gain improvements in these tasks not only requires skills from The Core but also contributes to achieving our success indicators. This insight goes back to Aristotle, who said, 'Excellence, then, is not an act but a habit'.

EXCELLENCE, THEN, IS NOT AN ACT BUT A HABIT

By focusing creativity, learning, and openness to failure on improving doing everyday tasks – the proverbial academic pit stops – success in everyday tasks influences our overall success. Accordingly, this chapter focuses on the pivotal role that developing good habits and systems around everyday tasks has in contributing to academic work.

TAMING EVERYDAY TASKS

The first step to optimizing everyday academic work and the time that these tasks take is to categorize and measure the time spent on this work (Drucker, 1967). Academic workers tend to work many hours (Misra et al., 2012). On average, those in the USA report working 55 hours per week (O'Laughlin and Bischoff, 2005); while Australian academics report working 50 hours per week (Winefield et al., 2008); and academics in Ireland 47 hours per week, the most in Europe (Kwiek and Antonowicz, 2013). But on what is this time being spent? The only way to accurately assess how you are spending your weekly time is to put tasks in your calendar and then use this as a basis for refining the mapping of your time to your priorities. In this way, your calendar becomes an essential 'knowledge' tool for mapping your time to your priorities.

From time to priorities

In Chapter 5, we argued that it was necessary to focus more on priorities than on time when doing academic work. Focusing more on time means that our sense of work progress or accomplishment results more from our views of ourselves doing tasks, how much time we spend on such tasks, and what the tasks are. More hours doing a task might lead to feeling accomplished but masquerades as effectiveness if these tasks do not map to priorities.

Focusing on your priorities in the time that you have brings a profoundly different focus to our daily lives. The usefulness of doing particular tasks is only ever evaluated in the context of whether these tasks progress stated priorities. Spending 1 hour on a task that helps to achieve a goal working toward accomplishing a priority is more effective than spending 100 hours on many tasks that have little effect on priorities (Table 11.1).

Table 11.1   Work: Time vs. Priority-Focused

Time-focused	Priority-focused
Doing 'stuff' that isn't linked to goals and priorities	Doing set tasks that link to goals and priorities with the intention of achieving success indicators
Hours invested	Goals met and priorities progressed
Nature of inputs	Nature of outputs
Accomplishment from actions	Accomplishment from results

Knowing and allocating your time: Calendar management

Do you still use a paper-based diary or calendar? Calendars in most workplaces are actually now electronic daily organizers (such as exist through most email platforms) rather than a traditional paper-based desk diary. These calendars are most often used in academic work to schedule particular types of academic tasks: meetings with others, classes to teach and seminars to attend. The shame of missing these various appointments with ourselves and others renders them important enough to get prompts in our daily calendars. The calendar is a prompt to be somewhere, doing something. Less commonly, are calendars used to schedule important academic work tasks, such as: student-marking, journal reviews, writing, reading, or creative time. Yet, this approach to the calendar misses most of the value that a calendar can bring to effectiveness. Calendars allow for us to know how we spend our time but then more proactively ensure that our time maps to our priorities.

Mapping time to priorities involves taking a frank look at what tasks you spend your time on and then making more conscious choices about what time is allocated to which tasks. This involves a subtle but profound reframing. While your calendar can be seen simply as a passive vehicle for scheduling events or meetings, it can be a proactive tool for setting and monitoring priorities: effectiveness in academic work is less about stating the tasks needing done but more about ensuring that priorities are enacted with tasks scheduled to time.

Put all tasks in your calendar

The first step to effective calendar management is to specify your priorities and then map these priorities to your own time, ensuring that your time always reflects your priorities.

First allocate particular time to tasks – minimally for each 30-minute chunk of work. If your habit is to answer emails sporadically throughout the day, then try to calculate how much time this takes and factor that in. Similar smaller tasks can be scheduled in 30-minute chunks. Larger tasks or groups of tasks can also be chunked into longer blocks of time.

This more detailed approach to time allocation is, in itself, time-consuming. However, when working days are cast as being formed of a series of 'tasks to time' in composition, provides an early indicator of where time is devoted and any disparities between our actions and our intended priorities. The nature of academic work as extreme knowledge work dictates that each minute could be spent doing a wide variety of different tasks and priorities. Some tasks make us feel busy in our work, but may not make us more effective or successful in our work because they don't reflect priorities. Seeing the root of effectiveness in academic work as time- and task-determined is far less justifiable than viewing effectiveness as arising from our ability to further priorities via tasks through the medium of time. As such, better utilization of the calendar as a tool for effectiveness arises not from monitoring time but by furthering work priorities in that time.

SHOW ME YOUR CALENDAR AND I WILL SHOW YOU WHAT YOUR PRIORITIES ARE

This re-visioning of your calendar may initially not seem natural. Spending more time on developing a more detailed calendar can itself scream of distraction. A useful mindset is to assume that unless a task is scheduled, then it's only a concept. Like the unsubmitted grant or manuscript, it has not yet been fully born. Effectiveness does not happen by magic or because of any special individual talent (Drucker, 1967) but when time maps, responds to, and furthers priorities (Sharma, 2006).

Calendars as value vehicles

Time should be allocated in your calendar for priority tasks first and everything else after these. Conceived in this manner, calendars become not only platforms for furthering priorities but also vehicles for expressing personal values. So, if family is your priority, allocate time to those activities first, such as family dinners, taking the kids to school and special events, and then slot in other tasks around those. Sometimes, priorities may clash and tasks that are more fixed in time, such as teaching a set class, may require that other tasks be accommodated elsewhere in the week. If tasks linked to our priorities are only allocated time after less important others, or, more likely, never allocated time at all, then they are far less likely to happen. Similarly, if reading, thinking, and writing tasks are priorities, time needs to be allocated to them before time is allocated to other tasks.

Issues around prioritization most often arise in our workshops when research and writing tasks are stated priorities but are not themselves subsequently allocated time in our daily schedules. This misalignment of priorities to time is a major contributor to ineffectiveness and frustration, often born of the assumption that writing or research will occur after or automatically around the other flow of time-thief tasks that need getting done.

Protecting your priorities

Utilizing your calendar and working to the tasks and priorities that it expresses requires being practically organized in mapping priorities to time, psychological determination, and a degree of comfort with work left uncompleted.

If you don't have control of your time, someone else will, and it takes active effort and time to keep control. Even time for this needs to be blocked in. Using your calendar more deliberately as a 'driver' for enacting your priorities and goals in tasks allows better assessment of how well your time is reflected in priorities. When you have some say in how your time is allocated, then you are also in a potential position of being in higher control of your effectiveness: a psychological shift from passenger to driver in controlling your time. In practice, this means always questioning whether tasks (old or new) fit in with your priorities before they are allocated time in your calendar. In instances in which tasks do not help achieve success indicators, ruthlessness is needed either to allocate minimal time or no time to that task in your calendar.

This inevitably means 'saying "no"' to some tasks. When these choices involve 'saying "no"' to new opportunities that arise, this can be challenging. It can involve disappointing others: journal editors in need of suitable reviewers, colleagues requiring supervisors, co-authors needing your input. It may involve disappointing yourself: not attending the tenuous conference in the sunny place that you always wanted to visit or forgoing the fix of checking your email or social media once more. If it does not fit in with your values and success indica-tors as expressed in your priorities, then it needs to get much less time in your calendar.

Inevitably, choices around prioritization are about making trade-offs: strategically weighing what tasks best further what is most important in our academic work. As economist Thomas Sowell wrote: 'There are no solutions. There are only trade-offs' (quoted in McKeown, 2014: 55). As such, getting more used to leaving work that could be done, never done or undone is a necessary step.

The psychological game of good calendar management

Your calendar is less like a calm sea and more like a raging battlefield. For your priorities to be successfully reflected via tasks and 'win' the required time in your calendar demands your dogged protection, focus, and determined action. The sense of work that we could do being deliberately left undone or even 'never done' is disconcerting but inevitable in extreme knowledge work. Spending allocated time to research writing, may leave emails, telephone messages and various other conversations unanswered. Time-thief tasks, like emails and meet-ings, never cease in academic workplaces. By nature, they go unfinished. Allocating less time, or even the most minimal time that we can sustain for them, is essential to effective academic work. Accepting this can be particularly challenging with a time-focused approach to aca-demic work (Table 11.1). As noted at the start of this chapter, this leads our focus to be more on inputs and on the psychological assurance that being occupied, busy, and doing these tasks brings. Leaving work undone, not done, or being done in minimal time is discomforting. We tell ourselves that this is indulgent, may look incompetent to colleagues and students, and that we're being unproductive.

We disagree, but it does require psychological strength. The wisdom of a priority-focused approach to work reminds us that prioritization is done to be more effective and successful in extreme knowledge work. The work that we don't do is as much a consequence of this as the work that we choose to do.

Workplace cultures that are time-focused tend not only to foster lower productivity via a combination of longer working hours and poorer results from the work that is done, but also to shame when one is seen publicly to prioritize other work over accepting invites to meetings or quickly responding to emails. However, such choices are not only just 'okay' but actually vital. Guilt, shame or a lowered sense of competency or commitment is not the answer and we cannot wait for 'free time' to magically appear to write, read, or allocate time for the personal things that we enjoy, family time or the enaction of any of our priorities. That time will never appear unless we make it so.

Dealing with the unexpected

As extreme knowledge work, academic work can be unpredictable with unexpected tasks becoming short-term priorities, such as a student in tears or proofs requiring annotation. The ability to identify such priority tasks from those tasks that are merely important can be used to shift priority tasks to other days and times. Crucially, priority tasks should not be deleted; rather, other tasks of lesser priority should be deleted to accommodate these priority tasks. Simple techniques like triaging your emails, meetings, and writing in 'urgent' and 'non-urgent' can allow unexpected priority tasks to be allocated time at the cost of delaying the less urgent work.

Tactics for time allocation

Various tactics can be used to aid effective calendar management:

- Taking time to manage your calendar each week or each morning.
- Blocking regular and re-occurring meetings in advance – try to block these meetings together into one day, if possible, or back-to-back so that more blocks are free for priority tasks.
- Colour-coding particular types of tasks by the main priority that they serve provides a ready visual indication as to how much time maps to priorities (Figure 11.1). If writing is one of your top priorities, you can then tell at a quick glance when analysing your calendar how much this is borne out in your actual time.

IF YOU DON'T HAVE CONTROL OF YOUR TIME, SOMEONE ELSE WILL

Better meetings

Meetings. Day after day, week after week. Surveys show that academics spend about one in every five working hours in a meeting (Ziker, 2014).

At our workshops – at all stages of academic work – more than any other single 'task', we hear of many frustrations about meetings in various forms. Meetings are too frequent, stop us getting to *real* academic work – especially writing, thinking, teaching preparation, and reading – and do not achieve their objectives often enough or quick enough. Meetings don't start on time, don't end on time or are a simple waste of time. Do meetings really work? Somewhat – but if meetings are allocated too much time in our schedules, and don't align with our priorities, the remaining time in each day to do the 'right' academic work is less. Fact.

There will always be some meetings that we are invited to that we must attend, either because of obligations to our students/workplaces or as a formal part of our role. Yet,

Weekly calendar — GMT-06

Time	Mon 6/12	Tue 7/12	Wed 8/12	Thu 9/12	Fri 10/12
6am		6 – 7 Exercise		6 – 7 Exercise	
7am					
8am	8 – Take Kids to School	8 – Take Kids to School	8 – Take Kids to School	8 – Take Kids to School	8 – Take Kids to School
9am	9 – Review Calendar, Priorities	9 – Review Calendar, Priorities	9 – Review Calendar, Priorities	9 – 10:30 Departmental Meeting	9 – Review Calendar, Priorities / 9:30 – Email
10am	9:30 – 12p To-Do List/Tasks	9:30 – 11 Reading Time	9:30 – 12p Research/Writing Time	10:30 – Review Calendar, Priorities	10 – 5p Research/Writing Time
11am		11 – 12p "Office Hours" for Students		11p – 12p "Office Hours" for Students	
12am	12p – 1p Reading Time	12p – 1p Lunch with Friend	12p – 1p Lunch with Colleague	12p – 1p Lunch Break	
1pm	1p – 4p Teaching & Prep Time	1p – Student Meeting / 1:30p – Student Meeting	1p – 4p Teaching & Prep Time	1p – 4p To-Do List/Tasks	
2pm		2p – 3p Research Team Meeting			
3pm		3p – Teaching Team Meeting / 3:30p – To-Do List/Tasks			
4pm	4p – 5p Email, Review Calendar	4p – 5p Email, Review Calendar	4p – 5p Email, Review Calendar	4p – 5p Email, Review Calendar	
5pm					
6pm					
7pm			7p – 9p Kids School Concert		7p – 10p Dinner with Friends
8pm	7:30p – 8:30p Yoga Class			8:30p – 10p Reading Time	
9pm					
10pm					

Figure 11.1 Mapping Time to Priorities via Calendar Scheduling

irrespective of the inevitability of meetings, many practices and factors can influence meeting effectiveness. Like many aspects of life, bad meetings are often blamed on others and it's reassuring to assume that we already know good meeting practices. However, like all self-work, good practices can and must start with ourselves. The following 'P's for better meetings can help and are discussed below: purpose and payoffs; participants; pre-work; plan; process; parking lot; post-meeting assessment; and post-work.

Purpose and payoffs

- Why has this meeting been called, or why am I calling this meeting?

  Be specific about the main outcomes that you and the other attendees minimally need for each meeting ahead of time. If you can list these in an agenda and prior to the meeting, this can avoid drifting 'off-topic'.

- What are the desired outcomes? How can they best be achieved?

  Different meeting formats may work for different purposes. Should the meeting be facilitated by a professional facilitator, a student, or chaired by you? This somewhat depends on the type of meeting but also on the likelihood of disagreement. Maybe a meeting is not the best means at all. Alternatives could be the provision of information via a conversation or telephone call, email or shared cloud-based document.

Participants

- Who has been invited to this meeting? Why have I been invited and can/should I contribute?

- Who am I inviting to this meeting? Can someone attend for me?

  Is every meeting attendee essential for every meeting? If not, consider asking others if they would rather pass. Remember, even if you are popular, don't assume that others need or want to attend your meeting. Value the time of others as if it were your own. Established academic workers, particularly those in administrative roles, have many necessary meetings but, sometimes, too, a curious urge to participate in meetings unnecessarily. Small issues are elevated to require meetings or it is assumed that the academic themselves must attend rather than another staff member. Ideally, make your de facto question, 'who could attend on my behalf?' and only if the answer is simply, 'no one' should the senior academic attend.

Pre-work

- As a meeting organizer, send out an agenda to attendees in advance.

  Use a template that includes the amount of time blocked for each item on the agenda and who will speak to or is responsible for each agenda item. You can even use the agenda to note action items.

Plan

- Make a plan for the meeting in advance if you are the organizer.

- Discuss default one-hour meetings. Can your meeting default change to 30 minutes?

  It's curious why 60 minutes has become the de facto length of meetings in many settings or situations. Really? What about 30 minutes or even 15 minutes? By being more sceptical about how much time is really needed, the amount of time spent away from other academic work in meetings can be dramatically reduced. This also often compels attendees to focus more and deviate less.

- As an invitee, read the agenda in advance.

  Ensure that you bring anything needed and have fulfilled any actions asked of you. Overall, be prepared beforehand.

Process

- If you are the organizer or meeting chair, use the appropriate process in the meeting.

  Examples: Some formal meetings may need minutes and formalized procedures, using Robert's Rules of Order (Robert, 2011); some meetings may suffice with just actions; whereas informal meetings may not need a formal chair or processes at all.

- Discuss the process with participants at the start of the meeting. Everyone should understand the process, plan and desired payoffs before starting.

Parking lot

- Stick to the agenda and put other items that are brought up in the parking lot instead of having them derail the meeting.

  The parking lot is used as a gathering place for 'off-track' or tangential items that can be covered at the end of the meeting as time permits or at another meeting if this is absolutely necessary. As creative and smart people, academic workers like to discuss, think and debate. We have seen high-level committees involving established academic workers charged with a particular task decline rapidly to discuss all manner of tangential issues that are beyond what the items they were charged with addressing. While potentially interesting, usually this is simply ineffective. Keep on track.

Post-meeting assessment

- Plan for a few minutes at the end of the meeting to get a sense from the participants regarding the meeting process. Were the right people here? For ongoing meetings: do we want to continue? What are the next steps?

  This is an important, yet rare, step. Soliciting feedback at the end of the meeting helps to ensure that everyone has the opportunity to contribute any final points and generally comment on how the process can be improved next time.

Post-work

- Plan 10 extra minutes in your schedule following a meeting or after a group of meetings to reflect (Harvard Business Review, 2006).

Meetings are not just work but also detract from work and create work. Allocating some time after meetings to do any work that resulted from the meetings allows loose ends to be tied. These follow-up tasks could include:

o   Writing a summary for your own purpose or for those who missed the meeting or need to know about the outcomes. Use the agenda if needed and simply write summary points as the meeting progresses against each item.

o   Record action items arising from the meeting on your to-do list.

o   Add future meeting dates or due dates to your calendar.

o   Make any needed follow-ups or add this to your to-do list.

o   If you were the chair or facilitator: How did it go? What could be done better next time? Good self-work around being open and reflective can make a big difference to improving this area of your own academic work.

Everyone can make a meeting's difference

Many aspects of effective meetings are easier in the role of organizer, chair or facilitator, but attendees can make a difference, too, for example, by:

•   Making suggestions to meeting organizers.
•   Discussing tools and effective meeting processes with colleagues and teams.
•   Being a good participant. Respect other people's time by being prepared and keeping the meeting on track. Consider the W.A.I.T. approach (Grogan, 2017) (Figure 11.2).

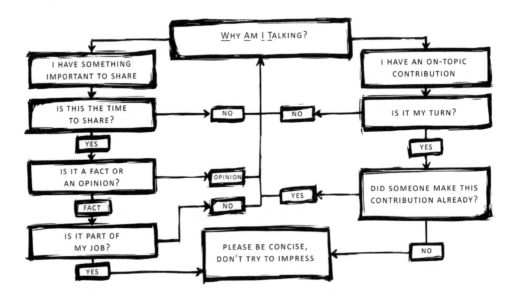

Figure 11.2   W.A.I.T. Approach to Being a Good Meeting Participant

Source: Grogan (2017)

Of course, academic work does not just happen between people, face-to-face, but is also increasingly done via screens (Decuypere and Simons, 2016). The main aspect of this mediated aspect of academic work we will focus on here is the dreaded email.

Managing email

If there's a gripe about modern academic work that is as common as the gripe about meetings, it's about email: its overload, its ubiquity, whatever the time of day or year, and its seeming centrality to getting so many academic work tasks done. How did academic work happen before email? How can it happen despite email? Indeed, research has shown that academic workers experience considerable stress around about email – and especially its high volume – with more stress being associated with more emails (Jerejian et al., 2013). Indeed, academic workers were more likely than other members of staff to receive higher numbers of emails (with the highest amount being in established academic workers) and read emails on evenings and weekends (Pagnata et al., 2015).

Kinman, commenting on this stress, concludes that there is 'increasing evidence that email overload and lack of respite from information and communications technology can lead to emotional exhaustion and cognitive failures' and has called for academics to 'develop e-resilience' (Reisz, 2016).

Despite the wide prevalence and costs of email to academic work, large surveys have found that academic workers seldom use deliberate email management strategies, such as filing, filtering, or deliberate inbox management (Pagnata et al., 2015). Perhaps this is because academic workers are more passionate about doing work perceived as being real academic work. However, we think that it is because this academic work is so important that email needs to be better managed in academic workplaces. So, how can we handle email better?

Develop a lens for email

First, put and keep email in its place. This recommendation is based on recognizing that email in itself is not a success indicator, a priority, or a goal, but is simply a tool which can be used to complete tasks; however, the risk is that we allocate too much time at the wrong times of day to email. Our approach is not to consider email inherently as real academic work, because while email never stops, it actually often prevents us from focusing on that which needs to be done to achieve our success indicators. Accordingly, email fits into a dubious category of being a task that serves but does not constitute a work-end or outcome in itself. Email is a time-thief because email is:

- Checked various times throughout the day, breaking up our workflow, creativity, and focus.
- Read and replied to even at 'peak performance' times of day (like first thing in the morning), when creativity is high.
- Associated with a ready but false psychological payoff of 'work done'.

Schedule time to do email

Schedule regular time for email in your calendar, because it is highly predictable that email will exist that needs to be attended to. Pick the 'right' time of day for you, ideally when your creativity is lowest. We believe that doing email isn't a priority task, therefore it shouldn't be scheduled during your most optimal times of day – the times where you have the most creativity or energy. Instead, schedule it for when you are more tired.

Don't reply to everything or everyone

Simply do not reply to emails unless an email *demands* this. Also, consider before you 'Reply All' if everyone else on the original email *must* know your response. For example, meeting availability requests usually don't need to go to the whole group of potential attendees but only to the person organizing the meeting. This shows thought for others; by keeping the volume of everyone else's emails a little bit less, we can help workplaces be less stressful.

Only send an email that is necessary

Send fewer emails. An implication of replying to emails only if it is necessary is to remember that if you want to receive less email, sending less is a good start. Some work matters are much easier resolved via a quick telephone call or face-to-face conversation rather than a chain of back-and-forth clarification emails. Consider that email is a communication means but may not always be the best one.

Do emails at set times

Allocate time in your calendar for email. A simple research-based solution to reduce email stress is just to check it less often (Kushlev and Dunn, 2015). Make a conscious choice to 'check email' less (i.e. reading or scanning emails outside of scheduled email time) and 'do email' more. 'Doing email' is a dedicated and scheduled work task in which you touch each email only once (see next point). 'Checking email' makes it harder to track what you have responded to, also, distracted by your email, you risk missing out on the non-screen world, such as interactions with others.

Touch each email once

Appreciate the difference between these two approaches and, if you can, touch email just once. If you 'don't have time' to do this one-touch management, then it is a sign that you are 'checking' – not 'doing' – email. Also, it may be that you aren't using scheduled time for doing email. When you 'touch' the email, be prepared to respond, file or delete it at that time.

Use email templates, filters, and priorities

Utilize ways that you can respond to emails quicker. If you write similar emails repeatedly, consider using an automated 'canned' response email template, which can be personalized quickly. All emails are *not* the same.

Email systems can automatically file emails as they arrive into your various work folders, and these automated systems can learn via your own filing and refiling what emails should go in which of your work folders. This helps to automatically triage emails by topic and sender. Further, consider using the 80–20 rule by replying only after a quick scan to identify the 20 per cent of emails that you received that most justify receiving prioritization in your responses; these emails should be the ones that contribute most to your own success indicators. Since you only have a scheduled amount of time for the task of doing emails, identifying and doing the most important emails first is preferable.

File and dump your email

Email inboxes are not to-do lists. Many workers tend to keep 'never-ending' inboxes because emails are not systematically deleted. This backlog of emails is both intimidating and also messy to search. If you currently have an enlarged inbox (ouch!) and there are too many emails to file, then do a 'mail dump', in which you file/archive all the emails that are currently in your inbox into a separate folder so that you can start from scratch, utilizing better email management habits.

Also, develop a systematic file folder structure to file different kinds of emails, depending on your various categories of academic work. For example, emails from students on each of your courses can all be filed into the same folder. Keep a 'to read' folder to file valuable reading that you shouldn't stop to read while you do your email but can revisit during the time that you have scheduled for reading.

Ruthlessly unsubscribe

Cut off emails at the source. This is a ready and easy means to begin to tame the volume of email you receive. If you find yourself always deleting emails from the same list-servers without ever reading them, then unsubscribe. This will reduce email clutter and the task of checking email will take less time.

Take pride in your email and its etiquette

Take pride in writing emails. As with any genre, clear and concise emails reflects well on you, your work, and your workplace. Small touches, such as the contents of a subject line, can be very helpful to others. Military personnel, for example, are encouraged to incorporate into subject lines keywords in caps to note the email's purpose (Sehgal, 2016), for example: INFO, REQUEST, or ACTION.

An important, yet final, point: never send emails that contain any content that you would not want printed in massive letters across your workplace building. Unlike an ill-advised verbal comment in the heat of the moment, emails are permanent, can be circulated by anyone without your consent, and don't have you ready at hand to qualify your intention or apologize.

OTHER SYSTEMS, ROUTINES, AND HABITS

Building systems, routines, and habits is at the heart of effectiveness. So far, we have addressed how to have better meetings and manage our email, but there are other common tasks that can be reduced via maintaining effective systems, routines, and habits. While developing these involves the investment of time, it is essential to do so, given the current challenges faced by academic workers.

To-do lists

To-do lists, as inventories of tasks needing done, won't help us do the right things, but they do help ensure that the right things get done (Allen, 2015).

While the notion of simply listing tasks needing to be done seems easy, most to-do lists fall down in a number of key areas:

- *To-do lists detail priorities and goals but not tasks*: A to-do list should be at the task level (see Chapter 5). Priorities and goals are too big to be 'checked off' a list and must be thought through and broken down into tasks.
- *We confuse quality with quantity*: How long or short our list is should not be a mark of academic honour or martyrdom. The most valid indicator of to-do list quality is how accurately our goals and priorities are reflected in the tasks on our to-do list.
- *To-do list tasks are not prioritized:* This risks not doing the right thing at the right time and not focusing on priority tasks first. Cleaning your home to avoid a much more important task like editing a rejected article for resubmission leads to a cleaner living space, but not to manuscript success. Related to this is not setting deadlines for these tasks. Deadlines are an important part of ensuring that these tasks are completed in the right time.
- *Gratification comes from 'checking off' the most number of tasks in a day*: This focuses on doing what might be fast or easy first in order to ensure the maximum number is checked off versus doing the priority tasks first.
- *Time is not allocated in schedules for completing tasks*: Tasks can't get done if you haven't allocated time for them.
- *Viewing the to-do list as a form of perverse torture*: A to-do list should be viewed as a helpful tool that supports effective work. Reading and rereading our list and then stressing about each single item that is not yet completed is unhelpful and can lead us to avoiding our to-do list altogether. However, if we don't look at our list, then we aren't using it for the good that it was intended, and then a negative pattern follows, in which the list grows ever longer.

Better to-do lists

Given these challenges, what can be done to better harness the to-do list? As with many things in academic work, the effective to-do list starts with the self.

Find a method that works for you

One option is to use an app on your phone or computer (see some examples in the Remarkable Resources section below). Apps often have built-in features to prioritize and set deadlines. Many calendar/schedule management programs (for example, Microsoft Outlook or Google Mail) have built-in features to create to-do lists. The benefit of these is that they are already integrated with your calendar, and reminders can be set up to show deadlines within your calendar. Others may prefer to keep a paper list. Be mindful that, unlike digital lists, time is needed to write and rewrite these lists as priorities and deadlines shift. If you prefer pen and paper, keep multiple lists on separate pages in your notebook that are broken down by level of priority. Trial and error is key to finding the best fit for you, so try something new. For us, working toward a plethora of goals in various work environments, it is a mixture of these approaches that over time we have found works best.

Prioritize your to-do list

Ask yourself: 'What are the three most important things I can do today that will help me ultimately to reach my success indicators?' When prioritizing, consider what is important versus what is simply urgent. A useful tool for this is the Eisenhower Matrix (Figure 11.3).

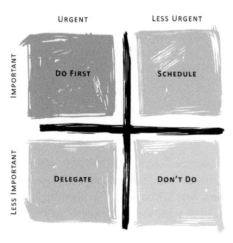

Figure 11.3   Eisenhower Matrix

Do a 'brain-dump'

If the list is only 'in your head', forgetting tasks is inevitable. Take time each day to do a brain-dump and list everything that you think should be on your to-do list. Once written on the list, these tasks can be prioritized, scheduled, or even eliminated if they are not deemed to be a priority at all.

Review your to-do list each day

While adding new tasks is inevitable, it is important to review your to-do list each day, so that you evaluate what tasks you will work on first (that is, prioritize) and make sure that you have scheduled time to accomplish them.

Using the Eisenhower Matrix

In a speech in 1954 to the Second Assembly of the World Council of Churches, former US President Eisenhower, who was quoting J. Roscoe Miller, President of Northwestern University, said: 'I have two kinds of problems: the urgent and the important. The urgent are not important, and the important are never urgent' (Eisenhower, 1954). This principle has been coined the 'Eisenhower Principle' because it is said to be how he organized his workload and priorities, with the understanding that we must focus our time on the tasks that are important without always being pulled to focus on the tasks that are urgent.

In this case, important tasks have an outcome that leads to us achieving our success indicators via our priorities and goals. On the other hand, urgent tasks demand immediate attention and are sometimes associated with achieving someone else's priorities and goals. They are often the ones that we concentrate on because the consequences of not dealing with them are or seem immediate. Establish which tasks are important and which are urgent to overcome the natural tendency to focus on unimportant urgent tasks during the time that is scheduled to complete tasks that will ultimately lead to achieving success indicators.

The Eisenhower Matrix (Figure 11.3) can discern where particular tasks on your to-do list should fall in terms of priority and even whether or not the tasks should be done. Of course, this tool should be used with reference to your success indicators, priorities, and goals from The Success Pyramid.

Important and urgent tasks

Ideally, no important tasks become urgent. But inevitably, circumstances change and unforeseen events transpire. Procrastination about academic work or leaving some tasks to the very last minute happen to others, too. While proactive planning can avoid these scenarios, allocate some 'buffer space' in your schedule to complete 'urgent' tasks to ensure that there is always time for such tasks and important but less urgent tasks. If you find that you have many urgent and important tasks, think about how these tasks could be scheduled ahead of time in future or what is causing your important tasks to become urgent.

Important but not urgent tasks

Important but not urgent tasks are the ones that are most likely to help you to achieve your success indicators via your goals and priorities. This is the important work that must be scheduled in order to ensure that it is completed.

Not important but urgent tasks

Not important but urgent tasks are the ones that most prevent us from achieving our goals. Often, these are tasks taken on in error and even regret. Could we have said 'no' to taking on this task, in the first place? Was this delegated to us but could have been avoided if we had kept to boundaries? Ideally, these tasks could be delegated or deferred so that they do not take us away from our important tasks. Sometimes, these tasks should be scheduled if they are reoccurring in nature. For example, student questions or requests might not be 'important' to achieving our goals for this week but this is often an urgent expectation as part of our roles. Therefore, scheduling office hours for students ensures that time is allocated and that important tasks are not interrupted.

Not important and not urgent

Not important and not urgent tasks should be avoided whenever possible. Some can simply be ignored or deleted from the to-do list. Others, which have been imposed or have been added to our to-do lists by virtue of others, should be re-evaluated. Consider if it is possible to politely decline. Be aware of why these items were part of your to-do list in the first place and how to avoid adding them in future.

Résumé and reference systems

Two additional priorities for academic workers, irrespective of discipline or stage, are keeping up-to-date personal résumés and references.

Résumés are often mentioned and used in academic workplaces (Semenza, 2014) but seldom discussed. These days, it is not uncommon for academic workers to have to keep two or even three different paper and online versions. Keep an up-to-date résumé containing accurate and comprehensive information on your academic work. Develop a system to manage your résumé(s) that is smooth and accurate – record all the work outcomes that are required. Establishing academic workers should seek good examples of résumé formats that are clear, clean and contain necessary information (Semenza, 2014), and establish their own versions. Updating periodically, such as every month or quarter, is better than leaving it for 6 or even 12 months. Establish a 'parking-lot' computer file and/or paper folder for quickly filing outputs. You are likely to need physical copies of abstracts, manuscripts, books, and teaching evaluations for job or promotion applications, so maintain good online and paper systems that allow your years of output to be documented.

Similarly, maintain one or more bibliometric/reference database(s) to help organize litera-ture, reading, and writing. These tasks have become much easier with technology. A number of widely available and relatively inexpensive reference management platforms exist along with a smaller number of less sophisticated but free open-access systems in the public domain.

The reference management systems can be used for a variety of purposes: for your own citations, to keep track of interesting reading or seminal articles or as a receptacle for citations for each project or a larger meta-library for all of your projects, reading, and writing. This meta-library is bigger and less likely to be confused with other libraries but all too quickly gets very large and unwieldy. The purpose of your system will dictate how you would organize the citations and the categories used and how many different databases you would set up. Start your bibliometric system early in your academic project or career rather than piece it together when all your reading, thinking, and writing is done. Develop good habits in your file man-agement and maintain good practices in file completion and management to allow the added value of a bibliometric system to be realized.

Why so obvious?

The high volume and wide prevalence of every task in academic work might suggest that academic workers would obviously prioritize doing this work effectively. Indeed, as we have shown, lots can be done to further this. Managing everyday tasks well – notably emails and meetings – may not be immediately attractive but allows other academic work to be done better. The science of marginal gains shows that these everyday tasks are integral to success.

As such, academic workers dismiss the costs of not doing everyday tasks well at their peril. Common sense, Voltaire mused, is anything but common. Consequently, it's common to dismiss or downplay the importance of improving in everyday tasks and/or focusing only on the more attractive tasks that teaching, research, and engagement provide. Arguably, this shows the need for more self-work, stemming from a mistaken identification of academic work with an identity ideal that precludes anything as humble as seeking to streamline and improve in everyday tasks. This is, we contend, neither intellectual nor ethical: it is akin to attempting the other tricky tasks of academic work with one hand tied behind your back. To do this extreme knowledge work, all advantages help, and managing everyday tasks in academic work can bring such advantages to the head, heart, and soul.

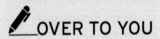 OVER TO YOU

Using the Eisenhower Matrix

Look at the to-do list that you are currently using or think about the tasks that you have been working on this week. Where do these tasks fall on the matrix in Table 11.2?

Table 11.2 Using the Eisenhower Matrix

	Important	Not Important
Urgent		
Not Urgent		

1. What changes do you need to make based on your findings? For example, are there tasks that should be deleted or actions taken to move tasks out of the Important and Urgent box?

═══ REMARKABLE RESOURCES ═══

Things (https://culturedcode.com/things)

This app can help you maintain your to-do tasks list from your phone, laptop, smart watch, or tablet. It's simple but has just enough features to help you do everything you need. Many other to-do list apps also exist; find one that works for you and integrate it into your daily life.

(Continued)

Trello (www.trello.com)

A versatile online 'productivity platform' that can be used to manage all manner of different projects, from simple personal to-do lists to complex long projects involving many other people and parts (https://trello.com). Simple to use and easy to access from your computer or smartphone, the adaptation of this platform is key to why so many project managers rely on it to meet their goals by getting the right tasks done.

SECTION 3

BRINGING IT ALL TOGETHER

For the great doesn't happen through impulse alone, and is a succession of little things that are brought together.

(Vincent van Gogh, 1882)

The challenges of academic work leave one breathless. Sometimes, feeling hopeless too. High work volume, astonishing diversity, growing casualization and high expectations amongst a million other things. For this, *all* you bring is this thing you call 'The Core'? And a pyramid? Just baubles to peddle against the biggest and most magnificent of challenges: to develop and share new knowledge, to do academic work? Indeed, that is exactly what we've brought. Not to undermine the scale, depth, or range of the immense challenges of academic work but to focus on those facets that will most likely see us through. The battles will never go away, challenging events beyond our control *will* happen. Life is often going to be far from perfect, but the right academic work can get done.

The demands of our urgent work cry out for attention. Now. But while a focus on those tasks give a sense of preoccupation and even work progress, this risks failing to recognize that academic work is extreme knowledge work and needs to be approached, accordingly. It seems less congruent with our instincts to prioritize developing The Core, use The Success Pyramid or to delve deep in order to explore values or do self-work: dwelling on these lacks immediacy or even seems indulgent. The never-ending academic work makes never-ending demands of the tasks to be done, to be done quickly and to be done quicker still. Don't dare step away from the tyranny of the work. However, it is by stepping away, delving deeper and then focusing down that helps the right academic work be done via the emergent powers of the various parts of The Core and The Success Pyramid. As ways of seeing, dealing with and doing the right academic work, these allow a foundation that better acknowledges the extreme knowledge work of academic work.

Each of the following academic worker's situations is used to illustrate how to apply the concepts detailed in this book, particularly around the nature of academic work, The Core and The Success Pyramid, and how these elements can be brought together in daily academic work challenges. These are, of course, tracings: pen pictures that remove and edit elements of humanity but represent some of the many who have participated in workshops that we have led over the years.

While the aim of this chapter is to illustrate the application of The Success Pyramid and The Core, we hope to convey the ways in which these can be applied – how their facets can influence each other to your benefit and offer solutions. It is less important what these solutions actually are; even around the same challenges identified in the chapter, different priorities will be important for different academic workers. What is more important is the practice of seeing your work in terms of The Success Pyramid and of seeing and setting your responses to presented challenges more in terms of The Core. While we suggest solutions to the challenges detailed in this chapter, you will have your own solutions to your own challenges using The Core: more than one is likely to solve any one particular challenge.

EMERGING ACADEMIC WORKER: THE DOCTORAL MILIEU

Michael is in the haze of his PhD. During the third year of his doctoral studies at a research-intensive university, now in his late twenties, he feels depressed and is not making any progress relative to others at the same stage. His initial zeal for doing doctoral work has waned into occasional enthusiasm, intermingled with beige periods of flatness, in which finishing seems so far off and the barriers to doing so interminable. *Make sure that you are seen to work long hours and don't admit to having a life outside*, is what he tells himself. Talk of time shortages, increased competitiveness and personal differences are endless and exhausting. Bleakness pervades during these times. *Why does everything take SO long? Why can't he get things done quicker?*

He knows he's not about to rush into a massively wrong career decision; he looks and listens a lot. He feels a lack of 'click' with his supervisors, who keep telling him to buckle down and that everything takes longer than expected. All of this, but also to make himself more competitive for jobs afterwards, he must not only finish his doctorate in time but he also needs to publish at least three papers on the way. When he thinks about his teaching and writing, the psychological tension takes him aback. His blood runs cold. *Why can't he be better?* He looks at what others do and tries to crib, borrow and steal good habits, but mostly the manuscript-writing and teaching prep still feel laborious in process and limited in outcomes. He wonders sometimes how he even ended up on the doctoral journey in the first place – let alone why he would choose academic work for a life. If he can't muster the hunger and happiness needed for his PhD, how could he ever contemplate a life doing this work? His university offers some courses on workplace skills and career development but, along with the other doctoral students, he struggles to plough on with the 'real work' for as much time as possible during waking hours.

He's not even sure that he wants to follow the academic route any more. What about a career in government instead? It seems a lot less about insane work expectations. He tried to broach his thoughts with a couple of older, salaried academic workers in his department whom he likes but got varied advice: that his path to an academic career is destined and he needs to focus, or to go with what he really wants to do. If only he knew. Being a doctoral student was supposed to be about exciting research and making a difference but it now seems a place of uncertainty and flux.

Commentary: Michael's Doctoral Milieu

Michael's challenges reflect acclimatization to the nature of academic work, and workplaces. His challenges speak to the difficulties of the overpowering norms to work longer and harder, and the worry about outputs, which lead to chasing shorter-term goals. What to stand for amidst the vicissitudes of academic work?

Doctoral study is the first exposure to the messy realities of academic work, workers, and the workplace. Work that has so many difficulties that don't readily label themselves. Supervisors who fight, not only with students but also with each other. No one telling you what the answer is or what to do. Issues, for Michael and all those involved in doctoral work, are about the realities of extreme knowledge work.

This seems theoretical but, in the mix, it is first about the challenges of the real world not presenting themselves with neat, inherent labels. This messy milieu is frequently written out and, as such, is unexpected. The doctoral process is represented as a *journey*, implying a sense of destination, apparent progress, momentum, and 'moving towards' that is often lacking in the reality of doctoral work (Thomson and Kamler, 2016) and written accounts of doctoral work. The Success Pyramid and The Core help provide inroads into this messy extreme knowledge work. Faced with a thousand choices about how and what we see, address and do, these suggest that Michael must first start with his chosen success indicators, goals, priorities, and tasks (see Chapters 3–5).

All too readily, the challenge of academic work also becomes about the self, and especially the self-work that we must do. Time and again at our workshops we hear, however, of the harsh, lonely, and drifting realities of doctoral study experiences. Although common, these are seldom shared for fear of being seen to be incompetent, or weak. Deeper still, vulnerability, self-doubt and concern over progress (both current and future) are common but equally taboo. Appearing competent or invulnerable to doubts, focusing on input efforts and working ever more hour stake precedence. Like Michael, this can leave us feeling simultaneously distressed but also unable to really see and enact any alternatives. The commonality of such challenges are as striking as they are difficult. These emotional and intellectual work challenges should be openly discussed with trusted others in academic workplaces.

Michael is grappling with the extreme nature of knowledge work at the doctoral stage. Intellectually *and* emotionally. The past securities of guaranteed outputs from effortful inputs have vanished. Effort no longer yields proportional output. Doing things, keeping busy or, in short, inputs, are seldom the problem – months of tasks can add little value if focused on the wrong tasks, goals, or priorities. But doing the right things requires the discipline to step back and hold our urge in check to rush in and 'do'. This is hard at the doctoral stage because so much is at stake, usually against a financial clock and ticking time. Few stages of academic workers' careers have as much at stake: foundations of qualification, specialization and attractiveness to employers are formed during this period. Moreover, the world is so full of others who look like they are getting on just fine and producing papers, presentations and kudos at every step.

Completing a values inventory (Chapter 2: Values in Academic Work) will help start to inform the ongoing conversation that Michael has over what he should stand for in his work. Thinking about his mid-term job market aims (notably, completing his doctorate and publications) will require using The Success Pyramid in order to prioritize his main success indicators: finishing his doctorate in five years and publishing credibly in the meantime. By focusing on developing The Core, if he can build at least two of the papers from his reading and thinking (Chapter 6: Creativity) around his methods and literature review, this would be a strategic 'double-word' score (Chapter 4: Doing the Right Things I), helping him develop his thesis but making him more competitive in the job hunt. Writing well (Chapter 10: Write Anything Better) will be key, so prioritizing further developing his ability to write methods publications offers a strategic stream of development. Investing time in developing his writing of manuscripts in relation to methods is an important priority. Reading past published methods papers and using a rhetorical approach or MARKET to develop the vision and content of his own will be more important than just rushing to write.

Mentors are often proposed as being useful aids in navigating the messiness of the academic milieu. Indeed, human work and relationships are key to getting academic work done. But it is not unusual to get different, conflicting or even bad advice from otherwise clever, well-intentioned and successful mentors. Advice in mentorship relationships is given from distinctive and not always well-informed perspectives. Broadening Michael's relational networks – particularly of mentors – is important, especially when he has relied on a small number of people immediately around him up to this point (Chapter 7: Human Work and Self-Work). Prioritizing building these broader relationships, even meeting one new person every couple of months who could be a potential mentor, is likely to help Michael get different perspectives on his academic work challenges: someone who, while not offering the same advice, would offer a range of perspectives on his situation. He could prioritize meeting people from complementary but different disciplines, inside and outside his workplace, with different styles/research methods, in different life stages. The challenges of academic work will not go away and academic jobs aren't for everyone. Michael needs to continue to reflect on and build his capacity to deal with extreme knowledge work. This will help address whether the academic career is right for him.

ESTABLISHED ACADEMIC WORKER: THE SQUEEZED MIDDLE

Lesley is seven years post-PhD and firmly ensconced in an academic career. She has a sense that this was and is right for her and intends to stay in academia for the rest of her life. After three short-term contracts, she has been in a temporary academic position for nearly six years and has been promoted once. Her contracts are usually six months to two years. While these contracts are short, her boss has always worked something out to make sure that she is kept on. This really gets her down. With her partner, she has two children (a son aged 12 and a daughter aged 5), who both play soccer twice a week. Her daughter just started piano lessons. Her time scarcity just went another notch higher and although she tries to juggle the driving, it always seems to her like she is absorbing all the family work and working later in the night or getting up at 5 a.m. to get some exercise and work in before everyone else awakes. Outside work, her partner is broadly supportive but is frustrated over how distracted she often is and why her employer can't seem to provide a longer contract. She's always feeling pressed, like her work is never done.

Lesley loves doing academic work and wants to do it as best she can. She thinks that it will get easier as the children get older. Workwise, her job involves a one-third blend of teaching, research, and engagement. She judges her work progress on developing her profile and résumé around teaching and research to have been steady. Trying to strike the elusive 'work–life balance', she feels on the precipice of compromising her personal and work life too much. She goes into work after dropping off her children at school and leaves at 4 p.m. sharp. Her family (especially her in-laws) comment on her working so much, and she can't help but think that her work colleagues are watching her, thinking that she is shirking by coming in later and leaving earlier. She used to feel guiltier but blocks out those feelings now.

Her publications tick along, her teaching is solid and she is involved in some decent committees, internally and externally. She wants to reach full professor status but she has received feedback that she needs to become more internationally known, especially by presenting her work in keynotes and prestigious international meetings. *But how to make travel plans, amongst everything else, to make this happen?* She wonders if there could be other routes to promotion. *There must be more than one path, right?* The thought of presenting more also makes her heart sink. Other people can be so exhausting and it's a part of her job that has never felt comfortable for her. That, and the dreaded networking. She feels that she has done okay with her smaller and more familiar group of collaborators. She knew that academic work was not easy, but wonders whether she is actually better off holding her life together and not pushing for promotion.

Commentary: Lesley's no-win situation

Academic work seldom occurs separately from our wider lives or roles. Extreme knowledge work means that our values, priorities, and tasks between work and non-work (so-called 'life') fuse, cross, and intersect. The rewards for academic work in the short- or mid-term are often not a permanent contract with a glossy salary. The combined effects of these are not just cognitive but emotional: we feel torn, strained, and compromised by the work and people that we feel so strongly for and about. The physical sensations of inadequacy, what Brown (2012) even terms 'shame', that arises from our struggles to fulfil work and home roles adequately are all too common and not confined by gender, age, or family structures.

Lesley's focus should orientate around self-work and prioritizing the right work, strategically. The realities of modern academic workplaces – increasing casualization, inequities in opportunity, pay and progression, and heavy demands around working hours – are unfair. Addressing these facets is important but also challenging in the middle of 'all the things'.

Inevitably, Lesley's time will always be filled and she will always feel pressed by the squeeze of work and home on her 1440 daily minutes. To tame this, Lesley's main success indicator (Chapter 3: Success and Its Indicators) – getting a permanent position with promotion – will need to inform her priorities mercilessly. To identify the tasks, goals, and priorities (Chapter 4–5: Doing the Right Things), she needs to accomplish to attain promotion, she has to discover whether she can counter her lack of capacity to present internationally with other options. The semi-occluded game of promotion in her workplace will need to be uncovered, not only by heavily scrutinizing the criteria but via talking to others, particularly those who have faced similar challenges or who have served on or made these decisions (Chapter 3: Success and Its Indicators). Good relationships with others will help these conversations to take place and will also help make them candid (Chapter 7: Human Work and Self-Work). This will better ensure that she can prioritize the right tasks and goals.

Working strategically – truly strategically – drawing on the insights of *Good Strategy/Bad Strategy* (Rumelt, 2011) so as to incorporate extreme focus, amplification and leverage to guide her priorities and tasks will be key to gaining disproportionally good outcomes from the time that she puts in, to particular tasks associated with her promotion (Chapter 4: Doing the Right Things). Her inevitable challenges about fitting all her tasks into 1440 minutes will also be aided by developing via The Core: perfecting the habits and systems that she has around everyday tasks (Chapter 11: Developing Better Habits and Systems for Everyday Tasks). As well as always seeking to improve the effectiveness and efficiencies around this, always prioritizing funds for keeping a research assistant to keep on top of these everyday tasks will allow her to prioritize focusing on the things that only she can do.

Lesley risks feeling tired and lacking in creativity because of the high volume and incessant nature of the demands on her at home and in work. Making choices to make it possible for Lesley to get away to focus on something beyond her immediate demands will be important, yet difficult to do. It will not happen by magic and she will have to enforce it. How can she do this while also retaining her sense of competency and sufficiency? How can she do this when her inbox, in-tray and work tasks overflow? It will be difficult but, by letting go and leaving 'it all' behind to do something else, this can help her regenerate her creative side (Chapter 6: Creativity: Adding the Vital Spark). Knowledge work, extreme as it is, needs the extra gears of the freshness that this provides. This is not work-shy but supremely work-pragmatic.

Finally, self-work also has a place in addressing some of the elements of academic work that Lesley feels are less congruent with her personality and predisposition – especially around building relationships with people whom she does not know (in her eyes, the dreaded 'networking') and presenting her work. Getting better and feeling better will not just happen. Seeing these 'zones' of her work as being amenable to improvement but also engaging in self-work and learning/development to improve comfort and then skill in these areas is important (Chapter 7: Human Work and Self-Work). Podcasts on networking, presenting, and work skills offer a means to engage with professional development resources when she is also fulfilling her other life necessities, such as exercise or driving (Chapter 8: Learning Success, Failure, and the Growth Mindset). When attending conferences to present, Lesley may find that harnessing insights from rhetoric will help her not only with presentations but also to connect with the different types of people whom she will meet in social situations (Chapter 9: Influence: Persuasion and Connection). This then exemplifies the added value of The Core: the notion that developing these core skills can benefit across a wide variety of different kinds of academic tasks. The puzzles and challenges of academic work – fair and unfair – will always be with her, but by focusing strategically there is much that she can do.

ESTABLISHED ACADEMIC WORKER: STEPPING OUT

Helen has been in the academic work game for 25 years. She's seen heads of department and deans – maybe seven or eight from her memory – come and go. The years pass. She still essentially enjoys her job as a full professor but with retirement now less than five years away, she is long past stressing about the small stuff of her work or bothering too much with other academic workers. But she also feels hollow ... *Is she just holding down a job until inevitable retirement?* She did hope to build something bigger once, in terms of her research, but it never seemed to happen.

Her teaching and research are not going to change much now. She gets consistently favourable evaluation on her work, and although she very much works in her comfort zone, she has developed good habits to ensure that the flow of every task needing done around her work is contained and well managed. She tends to work the same 45-hour week, and stretches research projects to keep work within these limits. She had thought that she was doing exactly what was expected of her: focusing down and engaging her students. However, her head of department approached her and confided that she believed that Helen was not engaged or inputting to the Department as much as she could be. That she was 'coasting' and not contributing enough to the growth of the Department. Helen was shocked to hear this: it made her immediately angry. She had spent years not being difficult with the administration and other colleagues and had kept her teaching and research afloat across all the ups and downs over the decades. This felt like a real betrayal to her and the thought of 'doing as she was told' and toeing the line made her recoil. She could barely comprehend the conversation that had taken place, wondering, *am I really disengaged like this?*

She reflected as hard on this as her overpowering feelings of hurt allowed. Helen had admittedly reconciled herself long ago to protect herself from other people's conduct or unreasonable expectations; she tries to keep out of the gaze of others and do the work she really wants to. This provides a space of solace to the craziness she often feels around her in her department; it gives her permission to have interesting relationships with her students. She really cares about the students and will miss them when she retires. Being around younger people, she finds, keeps her fresh and engaged, but she feels, too, the pressure to get her students 'done' quickly. She really feels that it is increasing and it's not a pleasant feeling. *What of their development?* The debates and discussions along the way and, above all, seeing the students grow – this is what gives her so much pride.

Beyond her teaching and research, Helen feels no inclination to get involved in administration or to work much with others. Things don't seem like they will ever be different in her department anyways, and no one seems to listen or to 'be' her type of person. She goes into the office now as little as she can get away with, and apart from a few nods and social niceties to those in the offices around her, she keeps to herself. The rot set in about ten years ago, when the government put the pressure on for a more corporate, managerial model: more 'deliverables' and 'impact'. Buzzwords like 'excellence', 'dynamic' and 'innovation' mask the micro-management appraisal culture that seems to pervade. That's not what she signed up for. Academic workers, the supposed super-heroes, are actually the super-regulated. Some weeks whizz by towards her retirement but mostly they plod. *How did her university and department come to this?*

Commentary: Helen's non-quandary quandary

Some of the biggest challenges that academic workers face arise because the right success indicators are not readily apparent or work is focused on passing time rather than success and priorities as per The Success Pyramid. The reasons for her hollow feelings don't readily present themselves in extreme knowledge work as symptoms of labeled problems. While there is a lack of insufficient happiness for Helen to provide deep fulfilment in her work, she has insufficient unhappiness to motivate the urgency to take steps to change course. What should she do different? Moreover, should she do anything different at all?

The sense of time passing by beyond success indicators is not uncommon. Academic workplaces that offer permanence around contracts may provide high levels of job security for senior staff. This protects and provides important stability to do academic work. Yet, over the long term, the individual academic worker makes decisions, day after day, year after year, over how to do their academic work, to a varying degree what this work is focused on and to what end. The vast majority of support for doing academic work remains focused on emerging academic workers at or close to the start of their careers on either side of the doctorate. Yet, the challenges of doing academic work and staying not only effective and successful but also happy over decades can be quite different. With so many factors at play – and so many other people, too – staying enfranchised, engaged and even excited about academic work is, indeed, a feat. With decades of experience, doing the right tasks is not a challenge for Helen, but pinpointing the right course via the right success indicators is Helen's challenge.

What are Helen's success indicators for the final few years of her academic career? Certainly, they are likely to be different to those that have come before. But is she really clear on these now? Once her time is done, it's done. The daily clock on her remaining work time counts down with each day. No one is going to set these indicators for her and these will not find her by magic. Even if her success indicators are more self-focused, identifying these more overtly will help her plan and use her time to prioritize better (Chapter 3: Success and Its Indicators).

Furthermore, finding the right success indicators involves something of a conundrum about what the issue is that Helen should address via her success indicators. While some may see Helen as being 'disengaged' and even 'difficult', she could be seen as being well focused on her priorities – true to her earlier career success indicators around teaching students well and retaining a sense of integrity and fit when academic workplace framings, priorities and expectations seem to change before her eyes. What from one perspective looks like calculated disengagement may be more about self-protection from the perceived 'values gap' that guide a person's academic work and those that are seen to be dominant in the working culture or evident in other people (Chapter 2: Values in Academic Work). That said, her emotions tell her that she is not happy. Something is wrong: this is not the life of academic work that brings her deep fulfilment. But what then?

Can Helen challenge herself to get and remain uncomfortable: to put herself more 'out there' in her department? To risk frustration and annoyance she anticipates with her colleagues but perhaps more meaningfully also contribute to the students' education in new and different ways – one of her most important success indicators. Doing so will require more self-work. This may be fruitful not only for herself but also for her workplace and colleagues: the most experienced academic workers can make dramatic and profound differences to academic work cultures, particularly when they share their own failures (Chapter 8: Learning: Success, Failure, and the Growth Mindset).

The apathy that she feels around her workplace is real and Helen is not sure exactly why she feels this so acutely. More self-work – particularly, reflection and openness to her own feelings – will help clarify what's contributing to her malaise. Building stronger relationships with others (Chapter 7: Human Work and Self-Work), including being far slower to judge their actions and motivations, may also ease her feelings of anger and negativity. Prioritizing building these stronger relationships with her colleagues presents risks and the potential for disappointment, but also for new insights and experiences with the people around her. While she is unlikely to find some mysterious utopian connection, the workable strain of others and herself may be more sustaining than stepping out of so much in her workplace.

If Helen's case, and any of the others', look messy, vague in parts and inconclusive in ending, that's because they are. The challenges that academic workers face in being and staying effective, successful, and happy can be clouded in ambiguity, and our own motivations can be hard to discern, evident more in our emotions in real situations than the stories we may tell others and ourselves. Our predicaments around work reflect not just ourselves but also the workplace contexts that we find ourselves in and the relationships that we have with others. In The Success Pyramid, a consideration of what success is to be for us and what then to prioritize and enact in goals and tasks will routinely serve us well, providing that it is linked to a nuanced consideration of our values. Developing self-work, human work, being creative, taming everyday tasks, seeking some influence, and learning as we go (all parts of The Core) provide a means to channel our efforts and to focus them on what matters most to us and meet the career-long challenge of being effective, successful, and happy in our work.

In summary, these three academic workers reflect parts of the different and vast types of challenges of academic work at different stages. The challenges for established academic workers tend to arise more from ambiguity around, or sheer misalignment of their success indicators with their work. Truly facing this requires courage, even during the late stages of your career, to be brutally honest about your values and whether your work still aligns with them. It's much easier just to let time go by. The success indicators during mid- and early careers tend to be more to the fore, but the time and energy to do them – particularly amidst the failures and constraints of academic work – is difficult.

It is less important here to come to the right answers for our three workers than to show how the concepts within The Success Pyramid and The Core can be used to overlay, interpret, and ask right but challenging questions of our own academic work and, most vitally, of ourselves.

12

WHAT NEXT...?

Never doubt that a small group of thoughtful, committed citizens can change the world; indeed, it's the only thing that ever has.

(Margaret Mead)

Writing is, indeed, discovery, and this book has been no exception. Completing it provided us with the opportunities to reflect anew on the future of academic work but also on reactions to its content and on our own academic work. As this book nears its end, we speculate here on the future of academic work and make space for introspections around the book itself.

However, we know that this book poses more hard questions than easy answers: we don't think that the secret in academia is slowing work down, getting personally more comfortable, or waiting for others to change. Readers who feel consistently piqued should recognize that strong reactions are always the most telling, and if this book opens space for debate, discussion, and disagreement, then this is not only a good thing but it is what academic workplaces need if they are to meet the changing needs of societies, students, and knowledge for the future.

THE FUTURE OF ACADEMIC WORK

If academic work seems challenging and vulnerable now, what of its future? What of, pointedly, the future of academic workers and workplaces? Few predicted how the world would change in 2017 – particularly the rise in power of so-called populist movements across Europe and the USA. This has led to major reductions in sector funding to academic workplaces, changes to funding eligibility for academic workers and both increased scepticism of, and urgency for, the process and fruits of academic work: knowledge, truth, and science (Judis, 2016). These seismic changes occur, perhaps not coincidentally, in times when workers and human work is in peril: up to 35–45 per cent of today's workers may be replaced in the workplace by robots in the next 20 years (BBC, 2016; White, 2017). While advances in technology and artificial intelligence research and innovation is driving this growth, these robots will have little need for traditional forms of academic learning.

Those students who remain will have grown up with Netflix on-demand models of consumption and are likely to seek and expect education when, where, and how they choose: unbundled, user-friendly and totally accessible via technology (La Belle, 2016). Platforms of learning that, compared to today, are much more data-driven and then more primed to be responsive to each student and offer higher perceived value for money (Alferovs, 2017).

It's hard to say what academic workplaces will look like in the mid-term decade, let alone in a distant future. The rising consumer costs of a degree education do not tally well with these trends. Everyday tasks, including responding to student emails, could be performed automatically using artificial intelligence assistants (Niemtus, 2017). To reduce costs further, the ever greater job casualization of academic workers (Chakrabortty and Weale, 2006) undermines both sustainability and ethics in academic workplaces. While research funding gets more competitive, so, too, do the expectations of academic workers diversify. Alt-metrics, fuelled by the perceived need for academic work to generate broader societal impacts, evolve to measure ever more aspects of teaching, research, and engagement.

These disruptive changes and the demands that these make on academic workers shed light on the benefits of approaches, such as those detailed in this book in The Success Pyramid and The Core, which focus on deeper skills and habits rather than on tasks. While the tasks of academic work and the expectations around them will surely change, we believe that the underlying skills and mindsets which help academic workers to do this extreme knowledge work will transcend.

NEXT STEPS: WHERE DO WE GO FROM HERE?

This book's content is likely to be used in different ways by different readers. We've covered topics that are conceptually simple but likely to provide a lifetime's worth of diverse challenges and learning. Incorporating your personal values in your work, 'doing the right things', and self-work remain some of the hardest challenges for any knowledge worker.

Likewise, individual personalities may either draw or repel you from particular facets of what we have addressed and recommended. As with life, for each of us personally, changes in some directions are relatively easy to do, whereas others will require our proverbial 'hell' to freeze over before we can face making those changes.

Don't implement or enact all the content of this book all at once. Rather, work to identify which facets will allow you to make at least some preliminary changes. Then act. This combats the allure of inspiration – a state in which generalized contemplation and emotions of change and improvement stand as 'warm and fuzzy' replacements for any form of subsequent personal action to change or improve. Pointedly: start now and start somewhere.

START NOW AND START SOMEWHERE

Your immediate changes could be as large and time-consuming as reformulating your success indicators and priorities for the next three years or could be as small and instantanious as removing all the email from your main inbox and archiving it to start anew. Changes, like this are more concrete – but some of the hardest changes are likely related to doing self-work around your own mindset, fears, and emotions. These still involve actions – and can be some of the changes that impact most on happiness, effectiveness, and success. Just keep progressing.

Don't expect your changes to have predestined or instant payoffs – as extreme knowledge work, academic work is not like that. Yet, however small, keep progressing and, as much as you can, lean into the discomfort of uncertainty about what could, might, or you worry will, happen. You may find some concepts or insights that had previously seemed incidental or peripheral to take on profoundly new significance or power. Because of this, revisit and reflect the various facets we have outlined when you feel called to. These still keep giving back to us in ways we don't expect.

Like any change in behaviour, mindset or established patterns, the challenge is not only starting but also sticking to it – particularly when academic workplaces and fellow workers contain so much noise around what our own work *should* look like. It can be hard to leave work on schedule, be seen to 'say no', make strategic choices, or write less but write better. It may seem easier to stay in our 'effectiveness closet' and remove all talk of aspiring to be happy from our workplace.

We encourage small groups or *communities of practice* of academic workers to get together to reflect on and discuss their mutual challenges around effectiveness, success, and happiness in their workplaces. Sharing with, and caring for each other around these concepts form important and sustaining elements to help avoid assimilation into ineffective work cultures. In time, these cultures can be resisted, and then changed by courageous individuals and groups. In many ways, this is what so many academic workplaces now need.

If you found this book useful, please share your thoughts, feedback, and stories of success, challenge, and failure with us and others via our Twitter account (@EffectiveAcad, #happyacademic) and webpage (www.effectiveacademic.com). Sharing learning in this way is immensely helpful and mutually beneficial. In our respective academic roles, workplaces, countries, and continents it reminds us each that we are never alone in and on our journeys. We can learn so much from sharing, discussing, and reflecting on our challenges to be effective, successful, and happy in academic work.

WHAT WE LEARNED DURING THE WRITING OF THIS BOOK

Books express their writers' experiences but shape their experiences, too. We wrote this book during one of the most unpredictable and challenging periods of our professional lives. A time that tested us more than we could have ever expected – and from so many directions. Stoical perspective is everything. No one died or was hurt: what really was the worst that could happen?

Yet, the intensity with which academic work occupies us, the passion that we have for *our* work and the struggles that we face with uncertainty, doubt, and vulnerability strike us anew. As we continued to develop and apply the concepts in this book, particularly around The Success Pyramid and The Core, what new insights emerged during our journey?

It's never just words

Each week, we *still* grapple with many of the challenging concepts and advice that we have described in this book. Vulnerability, fear, uncertainty, stress, anxiety, worry. These are *never* just words or part of follow-me phrases, but real and powerful human states. Other people's crises, questions, and experiences are never just words: they are as real, forceful, and dizzying for others as they are for us. We understand this more and better now than ever before. Returning to and remembering the physical and emotional sensations of these experiences brings empathy to our academic work and interactions with others.

Similarly, openness is not just a word. We may talk, cast up and challenge others 'to be open', but authentic practice of being and staying open remains elusive in the midst of strong emotions and intrusive thoughts. A journey rather than a destination, being open is never just a word. It is a constant challenge to the self to listen deeply, always question and step into the vulnerability of being and staying open.

Values are essential, especially when times are toughest

When academic life is at its toughest – when our workplaces and work pose the hardest questions and challenges to us in the most tiresome and mischievous ways – it's tempting to rail against the source of our all-too-real ills. Yet, amidst the noise, we found that there is never a more important time than our toughest times to make space to come back to what really is most important: personal values. Day by day, we strive to honour these values and use them to guide our minds and efforts in many ways. Even smaller, everyday tasks can rekindle 'energy' for work and provide much needed solace and re-founding. When it's hardest to draw on values, this is when values matter most.

It's tough because it is tough

The trials and tribulations of academic work and workplaces arise because of the extreme nature of this knowledge work. Working with others always brings challenges. Every day. With all that can go wrong and fail, nevertheless, expectations for us are high and so, so wide. Academic work is tough. If we expect academic work to be smooth, predictable and easy … such scenarios are best seen as exceptions, not expectations.

In our experience, this book is least likely to be read by those academic workers who most need to read it. That said, this book can, with certainty, stand to make a difference to this tough reality, replete as this is with uncontrollable factors, people, and events, because it is being read by the one person in the world who can, with certainty, enact its vision. You. This is what we each strive to enact each day, too.

Read your surprises

Our feelings and emotions can still surprise us. Reactions of high intensity are very challenging to live through but offer some of the most precious opportunities for learning. Intense reactions, from anger and frustration to doubt or fear, offer enticing possibilities of insight and self-growth. These come at times, however, when we are, by circumstance, less predisposed to be open or take time to find peace to scrutinize and explore our own reactions.

Similarly, instances when emotions and reactions surprise with their calmness provide opportunities for our learning. What is it that has contributed to this calmness? What self-work has brought us to this place? How can this help in other areas? Understanding what has helped make the difference is as important as understanding where things go awry. Learning occurs everywhere.

Practise, improve, progress OR fail, learn, try again

Others seem to have parts of academic life figured out more than I do. Familiar thought? Yet, be wary of this story – one will never know if it is true and it is also unlikely to help in your work. More than ever, we realize now that academic work involves a journey of continuous and hard learning. We experience this every day.

Academic work and workplaces are tricky, vexing, and sometimes overwhelming. There is so much that cannot be controlled. So many other people and *all* their issues. And we are putting so much of ourselves in the game, too. Being effective, successful and happy amidst the challenges of academic work is not about other people or even behaving naturally one-self. Focusing down on personal success indicators, not responding to what is easy (emails anyone?) and dwelling on self-work when others are difficult – these are continuously challenging. Learning to approach and do better is continuously challenging, too.

Much like meditation, it takes time, deliberative effort and ongoing failures to progress in The Core and The Success Pyramid. Development of your mindset and skills in the domains of The Core are likely to impact across the various tasks involved in academic work more readily. However, the full strategic power of your efforts, and the value of your time, will only become more fully realized when elements of The Core affect, leverage, and amplify each other. These effects are integral to the synergeries The Core captures – but may take time to develop and evolve. Our journeys have to be our own. Learning – even around the smallest of everyday tasks (Amabile and Kramer, 2011) – is more important than attaining any finalized sense of 'getting there' or 'reaching'.

If you struggle with the realities of being effective, successful, and happy in this work, then know that we, and almost all academic workers, do, too. The challenges of academic work are never-ending and will never end. Our struggles are far less a reflection of us being inept at this work than of being truly open to its realities, potentialities, and difficulties. Doing academic work well sets us the most personal of challenges to stay engaged, not only with others but particularly with ourselves. To learn and grow not only when it is easy and obvious, but especially when the lessons seem cruel and hard. To strive for good strategy, habits, and systems amidst the shifting sands and pressurized demands. And despite the noise, above all, continue to set our success indicators, priorities, goals, and tasks based on our values. This is academic work. And you have never been more ready for it.

REFERENCES

Aisenberg, N. and Harrington, M. (1988) *Women of Academe: Outsiders in the Sacred Grove*. Boston, MA: University of Massachusetts.

Aiston, S.J. and Jung, J. (2015) 'Women academics and research productivity: An international comparison', *Gender and Education*, 27(3): 205–20.

Aitchison, C. (2009) 'Writing groups for doctoral education', *Studies in Higher Education*, 34: 905–16.

Aitchison, C. and Guerin, C. (eds) (2014) *Writing Groups for Doctoral Education and Beyond: Innovations in Practice and Theory*. London: Routledge.

Aitchison, C. and Lee, A. (2006) 'Research writing: problems and pedagogies', *Teaching in Higher Education*, 11(3): 265–78.

Aitchison, C. and Lee, A. (2010) 'Writing in, writing out', in M. Walker and P. Thomson (eds), *Doctoral Writing as Peer Work: The Routledge Doctoral Supervisor's Companion*. London: Routledge, pp. 260–9.

Alferovs, A. (2017) 'The university of the future: Why universities should embrace learning analytics', *ITProPortal*. Available at: www.itproportal.com/features/the-university-of-the-future-why-universities-should-embrace-learning-analytics/ (accessed 2 November 2017).

Allen, D. (2015) *Getting Things Done: The Art of Stress-Free Productivity*. London: Penguin.

Alvesson, M. (2001) 'Knowledge work: Ambiguity, image and identity', *Human Relations*, 54: 863–86.

Amabile, T. and Kramer, S. (2011) *The Progress Principle: Using Small Wins to Ignite Joy, Engagement and Creativity at Work*. Boston, MA: Harvard Business Review Press.

Andriopoulos, C. (2001) 'Determinants of organizational creativity: A literature review', *Management Decision*, 39(10): 834–40.

Archer, L. (2008) 'Younger academics constructions of "authenticity", "success" and professional identity', *Studies in Higher Education*, 33: 385–403.

Arthur, M.R., Defillipp, R.J. and Lindsay, V.J. (2008) 'On being a knowledge worker', *Organizational Dynamics*, 37: 365–77.

Back, L. (2015) 'On the side of the powerful the "impact agenda" and sociology in public', *Sociological Review*. Available at: www.thesociologicalreview.com/blog/on-the-side-of-the-powerful-the-impact-agenda-sociology-in-public.html (accessed 2 November 2017).

Banks, G.C., O'Boyle, E.H., Pollack, J.M., White, C.D., Batchelor, J.H., Whelpley, C.E., Abston, K.A., Bennett, A.A. and Adkins, C.L. (2016) 'Questions about questionable research practices in the field of management', *Journal of Management January*, 42(1): 5–20.

Barnett, R. (2000) *Realizing the University in an Age of Supercomplexity*. Buckingham: Society for Research into Higher Education (SRHE) and Open University Press.

Barnett, R. (2011) *Being a University, Foundations and Futures of Education*. London: Routledge.

Barnett, R. (2013) *Imagining the University*. Abingdon: Routledge.

Bayles, D. and Orland, T. (1993) *Art & Fear: Observations on the Perils (and Rewards) of Artmaking*. Santa Cruz, CA: Imagine Continuum Press.

BBC (2016) 'Will robots replace workers by 2030?', *BBC News*. Available at: www.bbc.com/news/av/science-environment-38890905/will-robots-replace-workers-by-2030 (accessed 2 November 2017).

Becher, T. and Trowler, P. (2001) *Academic Tribes and Territories: Intellectual Enquiry and the Cultures of Disciplines*, 2nd edn. Buckingham: Society for Research into Higher Education (SRHE) and Open University Press.

Begg, M.D. and Vaughan, R.D. (2011) 'Are biostatistics students prepared to succeed in the era of interdisciplinary science? (And how will we know?)', *American Statistician*, 65: 71–9.

Berg, M. and Seeber, B.K. (2016) *The Slow Professor: Challenging the Culture of Speed in the Academy*. Toronto: University of Toronto Press.

Blackler, F. (1995) 'Knowledge, knowledge work and organizations', *Organization Studies*, 16: 1021–46.

Bogle, D., Dron, M., Eggermont, J. and van Henten, J.W. (2010) *Doctoral Degrees beyond 2010: Training Talented Researchers for Society*. London: League European Research Universities.

Bornmann, L. (2013) 'What is societal impact of research and how can it be assessed: A literature survey', *Journal of the American Society for Information Science and Technology*, 64(2): 217–33.

Bornmann, L. and Mutz, R. (2015) 'Growth rates of modern science: A bibliometric analysis based on the number of publications and cited references', *Journal of the Association for Information Science & Technology*, 66: 2215–22.

Bostock, J. (2014) *The Meaning of Success: Insights from Women at Cambridge*. Cambridge: University of Cambridge.

Boulton, G. and Lucas, C. (2008) *What are Universities For?* Leuven: League of European Research Universities.

Brown, B. (2007) *I Thought it was Just Me (But it Isn't): Telling the Truth about Perfectionism, Inadequacy and Power*. New York: Avery.

Brown, B. (2012) *Daring Greatly: How the Courage to Be Vulnerable Transforms the Way We Live, Love, Parent, and Lead*. London: Avery.

Brown, B. (2017) *Rising Strong: The Reckoning. The Rumble. The Revolution*. New York: Spiegel & Grau.

Brown, D. (2016) Happy: Why More or Less Everything is Absolutely Fine. London: Bantam Press.

Brown, S. (2015) *The Doodle Revolution*. London: Penguin Publishing Group.

Brown, T. (2008) 'Tales of creativity and play', TED Talk. Available at: www.ted.com/talks/tim_brown_on_creativity_and_play?language=en#t-915170 (accessed 2 November 2017).

Buzan, T. and Buzan, B. (1995) *The Mind Map Book: Radiant Thinking – Major Evolution in Human Thought*. London: BBC Books.

Cain, S. (2013) *Quiet: The Power of Introverts in a World that Can't Stop Talking*. New York: Broadway Books.

Campbell, A. (2015) *Winners: And How They Succeed*. London: Hutchinson.

Catmull, E. (2014) *Creativity Inc.: Overcoming the Unseen Forces that Stand in the Way of True Inspiration*. London: Random House.

Catto, J. (2016) *Insanely Gifted: Turn Your Demons into Creative Rocket Fuel*. London: Canongate.

Chai, K.T. (2015) 'Considering a clinical faculty role? Strategies for success', *Nursing*, 45(5): 23–6.

Chakrabortty, A. and Weale, S. (2016) 'Universities accused of "importing Sports Direct model" for lecturers' pay', *The Guardian*. Available at: www.theguardian.com/uk-news/2016/nov/16/universities-accused-of-importing-sports-direct-model-for-lecturers-pay (accessed 2 November 2017).

Christensen, C.M. and Eyring, H.J. (2011) *The Innovative University: Changing the DNA of Higher Education from the Inside Out*. San Francisco, CA: Jossey-Bass.

Clark, A.M. (2014) 'The gift of failure: Learning to provide better cardiac care', *Heart*, 100: 1221–2.

Clark, A.M. and Sousa, B.J. (2015) 'Academics, you are going to fail, so learn how to do it better', *Guardian Higher Education Network*. Available at: www.theguardian.com/higher-education-network/2015/nov/04/academics-you-are-going-to-fail-so-learn-how-to-do-it-better (accessed 2 November 2017).

Clark, A.M. and Thompson, D.R. (2012) 'Heart failure disease management programmes: A new paradigm for research', *Heart*, 98: 1476–7.

Clark, A.M. and Thompson, D.R. (2013) 'Successful failure: good for the self and science', *Journal of Advanced Nursing*, 63: 2145–7.

Clark, A.M. and Thompson, D.R. (2014) 'Succeeding in research: Insights from management and game theory', *Journal of Advanced Nursing*, 69(6): 1221–3.

Clark, A.M. and Thompson, D.R. (2015) '"But how many papers should I write …?" Making good choices about quality, quantity and visibility of academic publications', *Journal of Advanced Nursing*, 71: 1741–3.

Clark, A.M., Choby, A., Ainsworth, K. and Thompson, D.R. (2015) 'Addressing conflict of interest in non-pharmacological research', *International Journal of Clinical Practice*, 69(3): 270–2.

Clark, A.M., Redfern, J., Thirsk, L., Neubeck, L. and Briffa, T. (2012) 'What football can teach us about research and complex interventions', *British Medical Journal*, 345: e8613.

Clear, J. (2014) 'The value of marginal gains', *Lifehacker*. Available at: http://lifehacker.com/the-value-of-marginal-gains-1514453003 (accessed 2 November 2017).

Colzato, L.S., Szapora, A., Pannekoek, J.N. and Hommel, B. (2013) 'The impact of physical exercise on convergent and divergent thinking', *Frontiers of Human Neuroscience*, 7: 284. dx.doi.org/10.3389/fnhum.2013.00824.

Cortada, J.W. (1998a) 'Introducing the knowledge worker', in J. Cortada (ed.), *Rise of the Knowledge Worker*. Woburn, MA: Reed Elsevier, pp. xiii–xix.

Cortada, J.W. (1998b) 'Where did knowledge workers come from?', in J. Cortada (ed.), *Rise of the Knowledge Worker*. Woburn, MA: Reed Elsevier, pp. 3–21.

Cote, J.E. and Allahar, A.L. (2007) *Ivory Tower Blues: A University System in Crisis*. Toronto: University of Toronto Press.

Covey, S.M.R. (2006) *The Speed of Trust: The One Thing that Changes Everything*. New York: Free Press.

Csikszentmihalyi, M. (2008) *Flow: The Psychology of Optimal Experience*. London: Harper Modern Classics.

Darabi, M., Macaskill, A. and Reidy, L. (2017) 'A qualitative study of the UK academic role: Positive features, negative aspects and associated stressors in a mainly teaching-focused university', *Journal of Further and Higher Education*, 41: 566–80.

Decuypere, M. and Simons, M. (2016) 'What screens do: The role of the screen in academic work', *European Educational Research Journal*, 15: 132–51.

Deem, R. (2004) 'The knowledge worker, the manager-academic and the contemporary UK university: New and old forms of public management?', *Financial Accountability & Management*, 20: 107–28.

Defillippi, R.J., Arthur, M.B. and Lindsay, V.J. (2006) *Knowledge at Work: Creative Collaboration in the Global Economy*. Oxford: Blackwell.

Department of Defense (2002) Defense.gov News Transcript: DoD News Briefing – Secretary Rumsfeld and Gen. Myers, United States Department of Defense (defense.gov).

Dolby, R.G.A. (1996) *Uncertain Knowledge*. Cambridge: Cambridge University Press.

Drucker, P. (1963) 'Managing for business effectiveness', *Harvard Business Review*. Available at: hbr.org/1963/05/managing-for-business-effectiveness (accessed 2 November 2017).

Drucker, P. (1967) *The Effective Executive*. London: Collins.

Drucker, P. (1999) 'Knowledge-worker productivity: The biggest challenge', *California Management Review*, 41: 79–94.

Drucker, P. (2006) *The Practice of Management*. London: Harper.

DuBois, J.M., Anderson, E.E., Chibnall, J., Carroll, K., Gibb, T., Ogbuka, C. and Rubbelke, T. (2013) 'Understanding research misconduct: A comparative analysis of 120 cases of professional wrongdoing', *Accountability in Research*, 20(5–6): 320–38.

Dweck, C.S. (2006) *Mindset: The New Psychology of Success: How We Can Learn to Fulfill Our Potential*. New York: Ballantine Books.

Ebadi, A. and Schiffauerov, A. (2016) 'How to boost scientific production? A statistical analysis of research funding and other influencing factors', *Scientometrics*, 106: 1093–116.

Eisenhower, D.D. (1954) 'Address at the second assembly of the World Council of Churches', *The American Presidency Project*. Evanston, IL, 19 August, Speech No. 204.

Equality Challenge Unit (2016) 'Equality in higher education: statistical report 2015', *BMC Medicine*, 13: 232. Available at: www.ecu.ac.uk/publications/equality-higher-education-statistical-report-2015/ (accessed 2 November 2017).

Faigley, L., Graves, R. and Graves, H. (2006) *The Brief Penguin Handbook, First Canadian Edition*. London: Pearson Longman.

Farrazzi, K. (2005) *Never Eat Alone: And Other Secrets to Success, One Relationship at a Time*. London: Crown.

Ferguson, A. and Moritz, M. (2015) *Leading*. London: Hodder & Stoughton.

Fiedler, K. and Schwarz, N. (2016) 'Questionable research practice revisited', *Social Psychological and Personality Science*, 7: 45–52.

Firestein, S. (2016) *Failure: Why Science is so Successful*. Oxford: Oxford University Press.

Freedman, L. (2013) Strategy: A History. Oxford University Press, Oxford.

Frow, J. (2006) *Genre*. London: Routledge.

Gallo, P. (2006) 'This is why relationships still matter at work', *Forbes*. Available at: www.forbes.com/sites/worldeconomicforum/2016/03/16/this-is-why-relationships-matter-at-work/#5228b6bf83a2 (accessed 2 November 2017).

Garcia, H. and Miralles, F. (2017) *Ikigai: The Japanese Secret to a Long and Happy Life*. London: Penguin.

Gentry, R. and Stokes, D. (2015) 'Strategies for professors who service the university to earn tenure and promotion', *Research in Higher Education Journal*, 29: 1–3.

Gingras, Y., Larivière, V., Macaluso, B. and Robitaille, J. (2008) 'The effects of aging on researchers' publication and citation patterns', *Plos ONE*, 3(12): 1–8.

Goffee, R. and Jones, G. (2009) *Clever: Leading Your Smartest, Most Creative People*. Boston, MA: Harvard Business Press.

Goleman, D. (2013) 'The focused leader', *Harvard Business Review*, December. Available at: hbr.org/2013/12/the-focused-leader (accessed 2 November 2017).

Gornall, L. and Salisbury, J. (2012) 'Compulsive working, "hyperprofessionality" and the unseen pleasures of academic work', *Higher Education Quarterly*, 66: 135–54.

Graff, G., Birkenstein, C. and Durst, R. (2009) *They Say, I Say: The Moves that Matter in Academic Writing*. New York: W.W. Norton.

Greco, L., Kraimer, M., Seibert, S. and Sargent, L.D. (2015) 'Career shocks, obstacles, and professional identification among academics', *Academy of Management*. Available at: proceedings.aom.org/content/2015/1/12178.short (accessed 2 November 2017).

Greenhalgh, T. and Fahy, N. (2015) 'Research impact in the community-based health sciences: An analysis of 162 case studies from the 2014 UK Research Excellence Framework', *BioMed Central Medicine*, 13: 232. Available at: http://bmcmedicine.biomedcentral.com/articles/10.1186/s12916-015-0467-4 (accessed 2 November 2017).

Grogan, O. (2017) *Oisin Grogan: The $200 Million Business Coach*. Available at: www.200million coach.com (accessed 2 November 2017).

Guardian Higher Education Network (2014) 'Women in academia: What does it take to reach the top?', *The Guardian*. Available at: www.theguardian.com/higher-education-network/blog/2014/feb/24/women-academia-promotion-cambridge (accessed 2 November 2017).

Halleck, G.B. and Connor, U.M. (2006) 'Rhetorical moves in TESOL conference proposals', *Journal of English for Academic Purposes*, 5(1): 70–86.

Harvard Business Press (2006) *Giving Feedback*. Boston, MA: Harvard Business School Publishing Corporation.

Harvard Business Review (2006) *HBR Guide to Making Every Meeting Matter: Craft a Clear Agenda, Tame Troublemakers*, Follow Through. Boston, MA: Harvard Business Review Press.

Hegarty, J. (2014) *Hegarty on Creativity: There are No Rules*. London: Thames & Hudson.

Heifetz, R., Grashow, A. and Linksy, M. (2009) *The Practice of Adaptive Leadership*. Boston, MA: Harvard Business Press.

Heinrichs, J. (2007) *Thank You for Arguing: What Aristotle, Lincoln, and Homer Simpson Can Teach Us about the Art of Persuasion*. London: Three Rivers Press.

Helms, R.M. (2010) *New Challenges, New Priorities: The Experience of Generation X Faculty*. Cambridge, MA: Collaborative on Academic Careers in Higher Education (COACHE), Harvard Graduate School of Education.

Henkel, M. (2005) 'Academic identity and autonomy in a changing policy environment', *Higher Education*, 49: 155–76.

Henkel, M. (2007) 'Can academic autonomy survive in the knowledge society? A perspective from Britain', *Higher Education Research & Development*, 26(1): 87–99.

Henley, M.M. (2015) 'Women's success in academic science: Challenges to breaking through the ivory ceiling', *Sociology Compass*, 9(8): 668–80.

Henry, T. (2011) The Accidental Creative: How to Be Brilliant at a Moment's Notice. London: Portfolio.

Henry, T. (2013) Die Empty: Unleash Your Best Work Every Day. London: Portfolio.

Holiday, R. (2014) *The Obstacle is the Way*. London: Portfolio.

Horstman, M. (2016) *The Effective Manager*. London: John Wiley.

Hyland, K. (2002) 'Authority and invisibility: Authorial identity in academic writing', *Journal of Pragmatics*, 34: 1091–112.

Irvine, W.B. (2008) *A Guide to the Good Life: The Ancient Art of Stoic Joy*. Oxford: Oxford University Press.

Jerejian, A.C.M., Reid, C. and Rees, C.S. (2013) 'The contribution of email volume, email management strategies and propensity to worry in predicting email stress among academics', *Computers in Human Behavior*, 29: 991–6.

John, J.K., Loewenstein, G. and Prelec, D. (2012) 'Measuring the prevalence of questionable research practices with incentives for truth telling', *Psychological Science*, 23(5): 524–32.

John-Steiner, V. (2000) *Creative Collaboration*. Oxford: Oxford University Press.

Jones, B., Hwang, E. and Bustamante, R.M. (2015) 'African American female professors' strategies for successful attainment of tenure and promotion at predominately white institutions: It can happen', *Education, Citizenship and Social Justice*, 10(2): 133–51.

Judis, J.B. (2016) *The Populist Explosion: How the Great Recession Transformed American and European Politics*. New York: Columbia Global Reports.

Kamler, B. (2008) 'Rethinking doctoral publication practices: Writing from and beyond the thesis', *Studies in Higher Education*, 33(3): 283–94.

Kamler, B. and Thomson, P. (2008) 'The failure of dissertation advice books: Toward alternative pedagogies for doctoral writing', *Educational Researcher*, 37(8): 507–14.

Kamler, B. and Thomson, P. (2014) *Helping Doctoral Students Write: Pedagogies for Supervision*. New York: Routledge.

Katzenbach, J.R. and Smith, D.K. (2003) *The Wisdom of Teams: Creating the High Performing Organization*. New York: Harper Business Essentials.

Kegan, R. and Lahey, L.L. (2016) *An Everyone Culture: Becoming a Deliberately Developmental Organization*. Boston, MA: Harvard Business Review Press.

Kellaway, L. (2006) 'The thankless tasks of academia', *Financial Times*. Available at: www.ft.com/content/3544b206-a6f0-11da-b12c-0000779e2340 (accessed 2 November 2017).

Kimber, M. and Ehrich, L.S. (2015) 'Are Australia's universities in deficit? A tale of generic managers, audit culture and casualization', *Journal of Higher Education Policy and Management*, 37: 83–97.

King, M.M., Bergstrom, C.T., Correll, S.J., Jacquet, J. and West, J.D. (2016) 'Men set their own cities high: Gender and self-citation across fields and over time', *Physics and Society*. arXiv:1607.00376.

King, S. (2000) *On Writing: A Memoir of the Craft*. New York: Scribner.

Kinman, G. (2014) 'Doing more with less? Work and wellbeing and academics', *Somatechnics*, 4(2): 219–35.

Kinman, G. and Wray, S. (2013) *Higher Stress: A Survey of Stress and Wellbeing among Staff in Higher Education*. London: University & College Union.

Knights, D. and Richards, W. (2003) 'Sex discrimination in UK academia', *Gender, Work and Organization*, 10: 213–38.

Koay, D.L. (2015) 'Self-improvement books: A genre analysis'. PhD dissertation, University of Victoria, Victoria.

Kok, S.K., Douglas, A., McClelland, B. and Bryde, D. (2010) 'The move towards managerialism: perceptions of staff in "traditional" and "new" UK universities', *Tertiary Education and Management*, 16: 99–113.

Kolowich, S. (2016) 'The water next time: Professor who helped expose crisis in Flint says public science is broken', *Chronicle of Higher Education*. Available at: chronicle.com/article/The-Water-Next-Time-Professor/235136 (accessed 2 November 2017).

Kruse, K. (2015) *15 Secrets Successful People Know about Time Management: The Productivity Habits of 7 Billionaires, 13 Olympic Athletes, 29 Straight-A Students, and 239 Entrepreneurs*, 1st edn. Philadelphia, PA: The Kruse Group.

Kuntz, A.M. (2012) 'Reconsidering the workplace: Faculty perceptions of their work and working environments', *Studies in Higher Education*, 37(7): 769–82.

Kushlev, D. and Dunn, E. (2015) 'Checking email less frequently reduces stress', *Computers and Human Behavior*, 43: 220–8.

Kwiek, M. and Antonowicz, D. (2013) 'Academic work, working conditions and job satisfaction', in U. Teichler and E.A. Höhle (eds), *The Work Situation of the Academic Profession in Europe: Findings of a Survey in Twelve Countries*. Dordrecht: Springer, pp. 37–54.

Kyvik, S. (2012) 'Academic workload and working time: Retrospective perceptions versus time-series data', *Higher Education Quarterly*, 67: 2–14.

La Belle, C. (2016) 'Netflix and higher education: Leverage, leadership and talent development', *The Evolution*. Available at: evolllution.com/managing-institution/higher_ed_business/netflix-and-higher-education-leverage-leadership-and-talent-development/ (accessed 2 November 2017).

Lanham, R.A. (1991) *The Handlist of Rhetorical Terms*. Berkeley, CA: University of California Press.

Lazarus, R. and Folkman, R. (1984) *Stress, Appraisal and Coping*. London: Springer.

Lea, M.R. and Stierer, B. (2011) 'Changing academic identities in changing academic workplaces: Learning from academics' everyday professional writing practices', *Teaching In Higher Education*, 16(6): 605–16.

Lee, A. and Aitchison, C. (2009) 'Writing for the doctorate and beyond', in D. Bould and A. Lee (eds), *Changing Practices of Doctoral Education*. London: Routledge, pp. 87–99.

Lehrman, R. (2010) *The Political Speechwriters Companion: A Guide for Writers and Speakers*. Washington, DC: CQ Press.

Leith, S. (2012a) *You Talkin' to Me? Rhetoric from Aristotle to Obama*. London: Profile Books.

Leith, S. (2012b) *Words Like Loaded Pistols: Rhetoric from Aristotle to Obama*. New York: Basic Books.

Lesiuk, T. (2005) 'The effect of listening on work performance', *Psychology of Music*, 33: 173–91.

Levine, R., Lin, F., Kern, D., Wright, S. and Carrese, J. (2011) 'Stories from early-career women physicians who have left academic medicine: A qualitative study at a single institution', *Academic Medicine*, 86: 752–8.

Lipton, E. (2015) 'Food industry enlisted academics in G.M.O. lobbying war, emails show', *The New York Times*. Available at: mobile.nytimes.com/2015/09/06/us/food-industry-enlisted-academics-in-gmo-lobbying-war-emails-show.html?_r=0 (accessed 2 November 2017).

Lungeanu, A., Huang, Y. and Contractor, N.S. (2014) 'Understanding the assembly of interdisciplinary teams and its impact on performance', *Journal of Informetrics*, 8(1): 59–70.

Mackenzie, A. and Nickerson, P. (2009) *The Time Trap: The Classic Book on Time Management*. New York: AMACOM.

Malham, H.J. Jr. (2013) *I have a strategy: No you don't. An illustrated guide to strategy*. San Francisco CA: Jossey-Bass.

Manager Tools (2005) 'The art of delegation'. Available at: www.manager-tools.com/2005/08/the-art-of-delegation (accessed 2 November 2017).

Manager Tools (2006) 'Resolving Conflict'. Available at: www.manager-tools.com/2006/08/resolving-conflict (accessed 2 November 2017).

Manager Tools (2016a) Time (Priority) Management – Part 1 - HOF. Available at: https://www.manager-tools.com/2016/10/time-priority-management-part-1-hof (accessed 2 November 2017).

Manager Tools (2016b) 'Work family balance: Chapter 1 go home'. Available at: www.manager-tools.com/2012/08/work-family-balance-chapter-1-go-home (accessed 2 November 2017).

Manager Tools podcasts (2017). Available at: www.manager-tools.com (accessed 2 November 2017).

Matthews, D. (2015) 'Is industry funding undermining trust in science?' *Times Higher Education Supplement*. Available at: www.timeshighereducation.com/features/is-industry-funding-undermining-trust-in-science (accessed 2 November 2017).

Maxwell, J. (2011) *The 360 Degree Leader*. London: Nelson.

McAlpine, L., Jazvak-Martek, M. and Hopwood, N. (2008) 'Doctoral student experience: Activities and difficulties affecting identity development', *International Journal of Graduate Education*, 1(2): 136–49.

McArdle, M. (2014) *The Up Side of Down: Why Failing Well is the Key to Success*. London: Penguin.

McKeown, G. (2014) *Essentialism: The Disciplined Pursuit of Less*. London: Crown.

McMahon, D. (2006) *The Pursuit of Happiness: A history from ancient Greeks to the Present*. London: Penguin.

Metcalfe, A.S. and Gonzalez, L.P. (2013) 'Underrepresentation of women in the academic profession: A comparative analysis of the North American region', *NASPA Journal about Women in Higher Education*, 6(1): 1–21.

Misra, J., Hickes-Lundquist, J. and Templer, A. (2012) 'Gender, work time, and care responsibilities among faculty', *Sociological Forum*, 27(2): 300–23.

Moore, S. (2003) 'Writers' retreats for academics: Exploring and increasing the motivation to write', *Journal of Further and Higher Education*, 27: 333–42.

Moore, S., Neylon, C., Eve, M.P., O'Donnell, D. and Pattinson, D. (2016) 'Excellence R us: University research and the fetishisation of excellence', *figshare*. Available at: figshare.com/articles/Excellence_R_Us_University_Research_and_the_Fetishisation_of_Excellence/3413821 (accessed 2 November 2017).

Murnighan, J.K. (2012) *Do Nothing! How to Stop Overmanaging and Become a Great Leader*. New York: Portfolio/Penguin.

Musselin, C. (2013) 'Redefinition of the relationships between academics and their university', *Higher Education*, 65: 25–37.

Nadolny, A. and Ryan, S. (2013) 'McUniversities revisited: A comparison of university and McDonald's casual employee experiences in Australia', *Studies in Higher Education*, 40: 142–57.

Niemtus, Z. (2017) 'The automated university: Bots and drones amid the dreaming spires', *The Guardian*. Available at: www.theguardian.com/higher-education-network/2017/apr/04/the-automated-university-bots-and-drones-amid-the-dreaming-spires (accessed 2 November 2017).

O'Laughlin, E.M. and Bischoff, L.G. (2005) 'Balancing parenthood and academia: Work/family stress as influenced by gender and tenure status', *Journal of Family Issues*, 26: 79–106.

Omerod, P. (2007) *Why Most Things Fail: Evolution, Extinction and Economics*. London: John Wiley.

Pagnata, S., Lushington, K., Sloan, J. and Buchanan, F. (2015) 'Employees' perceptions of email communication, volume and management strategies in an Australian university', *Journal of Higher Education Policy and Management*, 37: 159–71.

Palmer, P.J. (2007) *The Courage to Teach: Exploring the Inner Landscape of a Teacher's Life*. San Francisco, CA: John Wiley.

Pare, A. (2009) 'Slow the presses: concerns about premature publication', in C. Aitchison and C. Guerin (eds), *Writing Groups for Doctoral Education and Beyond: Innovations in Practice and Theory*. London: Routledge, pp. 30–46.

Payne, E. (2016) 'Female scientists less likely to receive CIHR grants, stats show', *Ottawa Citizen*. Available at: ottawacitizen.com/news/local-news/female-scientists-less-likely-to-receive-cihr-grants-stats-show (accessed 2 November 2017).

Pencavel, J. (2014) *The Productivity of Working Hours*. Bonn: Institute for the Study of Labour.

Peters, S. (2013) *The Chimp Paradox: The Mind Management Program to Help You Achieve Success, Confidence, and Happiness*. London: Penguin.

Pink, D.H. (2005) *A Whole New Mind: How the Right-Brainers Will Rule the Future*. London: Riverhead Books.

Pitt, R. and Mewburn, I. (2016) 'Academic superheroes? A critical analysis of academic job descriptions', *Journal of Higher Education Policy and Management*, (38): 88–101.

Poynton, R. (2013) *Do/Improvise? Less Push. More Pause. Better Results: A New Approach to Work (and Life)*. London: Do Books.

Pressfield, S. (2002) *The War of Art: Break through the Blocks and Win Your Inner Creative Battles*. New York: Black Irish.

Pressfield, S. (2016) *People Don't Want to Read Your Sh*t: Why That is and What You Can Do about It*. London: Black Irish Entertainment LLC.

Reid, E. (2015) 'Embracing, passing, revealing, and the ideal worker image: How people navigate expected and experienced professional identities', *Organization Science*, 26(4): 997–1017.

Reisz, M. (2016) '"Email overload" risks "emotional exhaustion" for academics', *Times Higher Education*. Available at: www.timeshighereducation.com/news/email-overload-risks-emotional-exhaustion-academics (accessed 2 November 2017).

Ricca, C. (2012) 'Beyond teaching methods: A Complexity Approach', *Complicity: An International Journal of Complexity and Education*, 9: 31–51.

Robert, H.M. (2011) *Robert's Rules of Order Newly Revised in Brief*. Philadelphia: Da Capo Press.

Rolfe, G. (2013) 'Thinking as a subversive activity: Doing philosophy in the corporate University', *Nurse Education Today*, 14: 28–37.

Rumelt, R. (2011) *Good Strategy/Bad Strategy: The Difference and Why It Matters*. New York: Crown Business.

Ryan, S. (2012) 'Academic zombies: A failure of resistance or a means of survival?', *Australian Universities' Review*, 54(2): 3–11.

Sandberg, S. (2015) *Lean in: Women, Work, and the Will to Lead*. London: WH Allen.

Savigny, H. (2014) 'We need to talk about sexism in academia', *UK PSA Women & Politics Specialist Group*. Available at: psawomenpolitics.com/2014/12/10/we-need-to-talk-about-sexism-in-academia (accessed 2 November 2017).

Sawyer, K. (2013) *Zig Zag: The Surprising Path to Greater Creativity*. New York: Jossey-Bass.

Schell, P. (2014) 'Work less, do more, live better', *Times Higher Education*. Available at: www.timeshighereducation.com/features/work-less-do-more-live-better/2014929.article (accessed 2 November 2017).

Schon, D.A. (1984) *Reflective Practitioner: How Professionals Think in Action*. London: Basic Books.

Schwartz, T. (2010) 'The productivity paradox: How Sony Pictures gets more out of people by demanding less', *Harvard Business Review*, June.

Sehgal, K. (2016) 'How to write email with military pricision', Harvard Business Review, Available at: https://hbr.org/2016/11/how-to-write-email-with-military-precision?referral=00203&utm_source=newsletter_management_tip&utm_medium=email&utm_campaign=tip_date&spMailingID=16540896&spUserID=MTIwMzM4ODA5MjYS1&spJobID=960897061&spReportId=OTYwODk3MDYxS0 (accessed 7 November 2017).

Semenza, G.C. (2010) *Graduate Study for the 21st Century*. New York: Palgrave Macmillan.

Semenza, G.C. (2014) *Graduate Study for the Twenty-First Century: How to Build an Academic Career in the Humanities*. London: Palgrave Macmillan.

Senge, P.M. (2006) *The Fifth Discipline: The Art and Practice of the Learning Organization*, 2nd edn. New York: Crown Business.

Sharma, R. (2006) *The Greatness Guide: 101 Lessons for Making What's Good at Work and in Life Even Better*. New York: HarperCollins.

Silvia, P. (2007) *How to Write a Lot: A Guide to Productive Academic Writing*. Washington, DC: American Psychological Association.

Sinek, S. (2000) 'How great leaders inspire action', TED Talk. Available at: www.ted.com/talks/simon_sinek_how_great_leaders_inspire_action (accessed 2 November 2017).

Sinek, S. (2009) *Start with Why: How Great Leaders Inspire Everyone to Take Action*. London: Portfolio.

Smith, J. (2010) 'Forging identities: The experiences of probationary lecturers in the UK', *Studies in Higher Education*, 35(5): 577–91.

Smith, K.E. and Stewart, E. (2016a) 'The uneven impacts of research impact: Adjustments needed to address the imbalance of the current impact framework', *LSE Impact Blog*. Available at: blogs.lse.ac.uk/impactofsocialsciences/2016/07/25/the-uneven-impacts-of-research-impact/?utm_content=buffer94653&utm_medium=social&utm_source=twitter.com&utm_campaign=buffer (accessed 2 November 2017).

Smith, K.E. and Stewart, E. (2016b) 'We need to talk about impact: Why social policy academics need to engage with the UK's research impact agenda', *Journal of Social Policy*. Doi: http://dx.doi.org/10.1017/S0047279416000283.

Southwick, F. (2012) 'Opinion: Academia suppresses creativity', *The Scientist*. Available at: www.the-scientist.com/?articles.view/articleNo/32077/title/Opinion--Academia-Suppresses-Creativity (accessed 2 November 2017).

Sowell, T. (2007) *A Conflict of Visions: Ideological Origins of Political Struggles*, rev. edn. New York: Basic Books.

Sower, V.E., Duffy, J.A. and Kohers, G. (2008) 'Great Ormond Street Hospital for Children in London: Ferrari's Formula-One handovers and handovers from surgery to intensive care', in V.E. Sower, J.A. Duffy and G. Kohers (eds), *Benchmarking for Hospitals: Achieving Best-in-Class Performance without Having to Reinvent the Wheel*. Milwaukee, WI: American Society for Quality Press, pp. 171–90.

Sparks, B. and Bradley, G. (1991) 'A competency-based study of academic staff development needs', *Higher Education Research & Development*, 10: 165–75.

Spooren, P., Brockx, B. and Mortelmans, D. (2013) 'On the validity of student evaluation of teaching', *Review of Educational Research*, 83: 598–642.

Steiner, C. and Perry, P. (1997) *Achieving Emotional Literacy: A Personal Program to Increase Your Emotional Intelligence*. London: Bloomsbury.

Stone, D., Patton, B., Heen, S. and Fisher, R. (2010) *Difficult Conversations: How to Discuss What Matters Most*. London: Penguin.

Swales, J.M. (1990) *Genre Analysis: English in Academic and Research Settings*. Cambridge: Cambridge University Press.

Swales, J.M. (2004) *Research Genres*. Cambridge: Cambridge University Press.

Swales, J.M. (2009) *Other Floors, Other Voices: A Textography of a Small University Building*. London: Routledge.

Sword, H. (2012) *Stylish Academic Writing*. Harvard: Harvard University Press.

Sword, H. (2017) *Air & Light & Time & Space: How successful academics write*. London: Harvard University Press.

Syed, M. (2015) *Black Box Thinking: Marginal Gains and the Secrets of High Performance*. London: John Murray.

Tardy, C.M. (2003) 'A genre system view of the funding of academic research', *Written Communication*, 20(1): 7–36.

Tavris, C. and Aronson, E. (2015) *Mistakes Were Made (But Not by Me): Why We Justify Foolish Beliefs, Bad Decisions and Hurtful Acts*, 2nd edn. New York: Mariner Books.

Taylor, P. (2008) 'Being an academic today', in R. Barnett and R. Di Napoli (eds), *Changing Identities in Higher Education: Voicing Perspectives*. Abingdon: Routledge, pp. 27–39.

The Economist (1955) 'Parkinson's Law'. Available at: www.economist.com/node/14116121 (accessed 2 November 2017).

Thomson, P. and Kamler, B. (2010) 'It's been said before and we'll say it again: Research is writing', in P. Thomson and M. Walker (eds), *The Routledge Doctoral Students Companion*, pp. 149–60.

Thomson, P. and Kamler, B. (2012) *Writing for Peer Reviewed Journals: Strategies for Getting Published*. London: Routledge.

Thomson, P. and Kamler, B. (2016) *Detox Your Writing: Strategies for Doctoral Researchers*. London: Routledge.

Tight, M. (2009) 'Are academic workloads increasing? The post-war survey evidence from the UK', *Higher Education Quarterly*, 64(2): 200–15.

Times Higher Education Supplement (THES) (2016) 'Workload survival guide for academics'. 18 February. Available at: www.timeshighereducation.com/features/workload-survival-guide-for-academics (accessed 2 November 2017).

Times Higher Education University Workplace Survey (2016) *Times Higher Education*. Available at: www.timeshighereducation.com/features/university-workplace-survey-2016-results-and-analysis (accessed 2 November 2017).

Tuchman, G. (2011) *Wannabe U: Inside the Corporate University*. Chicago, IL: University of Chicago Press.

Twale, D.J. and De Luca, B.M. (2008) *Faculty Incivility: The Rise of the Academic Bully Culture and What to Do about It*. San Francisco, CA: Jossey-Bass.

Urban, T. (2016) '100 blocks a day'. Available at: https://waitbutwhy.com/2016/10/100-blocks-day.html (acces 2 November 2017).

van Gogh, Vincent (1882) *The Letters*. 274 To Theo van Gogh, 22 October. The Hague: Van Gogh Museum and Huygens ING.

van Lankveld, T., Schoonenboom, J., Volman, M., Croiset, G. and Beishuizen, J. (2017) 'Developing a teacher identity in the university context: A systematic review of the literature', *Higher Education Research & Development*, 36: 2.

Vostal, F. (2014) 'Academic life in the fast lane: The experience of time and speed in British academia', *Time & Society*, 24: 71–95.

Walker, G.E., Golde, C.M., Jones, L., Bueschel, A.C. and Hutchings, P. (2008) *The Formation of Scholars: Rethinking Doctoral Education for the Twenty-First Century*. San Francisco, CA: Jossey-Bass.

Ware, M. and Mabe, M. (2015) *The STM Report: An Overview of Scientific and Journal Publishing*. Lincoln, NE: University of Nebraska.

Watson, E. (2013) 'Introduction', in E. Watson (ed.), *Generation X Professor Speak: Voices from Academia*. Plymouth: Scarecrow Press, pp. vii–xxi.

Watt, J. and Robertson, N. (2011) 'Burnout in university teaching staff: A systematic literature review', *Educational Research*, 53: 33–50.

White, G.B. (2017) 'How many robots does it take to replace a human job?', *Atlantic*. Available at: www.theatlantic.com/business/archive/2017/03/work-automation/521364/ (accessed 2 November 2017).

Winefield, A.H., Boyd, C., Saebel, J. and Pignata, S. (2008) *Job Stress in University Staff: An Australian Research Study*. Sydney: Australian Academic Press.

Wood, M. and Su, F. (2017) 'What makes an excellent lecturer? Academics' perspectives on the discourse of "teaching excellence" in higher education', *Teaching in Higher Education*,

22(4): 451–66.

Woodhouse, H. (2009) *Selling Out: Academic Freedom and the Corporate Market*. London: McGill-Queens University Press.

Wuchty, S., Jones, B.F. and Uzzi, B. (2007) 'The increasing dominance of teams in the production of knowledge', *Science*, 316: 1036–9.

Ylijoki, O. (2013) 'Boundary-work between work and life in the high-speed university', *Studies in Higher Education*, 38: 242–55.

Zampetakis, L.A., Bouranta, N. and Moustakis, V.S. (2010) 'On the relationship between individual creativity and time management', *Thinking Skills and Creativity*, 5: 23–32.

Ziker, J. (2014) 'The long, lonely job of homo academics', *The Blue Review*, Available at: theblue review.org/faculty-time-allocation (accessed 2 November 2017).

APPENDIX 1

VALUES INVENTORY

Accountability

Achievement

Adaptability

Adventure

Affection

Altruism

Ambition

Authenticity

Balance

Beauty

Being Liked

Being the Best

Belonging

Care/Nurture

Collaboration

Commitment

Community

Compassion

Competence

Competition

Confidence

Connection

Contentment

Contribution

Cooperation

Courage

Creativity

Curiosity/Wonder

Dignity

Diversity

Duty

Education/Certification

Efficiency

Environment

Equality

Ethics

Excellence

Fairness

Faith

Family

Financial Stability

Forgiveness

Freedom

Friendship

Fun

Future Generations

Generosity	Love
Giving Back	Loyalty
Grace	Making a Difference
Gratitude	Openness
Growth	Optimism
Harmony	Order/Control
Health	Ownership
Hierarchy	Nature
Home	Parenting
Honesty	Patience
Honour	Patriotism
Hope	Peace
Hospitality	Perseverance
Humility	Personal Fulfilment
Humour	Power
Inclusion	Prestige/Image
Independence	Pride
Initiative	Productivity
Innovation	Recognition
Integrity	Reliability
Intimacy	Resourcefulness
Intuition	Respect
Job Security	Responsibility
Joy	Risk-Taking
Justice	Safety
Kindness	Security
Knowledge	Self-Discipline
Law/Rule	Self-Expression
Leadership	Self-Respect
Learning	Serenity
Legacy	Service
Leisure	Simplicity

Social Affirmation

Solitude

→ Spirituality

Sportsmanship

Stewardship

Success

Teamwork

Thrift

Time

→ Tradition

Trust

Truth

Understanding

Uniqueness

Usefulness

Vision

Vulnerability

Wealth

Well-Being

Wholeheartedness

Wisdom

Write your own:

INDEX

Note: Tables and figures are indicated by page numbers in bold print.